Re-membering the Body

FCCT | Free Church, Catholic Tradition

Barry Harvey and Bryan C. Hollon, editors

PUBLISHED VOLUMES:

Jeff W. Cary
Free Churches and the Body of Christ: Authority, Unity, and Truthfulness

Re-membering the Body

The Lord's Supper and Ecclesial Unity in the Free Church Traditions

Scott W. Bullard

CASCADE *Books* • Eugene, Oregon

RE-MEMBERING THE BODY
The Lord's Supper and Ecclesial Unity in the Free Church Traditions

Free Church, Catholic Tradition 2

Copyright © 2013 Scott W. Bullard. All rights reserved. Except for brief quotations in critical publications or reviews, no part of this book may be reproduced in any manner without prior written permission from the publisher. Write: Permissions, Wipf and Stock Publishers, 199 W. 8th Ave., Suite 3, Eugene, OR 97401.

Cascade Books
An Imprint of Wipf and Stock Publishers
199 W. 8th Ave., Suite 3
Eugene, OR 97401

www.wipfandstock.com

ISBN 13: 978-1-62032-017-4

Cataloging-in-Publication data:

Bullard, Scott W.

    Re-membering the body : the lord's supper and ecclesial unity in the free church traditions / Scott W. Bullard.

    Free Church, Catholic Tradition 2

    xii + 176 p.; 23 cm—Includes bibliographical references and index.

    ISBN 13: 978-1-62032-017-4

    1. Sacraments—Baptists. 2. Baptists—Doctrines. 3. Lubac, Henri de, 1896–1991. 4. McClendon, James William. 5. Jenson, Robert W. I. Title. II. Series.

BX6338 .B75 2013

Manufactured in the USA.

For Shannon

Verbum caro factum est, et habitavit in nobis; illi carni adjungitur ecclesia, et fit Christus totus, caput et corpus.

AUGUSTINE, ON THE EPISTLE OF JOHN, 1.2

Contents

Series Preface ix

Acknowledgments xi

1. Reconsidering Communion from a Free Church Perspective 1
2. James McClendon:
   The Supper as a Re-membering Sign in baptist Theology 13
3. Henri de Lubac:
   The Eucharist Makes the Church 59
4. Robert Jenson and the Gathered Body of Christ 98
5. The Eucharist Makes the (Free) Church:
   The New Baptist Sacramentalists and Ecclesial Unity 125

Bibliography 163
Index 173

Series Preface

Barry Harvey and Bryan C. Hollon, editors

WHY A BOOK SERIES entitled *Free Church, Catholic Tradition*? As he does on so many other occasions, Augustine eloquently articulates the benefits of engaging in the kinds of conversations that we hope it promotes. "Dear reader," he writes near the outset of *De Trinitate*, "whenever you are as certain about something as I am go forward with me; whenever you hesitate, seek with me; whenever you discover that you have gone wrong come back to me; or if I have gone wrong, call me back to you. In this way we will travel the street of love together as we make our way toward him of whom it is said, 'Seek his face always.'" Though Augustine's words here are addressed to individuals, the wisdom of what he says extends to the ecumenical spirit of our times. When set in this ecclesial context, his admonition provides both the content and the spirit that we hope will characterize this series.

The immediate context for this series is the growing number of scholars in Free Church communions who are interested in drawing upon the great tradition of the church catholic to deepen and enrich their own denominational heritage with its wisdom. We hope in particular that it will offer an effective means for getting the work of scholars from these church bodies into the wider theological conversation and that it will encourage others to join this conversation. The larger context is the modern ecumenical movement, which was given birth early in the twentieth century, developed in a variety of ways over the next several decades, and now in the twenty-first century has taken on new and diverse forms.

While ecumenism has many facets to it—ecclesiological, political, cultural—Jürgen Moltmann has helpfully identified its theological significance in his book, *The Church in the Power of the Spirit*. The ecumenical movement, writes Moltmann, has moved the churches away from the anathemas of the past, and ushered them down a path marked by dialogue and co-operation, culminating in toleration and the arguing out of differences within the one church. The ecumenical path, says Moltmann, leads theologically to living in council. He concedes that though the hope of an ecumenical all-Christian council, where Christianity would speak with one voice, is not at all likely in the foreseeable future, that hope nevertheless already sheds light on the present "wherever the divided churches are beginning to live in council with one another."

Living in council entails, on the one hand, consulting other churches and searching other traditions when asking questions affecting one's own communion. The days of returning always to the same dry wells to resolve internal problems and answer pressing questions are over. In particular, Free Churches that have entered into council with other churches are discovering new insights and fresh reservoirs of meaning. The *Free Church, Catholic Tradition* series has its first and most pressing *raison d'être* here, as more and more believers in these churches find ways of life and thought in the great tradition of the church that in their opinion are desperately needed in their own communions.

In addition, says Moltmann, living in council means intervening in the questions of other churches in an effort to cut through old provincial divisions. Though the idea of intervention may sound overly-intrusive (one thinks of reality television shows in which friends and family members perform "interventions" on loved ones who are addicted or otherwise caught up in ways of life that are not healthy), if it is in fact the case that the whole church is present in every individual church, what one body finds problematic or troublesome has important implications for the others: "it is then impossible to say that the controversy about papal infallibility is 'an internal problem for Catholics' or that the dispute about infant baptism is 'an internal problem for Protestants.'" Of course, if such interventions are not done prudently, carefully, humbly, and above all charitably, they will be of no avail.

The volumes in this series thus seek to cut across some of these well-established, though theologically problematic, divisions that have kept Free Church communions in particular from the riches of the Catholic intellectual, moral, and liturgical tradition, and to reconnect believers in these churches with the insights and wisdom of the church catholic. We also hope that Catholic theologians, together with Protestants from the magisterial traditions, would also find in the series a forum for shared inquiry with their "separated brethren," that together we might seek the face of God in the midst of our fragmented context.

Acknowledgments

I HAVE COME TO love the exercise of writing and editing a theological book, seeing it as a very small contribution to the upbuilding of the body of Christ. I have many to thank for this positive, if naïve, outlook. Knowing that many will be left out, I would first like to express my deepest thanks to Barry Harvey for his influence upon me while writing this book and for his editing. Without his patience, encouragement, and insight I could not have completed this task.

I would also like to express my gratitude to Ralph Wood, who first as teacher and then as supervisor introduced me to the work of Henri de Lubac and eventually allowed me to teach de Lubac to his finest undergraduate students and seminarians. Not long after this development, as churchmate and friend, he and a small group of others from DaySpring Baptist Church in Waco, Texas, became for me what de Lubac calls the *corpus verum*.

Additionally, the community of learners at Judson College in Marion, Alabama, should be thanked. Not only have I been given ample time, encouragement, and other forms of support from President David Potts to engage in research, to write and edit the work, and to present portions of chapters at conferences, I have been urged to complete the work by Judson's students and fellow faculty members. Religion major Paula Fendley asked me almost daily if I had worked on "the book," while Brianne Culp combed through pages and pages of footnotes and created the index. Most importantly, however, at Judson I have seen the Eucharist come to life for our campus community in the form of our "Weekly Communion" service each Wednesday afternoon. There, the students, faculty, and staff gathered together to pray for one another and the world, to sing, to read Scripture to one another, to serve the elements to one another, and to bless one another. That students like Christina Lee insisted on baking the bread and Miriam Hart and Laura Hyer shared their musical gifts so freely only deepened our appreciation of these moments. This service is attended by students, faculty members, and—appropriately—by members of our maintenance staff. Truly, I believe de Lubac's claim that "the Eucharist makes the Church," and I also believe that this truth is somehow manifested on the campuses of colleges all over the world.

There are many others to be thanked. Along the way, Stanley Hauerwas and Curtis Freeman first introduced me to Jim McClendon's work while I took the master of divinity at Duke University. Steven Harmon and Mikeal Parsons saw to it that my early work on McClendon got published. Moreover, as dear friends and fellow graduate students, Marc Nicholas and John Inscore Essick helped sharpen my thinking on the Eucharist and what it might mean to place McClendon in conversation with de Lubac, while Amber Inscore Essick's careful reading helped me revisit both grammatical and pastoral questions in the final stages of editing.

Finally, I would like to thank my family, who sacrificed much so that I could take the time to pursue something as odd as writing about a Louisiana Baptist and a French Catholic and their influence on a movement sometimes referred to as Baptist sacramentalism. We had heard of none of the aforementioned characters or "movements" when we began our life together, but because they have become a concrete reality in all of our lives through the Church, this project has served to enrich our lives, our care for one another, and our conversations. Truly, as the passage that undergirds this entire work states, in our experience "we who are many are one, for we all partake of the one loaf."

1

Reconsidering Communion from a Free Church Perspective

The Disappearance of the Eucharist's Unitive Function

THIS BOOK IS A Baptist retrieval of the Eucharist, or Lord's Supper, as a vital basis for the unity of the Church as the body of Christ. In the pages to follow, I argue that over the last two centuries a thick conception of the unity brought about by the Eucharist has greatly diminished. However, down through the centuries, the Church has said that this is a "sacrament"[1] that pulls members of the Church "godward" and, significantly, together as the body of Christ.[2] As Henri de Lubac once said, the social aspect of the Supper "is the constant teaching of the Church, though it must be confessed that in practice it is too little known."[3]

---

1. By "sacrament" the Church has historically meant a "visible word," a sign symbolic of grace that in some sense has already been conveyed, but which conveys grace to the participant by incorporating the participant into the Christian church. Through the Eucharist one is put into a proper relationship with the Divine and, importantly, with fellow members of Christ's body. A sacrament, then, is a practice that both signifies grace and is itself a mediator of the grace that is signified. Lutheran theologian Robert Jenson draws upon Augustine, Luther, and several other important Christian theologians to describe the term *sacrament* in this way. See Jenson, *Visible Words*, 10–11.

2. Irenaeus, *Against the Heresies*, V.2.3; Augustine, *On Christian Doctrine*, bk. 3, ch. 9; Augustine, *Commentary on Psalm 33*; Thomas Aquinas, *Summa Theologiae*, Tertia Pars, Question 75, esp. articles 1–5; Luther, *Large Catechism*, 92; Luther, "Babylonian Captivity of the Church," 256–57; Calvin, *Institutes of the Christian Religion*, IV.17.14, IV.17.33; Schmemann, *Eucharist*, 28–29, 194.

3. De Lubac, *Catholicism*, 82.

Re-membering the Body

I argue in the pages that follow that de Lubac's critique is true not only of his own tradition (Catholicism) but of the Church universal and especially of Baptists. Indeed, against the grain of the larger Christian tradition, Baptist and other "free church" theologians have not only traditionally neglected the unitive function of the Supper,[4] they have largely denied that anything "happens" in the Supper at all, positing a purely (or "merely") symbolic role for the Supper wherein the Supper has no unique power in pulling members of the Church either godward or together.[5] More than a few Baptist theologians, however, insist that the Supper is more than symbolic. In the words of James Wm. McClendon Jr., one of the most important Baptist thinkers in the twentieth century, the Supper is a "sign of salvation,"[6] and for McClendon "it is the nature of signs not only to betoken but to do something."[7] Consistent with de Lubac's claim about the social aspect being overlooked, however, McClendon skims over the unifying aspect of the Supper in his account of the Church's "signs" in his *Systematic Theology*. This slight is most notable in the section of volume 2 in which he champions a key part of his theological project—the solidarity of the Church. Ultimately, eucharistic unity is a parenthetical consideration for McClendon, summed up in one paragraph as "a (re-membering) sign."[8]

---

4. Definitions of "free church" vary widely. In this study, in addition to taking into account the manner in which theologians identify themselves, I follow the definition offered by Curtis Freeman, who says that "the Free Church tradition possesses at least five traits that may be understood negatively and positively: 1. freedom of the church (non-hierarchical order/congregational polity); 2. freedom of worship (non-prescribed liturgy/spiritual worship); 3. freedom of confession (non-binding confession/gathered community); 4. freedom of conscience (non-coercive authority/soul liberty); and 5. freedom of religion (non-established religion/separation of church and state)." See Freeman, "'To Feed Upon by Faith,'" 194.

5. It should be noted that in attaching the words *purely* or *merely* to the word *symbolic*, I am identifying interpretations that, in the words of Steven Harmon, "are radically reductionistic versions of the more robust theology of sacraments as symbols advocated by Huldrych Zwingli, for whom there was a real and inseparable connection between the sign and the thing signified." See Harmon, *Towards Baptist Catholicity*, 13. I will flesh out a fuller understanding of signs and symbols through the work of McClendon in chapter 2, and more briefly through fellow Baptist theologian Curtis Freeman in chapter 5 of this study.

6. McClendon, *Doctrine*, 379.

7. Ibid., 388.

8. Ibid., 402. Here the term *re-membering* is being used in direct contrast to the term *dismembering*. McClendon's understanding of the Supper as "a re-membering sign" is that this practice is an instrument through which God reconstitutes the dismembered body of Christ. In participating in the Supper, that is, members of the Church are both

In contrast to McClendon, whose view of the Supper is considered a lofty one within his own tradition, de Lubac regards the Eucharist as the very "heart of the Church."[9] Indeed, in a way similar to but stronger than what McClendon indicates when he describes the Supper as a re-membering sign, de Lubac argues that the early Church's understanding of the relationship between the Eucharist and the Church's unity was that "the Eucharist makes the Church."[10] As a continuation of Paul, who proclaims that "we who are many are one body, for we all partake of the one loaf" (1 Cor 10:17), we encounter this theme in patristic literature, wherein the Church's participation in the Supper is crucial for becoming Christ's body.[11]

De Lubac contends that the point of the body imagery is the unity of the Church, the ecclesial body of Christ. Indeed, he points out that as recently as Aquinas, it was the ecclesial body that was understood as the "real presence" of Christ in the world as a result of its participation in the Eucharist, while the Eucharist itself was said to be the "mystical presence"— "mystical" not because it was a misunderstood or "optional" concern, but because it was that body which lessened the temporal *caesura* between the ecclesial body and the historical body of Christ.[12] As William T. Cavanaugh says, the Eucharist, as the *corpus mysticum*, "insures the unity between the two times and brings the Christ event into present historical time in the church body," the *corpus verum*.[13]

---

reminded that they are "members of one another" in the body of Christ (Eph 4:25), and in fact *are made* members of one another.

9. De Lubac, *Splendor*, 78.

10. De Lubac, *Corpus Mysticum*, 88.

11. Augustine, *Confessions*, 7.10.16; Chrysostom, "Homilies on 1 Corinthians 10:16,17," 197.

12. De Lubac, *Corpus Mysticum*, 256.

13. Cavanaugh, *Torture and* Eucharist, 213. Though we will look at the early and medieval understandings of the *corpus Christi* in chapter 3, de Lubac and Cavanaugh (through de Lubac) are here retrieving the doctrine of the threefold body of Christ: the historical body (which walked the shores of Galilee and is now at the right hand of the Father), the ecclesial body (preeminently referred to as the *corpus verum*, or true body of Christ, in patristic literature), and the eucharistic body (the *corpus mysticum*, or mystical body of Christ). They argue that the Eucharist (*corpus mysticum*) makes the Church (*corpus verum*) in erasing the gap between the Church and the historical body. Cavanaugh says that in the oldest understandings of the threefold body, "the sacramental body and the church body are closely linked, and there is a 'gap' between this pair and the historical body. The Eucharist and the Church . . . are together the contemporary performance of the historical body, the unique historical event of Jesus" (Cavanaugh, *Torture and Eucharist*, 212).

Lutheran theologian Robert Jenson acknowledges and even occasionally employs de Lubac's claims, and yet he more frequently points out that while there is scriptural warrant for referring to the Church and the Eucharist as Christ's body, many Protestants and members of free churches believe that too much emphasis upon the Church and Eucharist as Christ's body invites a certain overestimation of the Church's position in relation to the triune God.[14] Jenson therefore attempts to carefully articulate a view of the Eucharist as effecting the body of Christ without absorbing the Church into the Trinity. Whether he succeeds in this endeavor is often debated, and yet I argue that Jenson—due primarily to his being a Protestant situated in North America—helps the contemporary Western reader see more clearly than does de Lubac why it is legitimate and utterly necessary to speak of an ecclesially embodied Christ.

Why McClendon?

In the pages that follow, I shall contend that most of what is needed for an argument for eucharistic unity is in place in McClendon's work, a unity that would not simply improve ecumenical relations but that would, as the work of Cavanaugh claims, ultimately enable the Church catholic to see itself as a body—and one capable of resisting the impulses that have gripped the world around it.[15] However, I shall also argue that while McClendon has moved beyond a purely symbolic notion of the Supper, he fails to capitalize fully upon his understanding of the Supper in calling the Church to be "one." To modify this shortcoming in McClendon's theology specifically, and in free church theology more generally, I want to add to the discussion on the relationship between the Supper and the Church's unity the voices of de Lubac, Jenson, and finally, a new generation of Baptist theologians who employ all three of these thinkers[16]—along with many others—in order to

---

14. Jenson, *Visible Words*, 33, 37.

15. Cavanaugh, *Torture and Eucharist*, 4, 14, 205. Employing the research of de Lubac extensively for his own constructive and contemporary political theology, Cavanaugh wants to insure, for example, that in talking about eucharistic unity we avoid the temptation to become "sentimental." Just as Paul's call for unity to the Corinthians contained more than a hint of anger, contemporary Christians need to take seriously the idea that when we talk about a unity rooted in the sacraments we are doing much more than singing a "feel-good hymn." See Cavanaugh, *Torture and Eucharist*, 235.

16. Like McClendon, these are primarily twentieth-century figures, and according to McClendon's own typology, their traditions represent the two types of ecclesiologies that

affirm sacramentalism within and for the life of Baptist churches.[17] This is quite important, for as I shall show in chapter 2, Baptist churches largely consider themselves groups of like-minded individuals who are voluntarily associated with one another. This is a thoroughly modern self-understanding and one that I shall argue is finally incompatible with the biblical understanding of the Church. That the Church is the "body of Christ" means that the Church is a (one) living reality, more than a name for a human institution made up of like-minded or coincidentally similar individuals. Biblical Christianity reminds us that this oneness comes about through the sacraments—especially for St. Paul we are "baptized into the body" (1 Cor 12:3), "we who are many are one body, for we all partake of the one loaf" (1 Cor 10:17).

---

stand in contrast to one another and (importantly) to the "baptist" type as well. Though long conflated with Protestants, "baptists" have their roots in "sixteenth-century Christian radicals" and represent "a third type of Christian community, a third understanding of 'church.' It is local, Spirit-filled, mission-oriented, its discipleship always shaped by a practice of discernment" (McClendon, *Doctrine*, 45, 343). According to McClendon, among the many contemporary groups with baptist roots are "Disciples of Christ and Churches of Christ, Mennonites, Plymouth Brethren, Adventists, Russian Evangelicals, perhaps Quakers, certainly Black Baptists (who often go by other names), the (Anderson, Indiana) Church of God, Southern and British and European and American Baptists, the Church of the Brethren, perhaps some Methodists, Assemblies of God, assorted intentional communities . . . [and] missionary affiliates of all of the above" (McClendon, *Ethics*, 34–35).

17. Among Baptists attempting to recover a sacramental understanding of the Lord's Supper are Molly Marshall, Phillip Thompson, Curtis Freeman, Elizabeth Newman, Barry Harvey, and John Colwell. Steven R. Harmon takes note of these thinkers, whose thought on the Supper will be examined in chapter 5, in *Towards Baptist Catholicity*, 13–14. Indeed, in the same series of which Harmon's book is a part—Studies in Baptist History and Thought—Thompson, Harvey, Newman, and Freeman have essays in a volume titled *Baptist Sacramentalism*, wherein each of them advocates a "sacramental" interpretation of the Supper. Newman, especially, sees the need for a more sacramental understanding of the Supper in connection with the need for a thicker conception of unity, hoping for "an account of the Lord's Supper that might allow Baptists (and perhaps some others) to embrace a more sacramental understanding of this practice, and thus, I would also say, a more catholic understanding." See Newman, "Lord's Supper," 214. See also Ralph C. Wood's call for a "catholicized evangelicalism," which includes a more prominent place for the Supper in free churches, in his *Contending for the Faith*, 80–81, 187. In the final chapter I will also engage the work of Mark Medley, professor of theology at the Baptist Seminary of Kentucky. His "'Do This': The Eucharist and Ecclesial Selfhood" is very similar to de Lubac's project in that it sees the Eucharist as that which makes us "members of one another" in such a way as to image the perichoretic relations of the Trinity.

McClendon points the way forward for Baptists and other free church traditions to a high view of both the Supper and the Church within the framework of his "baptist type of ecclesiology," an overturned hierarchy in which the emphasis is placed upon local congregations.[18] However, I will ask whether a free church ecclesiology can survive the radically communal faith valued so highly by McClendon without a rich and fulsome understanding of the Eucharist. Is the unity for which McClendon calls possible within the framework of a "free" ecclesiology? This is one question being asked with increasing frequency by free church theologians,[19] and by employing de Lubac and Jenson, I shall argue that a eucharistic construal of the unity of the Church is necessary to sustain McClendon's understanding of the Church as a "convictional community."[20] Membership in the Church, for McClendon, is intrinsic to the Christian life. In his work it is the Church that ensures that its members live up to the expectations of the Christian faith—a practice he calls "watch-care."[21] This and other communal understandings of the Church cannot be sustained, however, if his Baptist descendants continue to imbibe the modern and postmodern notion that the Church is just another voluntary society rather than see themselves as "members of one another" through the Eucharist and other churchly practices.

Methodology

I will employ throughout a methodology of "tradition-based" rationality, subscribed to in varying degrees by McClendon, de Lubac, and Jenson. These three theologians, in line with many of the twentieth-century's most notable philosophers, all believe that "human knowledge is never without an *a priori*," indeed that "man is made in such a way that he cannot give

---

18. McClendon, *Doctrine*, 351, 379.

19. For examples of such questions, see Pinnock, "Physical Side of Being Spiritual," 12–13. See also George, "Sacramentality of the Church," 30–31, and Holmes, "Towards a Baptist Theology of Ordained Ministry," 255.

20. McClendon's use of the term *conviction* is a technical one. Convictions are "persistent beliefs such that, if X (a person or a community) has a conviction, it will not easily be relinquished and cannot be relinquished without making X a significantly different person (or community) than before." See McClendon and Smith, *Convictions*, 87; cf. McClendon, *Ethics*, 23; McClendon, *Doctrine*, 29.

21. McClendon, *Ethics*, 52.

meaning to something without choosing his perspective."[22] Accordingly, they are critical of the theological methods of most modern theologians, which they contend assume an ahistorical, disincarnate, and decontextualized objectivity, following a turn that has taken place in philosophy in the last century. To name two of many, Hans-Georg Gadamer and Alasdair MacIntyre have argued that the Enlightenment's aspiration to provide a foundation for human knowledge transcending historical, linguistic, or cultural contexts has failed.[23] Since this study examines authors who write primarily for members of a particular tradition, these insights shall guide this study.

According to Gadamer, human knowing always takes place from within particular "horizons" of tradition and language. Persons are shaped intellectually and morally by the particular languages and traditions within which they exist. Because of this posited imbeddedness of all human thought, Gadamer rejects the Enlightenment's claim of having secured a pure objectivity and consequently the best methods of intellectual inquiry. He thus claims that "the fundamental prejudice of the Enlightenment is the prejudice against prejudice itself, which denies tradition its power."[24] While for Gadamer it is important to be aware of one's own biases, human understanding is "to be thought of less as a subjective act than as participating in an event of tradition."[25] Understanding the value of an ancient theatrical play, for example, requires one not only to understand the impact of the play on its original audience, but to "take account of that other normative element—the stylistic values of one's own day—which . . . sets limits to the demand for a stylistically correct reproduction."[26]

Although his differences with Gadamer are significant, MacIntyre has also argued in favor of "tradition-based" reasoning. According to MacIntyre, a tradition is "an historically extended, socially embodied argument, and an argument precisely in part about the goods which constitute

---

22. De Lubac, *Theological Fragments*, 39.

23. Though these two thinkers share something of a perspective on this question, they have widely varying positions on many other issues.

24. Gadamer, *Truth and Method*, 270. The use of "prejudice" here is a technical one, and Gadamer guards against using the term solely in a negative sense. "Prejudice" refers to any "judgment that is rendered before all the elements that determine a situation have been finally examined."

25. Ibid., 290.

26. Ibid., 310.

Re-membering the Body

that tradition."[27] Intellectual and moral reasoning necessarily draw upon the resources of particular traditions, which develop over time as their formative texts are brought to bear on new contexts. New contexts often lead to epistemological crises within traditions, and traditions overcome these crises by drawing upon their own resources, and, importantly, by prudentially appropriating insights from other traditions.[28] In line with this methodology, I hope to appropriate for Baptists—especially for McClendon and those contemporary theologians whom he has influenced—the insights of the Catholic and Protestant traditions on the Eucharist and its vital connection to the unity of the Church.

This study may therefore be seen as a continuation of the Church's "ongoing conversation" about the Supper as a formative practice of the Church. The study will draw upon Scripture and the Christian tradition as authoritative sources, though the authority of a particular patristic figure, for example, might be examined and questioned to a greater or lesser extent than another. In a sense, then, the study is also in line with what McClendon calls "theology": an ongoing and self-involving struggle in the discovery, understanding, and transformation of the convictions of the Church, "including the discovery and critical revision of their relation to one another."[29]

Overview of Chapters

The study will include five chapters. Following this explanation of the main thesis, methodology, and remaining chapters, in chapter 2 I first contextualize McClendon with an overview of earlier free church theologians' work on the Supper, including examples from Anabaptist and early British Baptist thought that may be read as "sacramental,"[30] or, at times, as hinting

27. MacIntyre, *After Virtue*, 222.
28. Ibid., 276.
29. McClendon, *Ethics*, 23.
30. McClendon believes that Anabaptists such as Pilgram Marpeck and Balthasar Hubmaier are his "baptist ancestors," and they seized upon the unitive aspect of the Supper in their point that, since the ascension, the Church has been and is now the "real" presence of Christ, the incarnation's "prolongation in history through the life of the church" (see Rempel, *Lord's Supper in Anabaptism*, 69). For Marpeck, in the Supper—practiced weekly—persons come together into one body both physically and mystically, becoming the body of Christ for the world (Rempel, *Lord's Supper in Anabaptism*, 148). In seventeenth-century England, Baptist Thomas Grantham practiced weekly communion

at a sacramental vision. This exercise will demonstrate the many traditions upon which McClendon draws in coming to understand the Supper as a "powerful practice" that is more than merely symbolic.[31] The chapter will go on to unveil in great detail McClendon's understanding of the Supper as "a re-membering sign" and connect this theme with his understanding of the unity of the Church.[32] I will argue that McClendon's work emphasizes both that the Supper "does something" and that there is indeed an ever-present need for Church unity, but finally that these considerations are too often disconnected in his work. In *Doctrine*, he does take note of the ancient affirmation that the Supper effects the unity of the Church, that this rite is a sign wherein members of the Church experience "reconstitution, being made part of the whole,"[33] and yet these potentially rich passages are not fully expanded. Moreover, since McClendon ultimately backs away from using the language of sacrament in relation to the Supper, this chapter will ask whether there is another sense in which McClendon's understanding of what Baptists have traditionally called the "ordinances" does not go far enough.

Chapter 3 will offer de Lubac's work on the Eucharist and the unity of the Church as a way of developing more fully some of McClendon's embryonic ideas. I argue there that de Lubac's work can go farther than McClendon's precisely because it takes better advantage of the tradition's resources, which mine Scripture in order to emphasize the unity necessary for living the radically Christian existence for which McClendon calls.[34] According to de Lubac, "the Eucharist makes the Church," and this is an ancient mindset that was present from the beginning but became deemphasized in the

---

and spoke of it as "sacrament" and unitive (Grantham, *Christianismus Primitivus*, 95). Grantham's use of sacraments is noted often by McClendon, but ignored is Grantham's connection of the Eucharist and the unity of the Church until McClendon's friend and mentee Curtis Freeman points out Grantham's emphasis on the Supper as a source of ecclesial oneness. As Philip Thompson says, for Grantham, "'common prayers and due use of the sacraments' . . . were both critical in preservation of the social world of seventeenth-century England." See Thompson, "Sacraments and Religious Liberty," 43.

31. McClendon, *Ethics*, 218; cf. McClendon, "Practice of Community Formation," 94.

32. McClendon, *Ethics*, 218.

33. McClendon, *Doctrine*, 402.

34. See, for example, de Lubac's *Catholicism*, which draws deeply upon Scripture and patristic figures even when addressing what de Lubac often called "the present situation." Originally published in 1938, it is widely agreed that his subsequent works "grew from its individual chapters much like branches from a trunk." See von Balthasar, *Theology of Henri de Lubac*, 35.

second millennium of the Church's existence as a result of the transubstantiation controversies.[35] De Lubac thought that the Church should return to an understanding that "the Eucharist makes the Church" in order to better articulate the unique unity of the Church as an alternative to the humanism of the twentieth century. His retrieval of the Eucharist as unitive shaped much of the proceedings of Vatican II and documents that resulted from the Council, and subsequently influenced much of late twentieth-century theology.[36] Indeed, the *Catechism of the Catholic Church* now includes the phrase "the Eucharist makes the Church."[37]

McClendon's awareness of this traditional understanding and use of the Supper[38]—coupled with the fact that the Eucharist as a unitive act constitutes a portion of the Christian narrative believed even by some of McClendon's "baptist ancestors"—makes his lack of emphasis in this area troubling, especially since he wrote a comprehensive systematic theology. De Lubac's more fully formed explication of the meaning of the Eucharist will serve to greatly enrich contemporary readers of McClendon, especially those interested in his ecclesiology and his contribution of the Supper as a re-membering sign. Moreover, in the end, de Lubac and those who have employed his insights will provide Baptists with some perspective in showing what a truly sacramental theology looks like.

Chapter 4 will argue that Robert Jenson's thought is a thoroughly sacramental theology from a Protestant perspective, and one that responds to concerns most often raised by Protestants and members of free churches who are skeptical of sacramentalism. For Jenson, just as for McClendon and de Lubac, the Pauline Epistles are central to the formation of the concept of the Church. In addition to his multiple references to 1 Cor 10:17, Jenson frequently cites Paul's naming the Church "the body of Christ" (1 Cor 12:27), and notes that this body is the Church universal. He emphasizes, moreover, that the Eucharist is a pivotal component in the unity of

---

35. For a discussion of the understanding of the ecclesial body as *corpus verum* and the altar elements as *corpus mysticum*, and the post-twelfth-century inversion of this understanding, see de Lubac, *Corpus Mysticum*, 34–39. This inversion is also summarized in Cavanaugh, *Torture and Eucharist*, 212–13.

36. See von Balthasar, "Achievement of Henri de Lubac," 42; Ratzinger (now Pope Benedict XVI) in his foreword to *Catholicism* (12); Rowland, *Culture and the Thomist Tradition*; Milbank, *Suspended Middle*, 7; D'Ambrosio, "Ressourcement Theology, Aggiornamento, and the Hermeneutics of Tradition," 533; Chantraine, "Cardinal Henri de Lubac (1896–1991)," 297–303.

37. *Catechism of the Catholic Church*, 1396.

38. McClendon, *Doctrine*, 402. Cf. *Ethics*, 31.

the Church,[39] showing that this was true for Paul and John in Scripture, and for Chrysostom, Aquinas, and Luther as a result of their readings of Scripture.[40] Finally, Jenson articulates an understanding of the Church as the "true" body of Christ while attempting to avoid conflating the Church with the second person of the Trinity. As stated above, whether he succeeds in avoiding such absorption is a major source of contention, and this question is addressed in the final pages of chapter 4. For now it will be sufficient to say that for Jenson, at her best the Church sees herself as an extension of the incarnation into history, and in part as a result of the Eucharist.[41]

In chapter 5, the study concludes by showing that McClendon is deeply connected to a later group of Baptist theologians who agree that the Church bound together in the Eucharist is not an unfree church, but rather the opposite.[42] McClendon gestures toward a sacramentalism that is more fully embraced by his students and others whom he has deeply influenced—a group I shall call "the new Baptist sacramentalists"—and these contemporary authors show that one vital way for Baptists to proceed in conversations about the unity of the Church will be to consult Protestant and Catholic sources that have developed a deep connection between the ecclesial body and the eucharistic body. The goal of the study is not to dissolve theological or practical differences between Baptists, Protestants, and Catholics, although neither is it solely to clarify those differences. In the end, I hope to bring forward a sacramental alternative for Baptists seeking to ground their quest for unity in biblical theology, and to do so precisely by mining the traditions of other sources that root their sacramental theologies in Scripture.

The Significance of McClendon

McClendon has been one of the most influential theologians in the development of a new generation of Baptist theologians. His commitment

39. Jenson, *Systematic Theology*, 1:204–6.
40. See Jenson, "Church and the Sacraments," 215, 222.
41. Jenson, *Systematic Theology*, 1:205.
42. Hence McClendon's use of *imago Dei* as a basis for the Church's unity and his retrieval of his Baptist (or "baptist") ancestors' use of the Supper. Claiming that humans are created in the image of God means for McClendon that humanity was created in the image of perfectly and mutually indwelling *hypostases*, and is therefore not a claim solely intended to support the intrinsic value and sovereignty of the individual, but one that indicates that humans were created to live in community. See McClendon, *Doctrine*, 448; McClendon, *Witness*, 378.

to "the way" of Scripture and the Christian narrative produced one of the finest bodies of work among twentieth-century Baptists. This display of a few eucharistic themes is not intended to slight his work on unity, nor to idealize the practice of the Eucharist in divided churches, but to show how all ecclesiology should incorporate the Eucharist.[43] Indeed, I make the claim that the lack of a sacramental understanding of the Supper has led to its being practiced only a few times per year in Baptist churches, and that this infrequent practice has led to a lack of actual unity among Baptists.[44] Elizabeth Newman, a Baptist whose work I will examine in the final chapter, puts it well when she says that for early Baptists, "as symbol became emphasized over against reality, the practice itself atrophied. Thus many Baptists and other communions came to celebrate the Lord's Supper only a few times each year."[45]

McClendon traces some of these themes in his writing, and even did so in the pulpit; as interim pastor of a divided Baptist church in California, he urged the congregation to move from a quarterly observance of the rite to a monthly observance.[46] In so doing, he adds some significant aspects to the free church tradition, and indeed I hope to demonstrate that his use of sign theory in his work on the Supper was groundbreaking for twentieth-century Baptists, not to mention way ahead of its time. The work of those whom he taught, wrote with, and influenced in many other ways is proof that, in addition to his own major contributions, McClendon is a pivotal figure in Baptist history and thought. There is no doubt, for example, that the relatively new and important *Baptist Sacramentalism* volumes that have been released in the last few years would have looked much different without McClendon's good work, even though their articles were written and published after his death.[47] Thus, it is without further delay that we turn our attention to the work of James McClendon and the theologians who set the stage for and otherwise influenced his understanding of the Supper.

---

43. Indeed, the sheer length of chapter 2 is indicative both of the importance and genius of McClendon's contribution to the Baptist discussion on the relationship between the Supper and the Church's unity.

44. McClendon, *Doctrine*, 445.

45. Newman, "Lord's Supper," 217.

46. See McClendon, *Making Gospel Sense*, xix.

47. In chapter 5, I will explore extensively McClendon's influence upon the contributors to the *Baptist Sacramentalism* volumes, focusing especially upon volume 1.

2

James McClendon

The Supper as a Re-membering Sign in baptist Theology

Introduction

JAMES MCCLENDON'S UNDERSTANDING OF the Lord's Supper as a "sign" is one of the most important theological contributions by a twentieth-century Baptist theologian working in North America,[1] especially since, as indicated in chapter 1, Baptists have largely said that the Lord's Supper is a "symbol" or "a mere symbol."[2] According to a purely symbolic view, the Supper outwardly symbolizes grace already conveyed inwardly by other means,

---

1. The reader should be aware that although this is a large claim, this project suggests in the end that while important in and of itself, McClendon's understanding of the Supper also clears the way for a relatively young and influential set of Baptist theologians who affirm a sacramental understanding of the Supper.

2. That Baptists have largely spoken of the Supper as purely a symbol is a claim that is widely agreed upon by sacramentalists and non-sacramentalists alike. See, for example, Leonard, *Baptist Ways*, 8. Leonard was commissioned by the Board of Managers of the American Baptist Historical Society to explore baptist identity in a volume that could replace Robert G. Torbet's *History of the Baptists*—a volume that was issued in three editions and served as an authoritative source for over half a century. Elizabeth Newman, professor of theology at the Baptist Theological Seminary at Richmond, has also concurred with this assessment ("Lord's Supper," 214–15). Curtis Freeman notes of the sacramental theories of Baptists that "for Baptists now as then, sacramentalism is rarely a live option," and that in contemporary Baptist life "it is not an overstatement to say that a 'sub-Zwinglian' theology of the Lord's Supper has become entrenched as a *de facto* orthodoxy among Free Churches" (see Freeman, "'To Feed Upon by Faith,'" 196, 206). See also Wayland, "Lord's Supper, Administration Of," 794.

and it further serves to remind Christians of Christ's sacrifice and their own faith commitments. On the other hand, by "sacrament" the Church has historically meant a "visible word"[3] that, whether spoken or acted, is "gospel-communication."[4] As such, a sacrament both signifies grace and is itself a mediator of the grace that is signified.[5] It is a sign through which God conveys grace to the participant by incorporating her or him into the Christian church, therefore putting the participant into a proper relationship with the Divine.[6]

In the pages that follow I will offer an account of the theology of McClendon as an example of a Baptist on the verge of being "sacramental," and one who connects his understanding of the Supper to his call for ecclesial unity. After contextualizing him by shedding some light on the almost five-hundred-year-old "free church" discussion about the Lord's Supper, I will explain what McClendon means by the term *sign*. His use of the term is a technical one, indebted to a long tradition of language about "signs" and accompanied by a thorough understanding of a theory of communication called "speech act theory" as it was articulated by J. L. Austin.[7] I will then explain how for McClendon an understanding of the Supper as a sign of "remembrance" does not stand opposed to belief in Christ's real presence in the Supper,[8] though the term *real presence* will have to be qualified. Having illustrated that the Supper is a sign in which God is present and active, I will move to an examination of the ways in which the Supper, sometimes called "a *re-membering* sign,"[9] contributes to an understanding of the unity of the church in McClendon's work. I will argue along the way that among twentieth-century Baptists living in North America, McClendon sees in a unique way the necessity of a retrieval of the connection between the Lord's Supper and the unity of the church.

---

3. Augustine, *In Joannem*, 80.3.
4. Jenson, *Visible Words*, 11.
5. Algerius, *De Sacramentis*, I, c. 5 (*PL* 180, 753 B).
6. Conner, *Christian Doctrine*, 273.
7. McClendon, *Doctrine*, 388.
8. Thus does he note that in dealing with the signs, "we come to an uncomfortable part of the systematic task" (see McClendon, *Doctrine*, 373).
9. Ibid., 402.

"baptist" Backgrounds: Mere Symbol, Symbol, and Sign

In order to arrive at an understanding of the significance of McClendon's work on the Supper, his career and writing must be set against the background of other major free church thinkers.[10] That free church theologians (and laypersons) have typically held the "purely symbolic" view of the elements is a claim affirmed even by free church theologians attempting to recover a sacramental view of the Supper.[11] Many early Anabaptists were martyred for refusing to affirm that the bread and the wine were truly the body and blood of Christ. Baptist theologian Timothy George relates that when sixteenth-century Anabaptist West Friesland was asked "'What do you hold concerning the sacrament?' he famously replied 'I know nothing of your baked God.'"[12] Another Anabaptist martyr, when asked just prior to her execution about the nature of Christ's presence in the Supper, responded, "What God would you give me? One that is perishable and sold for a farthing?"[13] She also told a priest that morning that if the bread truly was Christ's body, then he daily crucified Christ in consuming the bread.[14]

Given these words from McClendon's "baptist" ancestors, it is little surprise that most members of free churches currently living in North America, along with their ancestors, have largely said that what other traditions refer to as sacraments can be reduced not only to "symbols," but also

---

10. "Free church" and "baptist" are often used interchangeably in McClendon's work and in this study, primarily because McClendon thinks he and all Baptists are deeply connected to what he calls the "radical wing" of the Reformation. The pages that immediately follow will therefore discuss beliefs and practices of the Supper described in early Anabaptist thought as well as the work of important Baptist thinkers from the seventeenth to the twentieth century, with reference to the ways in which these theologies of the Supper contribute to their ecclesiologies. As McClendon says in his seminal work *Biography as Theology*, "I am a *radical* Christian. 'Christian'—that pays tribute to Augustine and Edwards, to Schleiermacher and Barth, and to all who challenge pat solutions, proximate loyalties, as idolatrous. 'Radical'—that affirms my solidarity with experience-saturated believers: with Anabaptists so little known, with revivalists and pietists, with Pentecostalists and communal celebrants of many sorts" (69–70). For a secondary source on McClendon and the *baptist* type, see Finger, *Contemporary Anabaptist Theology*, esp. 67–68.

11. See again Newman, "Lord's Supper," 214–15; Freeman, "To Feed Upon by Faith," 196.

12. George, "Spirituality of the Radical Reformation," 348.

13. Ibid.

14. Ibid.

to "mere symbols."[15] To speak of baptism for a moment, McClendon acknowledges that for most Baptists "baptism only 'represents' or 'symbolizes' conversion independent of baptism and prior to it."[16] To support his claim, one has to look no further than the influential Augustus Hopkins Strong, who wrote just before the dawn of the twentieth century that "baptism symbolizes the previous entrance of the believer into the communion,"[17] or the perhaps equally influential Edgar Young Mullins, who in the twentieth century agreed that baptism is "the outward sign of an inward change which had already taken place in the believer."[18] Such words affirm the position traditionally held over against the idea that baptism is a sacrament that conveys grace to the participant by incorporating the participant into the church, therefore putting the participant into a proper relationship with the Divine.[19]

Strong and Mullins—when they can be prompted to speak of it at all—apply this same language to the Supper. Strong seems to bring up the Supper in his systematic works only to explain what it is *not*—namely, to point out that the Catholic position is erroneous because it holds that "by a physical partaking of the elements, the communicant receives saving grace from God."[20] Mullins affirms a purely symbolic view of the Supper,[21] and this, combined with his emphasis on the primacy of the individual and the identification of "soul competency" as Baptists' primary contribution to religious history, means that he also rarely, if ever, links the unity of the church to the Supper.[22] This, as I shall argue below, is out of concert not only with the larger Christian tradition, but even with many of his Baptist predecessors.

---

15. See chapter 1 of this study.

16.. McClendon, *Doctrine*, 388. It should be noted that while I concede that Baptists have largely viewed baptism and the Lord's Supper in this way, as I attempted to show in chapter 1 there has been a vital (and, I contend, larger than is usually imagined) strand of Baptists who hold to a sacramental understanding of baptism and the Lord's Supper, and therefore to a sacramental understanding of the church. Persons who have traced these histories, and who therefore have authored works on the connection between the Supper and the Church, are the subject of chapter 5.

17. Strong, *Systematic Theology*, 527.

18. Mullins, *Christian Religion in Its Doctrinal Expression*, 384.

19. Strong, *Systematic Theology*, 273.

20. Ibid., 543.

21. Mullins, *Axioms of Religion*, 543.

22. Ibid., 45–58.

A Symbol, but Not "Merely"

"Merely symbolic," however prevalent a description of the Supper among persons identified as "baptists" by McClendon, is not the only description of the Supper employed by Baptists.[23] There is a strand of free church thinkers whose sacramental theologies are closer to the understanding of the Supper articulated by the Reformer Huldrych Zwingli, who, though he has been interpreted as giving a "merely" symbolic interpretation of the sacraments, emphasized not only that the Supper was "a memorial of a sacrifice," but also that the rite "was not the Supper . . . unless Christ is there."[24] As H. Wayne Pipken's translations and close studies of Zwingli's original writings have revealed, Zwingli denied any sense of Christ's physical presence but at no point denied what he called Christ's spiritual or true presence.[25] Indeed, the presence of Christ was indicated in each believer's partaking of the elements of bread and wine in faith. This Zwinglian understanding of the Supper becomes evident in the thought of W. T. Conner, who, interestingly, was Mullins' student and McClendon's teacher, as well as a major Baptist thinker whose influence and writing peaked during the middle decades of the twentieth century. Similar to Mullins in that he wrote very little about the Supper, Conner makes no references to the Supper in his *System of Christian Doctrine* (which he dedicated to Mullins), although there one can glean that he held to a symbolic view of baptism. Later, in the same work, Conner writes of baptism and the Lord's Supper that "these two ceremonies are pictorial representations of the fundamental facts of the gospel and of our salvation through the gospel. Over against this view is the view of the Roman Catholic Church that these two ordinances, with five others, are 'sacraments' that convey grace to the participant."[26] Conner, however, does not dismiss the Supper as *merely* symbolic in this later work, carefully noting that a symbolic view of the elements "does not deny the

---

23. Haykin, "'His Soul-Refreshing Presence,'" 177; Thompson, "Sacraments and Religious Liberty," 39; Freeman, "'To Feed Upon by Faith,'" 207. Ernest Payne, considered the mid-twentieth century's authority on English Baptist historical studies, even argued that no one understanding of the Supper can lay claim to being the dominant Baptist perspective (see Payne, *Fellowship of Believers*, 61).

24. Zwingli, "Exposition of the Faith," 260.

25. Pipken, *Zwingli*, 10–11. See also Stephens, "Theology of Zwingli," 90–91. It is Pipken's study, along with his own reading of Zwingli, that has led Freeman to differentiate between Zwinglian and what he calls "sub-Zwinglian" (or *merely* symbolic) understandings of the Supper. See Freeman, "'To Feed Upon by Faith,'" 209.

26. Conner, *Christian Doctrine*, 273.

spiritual omnipresence of Christ, but it does deny that Christ is present in the bread and wine of the Supper any more than he is present in any other material substance."[27]

Coming to a similar conclusion, Baptist scholar Dale Moody notes in *The Word of Truth* that the Catholic belief that Christ is physically present in the transubstantiated bread and wine is not biblical,[28] but that a credible group that includes Luther and Calvin has maintained that the elements are nonetheless "more than mere symbols."[29] Moody does not combat the views of this group, and later notes that "1 Corinthians 11:24ff and Luke 22:19 use the strong word *anamnesis*, translated 'remembrance' or 'recollection,' and this is much stronger than the word for 'memorial'. . . . Remembrance has reference to an event in the past that is recalled with such power that it brings a blessing into the present."[30] Importantly, this "blessing" for Moody includes not only union with God but the unity of all who participate in the Supper. He therefore allots equal space in this text to the fellowship with God and the fellowship among persons that takes place when they participate in the rite. Moreover, he laments the loss of the practice of church members confessing sins to one another before participation in the Supper.[31] Thus does Moody sound a call similar to the later and ultimately sacramental Baptist theology that we will discuss in the final chapter.

Sign Leading to Sacrament

John Calvin also has his imprint on the views of the sacraments in free church theology. Calvin believed that the bread and wine were "signs . . . which represent the invisible food which we receive from the body and blood of Christ."[32] Of the Roman Catholic position, he said, "they place Christ in the bread, while we do not think it lawful for us to drag him from

---

27. Ibid., 287.
28. Moody, *Word of Truth*, 470.
29. Ibid. Moody is not entirely accurate on this point, as Luther, though he believed that one who did not participate in "the sacrament" could not call oneself a Christian, on at least one occasion refers to the bread and wine as "merely outward signs . . . incomparably less important than the thing symbolized" (see Luther, "Pagan Servitude of the Church," 260).
30. Ibid., 470. Cf. Moody, "New Testament Significance of the Lord's Supper," 93.
31. Ibid., 472–73.
32. Calvin, *Institutes of the Christian Religion*, IV.17.1.

heaven,"[33] though he adds that one should "never subscribe to the falsehood that Christ is not present in the Supper if he is not secreted under a covering of bread."[34] Christ's body is surely for Calvin "in its place" (in heaven at the right hand of the father),[35] but the bread and wine are signs of Christ's body and blood that, if partaken of in faith,[36] open our souls and join us to Him who is in heaven, giving us an "increase in faith."[37] His emphasis is that we are not to place "confidence" in the sacraments or ourselves (thus it is not our faith that makes Christ present), but that "God . . . makes them effective."[38]

Free church sacramental theology has been heavily influenced by Calvin's understanding. While a number of Anabaptists were martyred for their refusal to affirm Christ's presence in the communion elements, some of these radical reformers held that Christ was in some sense present in the "signs" of the bread and wine. Balthasar Hubmaier maintained a robust account of the Lord's Supper as a "sign," one constituted by the "symbols" of the bread and wine. These signs, for Hubmaier, are objects that help believers remember Christ's sacrifice, and in pointing to Christ they make Christ present to the believers' church and generate believers' activity.

Hubmaier's view of the Supper also maintains a deep connection between the rite and the unity of the church. Hubmaier says that the elements of bread and wine are "the body of Christ in remembrance,"[39] but also that

> the bread and wine are word symbols of his love, by which we remember how he, Christ, was our Christ, and how we also are always to be Christ to one another. It is a sign of Christ's broken body because believers commit to allow their bodies to be broken for one another: "Thus as the body and blood of Christ became my body and blood on the cross, so likewise shall my body and blood become the body and blood of my neighbor, and in time of need theirs become my body and blood, or we cannot boast at all to be Christians."[40]

33. Ibid., IV.17.31.
34. Ibid.
35. Ibid., IV.122
36. Ibid., IV.14.9.
37. Ibid.
38. Ibid., IV.14.17.
39. Hubmaier, "Simple Instruction," 324.
40. Hubmaier, "Several Theses Concerning the Mass," 74–75.

Re-membering the Body

In seventeenth-century England, General Baptists articulated a sacramental understanding of the Supper. Their "Orthodox Creed" (1678) states that just as Israel "had the manna to nourish them in the wilderness to Canaan, so we have the sacraments, to nourish us in the church and in our wilderness-condition."[41] In General Baptist Thomas Grantham's *Christianismus Primitivus*, the Supper is instituted by Christ "to keep himself in the remembrance of his chosen disciples,"[42] but also so that his body and blood can be "fed upon by faith."[43] Grantham maintains, moreover, in significant sections in his work, that a portion of the grace conveyed in the Supper lies in the unity of the church. In a section of *Christianismus Primitivus* titled "The Lord's Table Teaches Unity," Grantham notes that it is the Supper in which "Christ gathers his people together at his own Table as one family."[44] Thus is the Supper a vital basis of church unity, not "inferior to any doctrine in the gospel tending to preserve the unity of the Church of God. Hence it is expressly called the communion of the body and blood of Christ."[45] Scholars have taken note of Grantham's connection between the Supper and the unity of the church, noting that while anti-sacramentalism swirled around him, the practice of the Eucharist—still offered on a weekly basis for Baptists in this era—was one that strengthened and unified the body of Christ. This is important, since these Baptists saw ecclesial oneness as necessary to resist the state church in seventeenth-century England,[46] and, as we shall see in chapter 3 through the work of William Cavanaugh, unity is especially vital to ecclesial bodies that seek to resist other, oppressive bodies.[47]

---

41. "The Orthodox Creed," Article 19.

42. Grantham, *Christianismus Primitivus*, 93.

43. Ibid., 94.

44. Ibid., 95.

45. Ibid., 94.

46. Thompson, "Sacraments and Religious Liberty," 47. John D. Inscore Essick has shown that for much of Grantham's career the General Baptists were often held in suspicion, and sometimes in contempt, by the English throne. Essick, "Messenger, Apologist, and Nonconformist," 169.

47. For example, using the Chilean government of the 1960s and 1970s as a prime example, Cavanaugh focuses on torture as a "results-oriented" practice and social strategy of the State that creates fearful and isolated bodies disciplined to serve the purposes of the State. Indeed, Cavanaugh says that it is not simply that torture isolates individuals, thereby making them fearful, but that torture itself has as its aim "the very creation of individuals," isolating persons' bodies so as to dismantle social, or bodily, rivals of the nation-state (see Cavanaugh, *Torture and Eucharist*, 3, 34–35). It is not a stretch to say that the fearful environment that often characterized seventeenth-century England

Moving ahead to the twentieth century, another British figure (and importantly, one who wrote around the time of Conner), Robert C. Walton, was an influential Baptist who offered a view of the Supper that contrasts with Conner's. For Walton the Supper does represent our salvation and the nature of the Christian life, but the function of the rite does not end with symbolism. For him, "the Lord's Supper is also a means of grace and the Real Presence of Christ is manifested therein. To interpret the Supper as a memorial feast and no more is to reduce it to a method of auto-suggestion. Sacraments are not only symbols: they are also instruments. They tell the truth and convey the grace. They speak, but they speak with power."[48]

Walton also recognized clearly the relationship between the sacrament of the Supper and the unity of the church. Deeply concerned that a "new individualism" had thoroughly and negatively affected British Baptists since the rise of the industrial revolution,[49] and writing just after World War II had destroyed much of western Europe, Walton held that as sacramental, the Lord's Supper was a vital basis for the unity of the church universal (which, for Walton, must always precede the denomination or local congregation). In his view, the "confident individualist" so prominent in twentieth-century Baptist thought must always be moderated by the "gathered community," the church summoned to the Lord's Table together,[50] "wherein all the members are one."[51]

"Signs" in the Theology of James Wm. McClendon Jr.

Like Grantham, Walton, and others, McClendon pushes beyond a purely symbolic view of the Supper and articulates an emphasis upon the unity

---

created the same need for unity among religious Separatists.

48. Walton, *Gathered Community*, 170. The gap between the sacramental views of the Supper articulated by Grantham and Walton is wide, to be sure, and I am in no way arguing that a sacramental view of the Supper has been the majority position throughout Baptist history. As to when the sub-Zwinglian view came to preeminence, Michael A. G. Haykin argues that "the view that the Lord's Supper is primarily or merely a memorial only began to become widespread in Calvinistic Baptist circles during the last quarter of the eighteenth century" (Haykin, "'His Soul-Refreshing Presence,'" 188). For his part, Walton is neither sub-Zwinglian nor Zwinglian—the language of "instrument" is the language of Thomas Aquinas (Aquinas, *Summa Theologiae*, 3.60.2).

49. Walton, *Gathered Community*, 110–17.

50. Ibid., 111.

51. Ibid.

realized—or at least pointed to—in this practice. McClendon, however, offers a more extensive explanation of signs and symbols than does Walton,[52] and he notes that the Supper is "a re-membering sign" of the church in that, as one of the powerful practices of the gathering church, it "reconstitutes" the church.[53] Among twentieth-century Baptists who lived and worked primarily in North America, McClendon's understanding and development of the Supper merits scholarly attention because he, unlike his teacher Conner and the majority of other contemporary Baptists, came closest among major Baptist thinkers to seeing in the tradition of his baptist ancestors and other traditions the need for, and the path to, a eucharistic unity of the church.[54]

Sign-Acts

In order to understand McClendon's view of the Supper as a sign of the church, one must also be familiar with his use of speech act theory. While the reader should keep in mind throughout the chapter that for McClendon analyzing the "signs" or "sign-acts" of the church is not the same as analyzing the signs of any other community (since the signs or sign-acts of the church are the acts not only of humans but also of God[55]), McClendon notes early on in his *Convictions* that for all communities and persons, there are "speech acts that are especially revealing of convictions,"[56] acts that proclaim and indicate what a community or person persistently believes.[57] In McClendon's framework "speech acts" can be grouped under a

---

52. Though Walton, who is a British Baptist, along with Hubmaier, an early Anabaptist whose relationship to contemporary Baptists is widely disputed, also significantly unpack their understanding of signs.

53. McClendon, *Doctrine*, 402.

54. Curtis Freeman, research professor of theology and director of the Baptist House of Studies at Duke University Divinity School, is at least one contemporary scholar who agrees with this assessment (see Freeman, "'To Feed Upon by Faith,'" 209).

55. McClendon, *Doctrine*, 389.

56. McClendon, *Convictions*, 17. This text was co-authored by McClendon and philosopher James M. Smith under the title of *Understanding Religious Convictions* in 1974 and revised and released under its current title in 1994. It foreshadows his methodology for the remainder of his career.

57. In McClendon's work the term *conviction* is also carefully defined. Convictions are beliefs, but beliefs held particularly tightly, defining who a person is. McClendon understands that "having a relatively fixed character is one aspect of having convictions," since convictions are "persistent beliefs such that, if X (a person or a community) has a

James McClendon

larger category called "sign-acts"—acts that, whether written or verbalized, have the ability not only to describe something but to do something. McClendon joins Austin in likewise describing these acts as "performatives":

> Perhaps the place where we most readily recognize performatives is in legal documents. After certain necessary preliminaries, we may find the document saying, I hereby donate my ranch to my step-daughter Susan. This is, as lawyers say, the operative, or as we shall say, the performative clause. The action of the verb (in this case, "donate") is not described by the performative clause, it is accomplished. To execute such a document, in the appropriate circumstances (you being of sound mind, not under duress, actually having a step-daughter named Susan, the ranch being your own, etc.)—to execute it is to donate the ranch to your step-daughter.[58]

In *Doctrine*, McClendon shows how written words on the door of his seminary office function as performatives: "I put a sign on my office door: 'Students are welcome.' It employs some symbols, namely letters and words, in order to *do* something, in this case, to welcome the students who read it."[59]

While the above quotes are examples of written performatives, McClendon notes also that "one can donate *viva voce*, and most performatives are *viva voce*."[60] Just like written performatives, for McClendon and the sources he draws upon, these "verbal performatives do what they say."[61] Within the community of the church there are several examples of verbal performatives, and many of these are closely tied to belief in the church's unity.

A number of these performative utterances are given by McClendon in his essay "Baptism as a Performative Sign," along with citations of legal documents like the one above, including "'I (hereby) take this woman to be

---

conviction, it will not easily be relinquished and cannot be relinquished without making X a significantly different person (or community) than before" (McClendon and Smith, *Convictions*, 87, 174; cf. McClendon, *Ethics*, 22–23, and McClendon, *Doctrine*, 29). Christian theology, then, is an ongoing and self-involving "struggle" in "discovery, understanding, and transformation of the convictions of a convictional community, including the discovery and critical revision of their relation to one another and to whatever else there is" (McClendon, *Ethics*, 17, 23).

58. McClendon, "Baptism as a Performative Sign," 409.
59. McClendon, *Doctrine*, 388.
60. McClendon, "Baptism as a Performative Sign," 409.
61. Ibid.

my wife' [spoken in a wedding ceremony]" as one such speech act.[62] Significantly, for the church "Christian baptism, as it is understood by the Baptist theologians just surveyed, and as it ought to be understood, is a performative sign . . . It is also a 'word' from the church to the candidate, a 'word' in which the church says something like: 'We receive you as our brother in Christ.' And it is a 'word' from the candidate to the church, a 'word' in which the candidate says something like: 'Brethren, I take my place in your midst. Receive me!'"[63]

Clearly for McClendon, baptism is a significant speech act in the language of the church in that it is the means by which the church receives its members. If, as noted above, speech acts reveal the tightly held beliefs of a community (in this case the church), then revealed here is the conviction that in baptism, something has changed, something has happened: a person who was not previously a member of the church has, in the speech act or sign-act of baptism, become a member of the body of Christ.[64]

The above passage is crucial not only because it helps the reader understand what McClendon, as a Baptist writing primarily in the latter third of the twentieth century, means when he talks about "signs," but also because of the way in which the reader begins to see the ways in which McClendon's understanding of baptism contrasts with much of Baptist theology of the same period. As noted above, Baptists living in North America during this period, along with their ancestors, largely said that baptism and the Lord's Supper are "symbols" or "mere symbols."[65] Indeed, McClendon acknowledges that for most Baptists "baptism only 'represents' or 'symbolizes' conversion independent of baptism and prior to it."[66] Again, one has

---

62. Ibid.

63. Ibid., 410. Though above I acknowledged McClendon's qualifier about the danger of linking speech act theory to the sacraments of the church because of the presence of God as an actor, here a much younger McClendon does not seem to recognize God as one of the actors.

64. There is a lack of clarity as to whose action brings about the change in the baptized, but I will refrain from making a critique at this point. I do so because this study is primarily concerned with the Supper, and the example of baptism here serves as a way of introducing McClendon's understanding of signs to the reader. Moreover, the criticisms I would offer here will all be raised when we come to the Lord's Supper.

65. See chapter 1.

66. McClendon, *Doctrine*, 388. It should be noted that while I concede that Baptists have largely viewed baptism and the Lord's Supper in this way, as I attempted to show in chapter 1 there has been a vital and surprisingly thick strand of Baptists who hold to a sacramental understanding of baptism and the Lord's Supper, and therefore

James McClendon

to look no further than the influential Strong[67] or Mullins[68] to see that the traditional Baptist view is often held over against the idea that baptism is a sacrament.[69] Also crucial here is the communal nature of baptism in McClendon's thought. While many Baptists think of salvation on a purely individualistic level—a private transaction between the individual and the Divine—for McClendon this "sign of salvation" is indeed salvific precisely because it incorporates a person into the body of Christ.[70]

Beyond "Mere Symbolizing": The Lord's Supper as a Sign-Act

As with baptism, McClendon turns to speech act theory in order to flesh out the meaning of the "sign" called the Lord's Supper, or the Eucharist, within the context of the biblical narrative and the narrative of the Christian church.[71] He calls the Lord's Supper (quite intentionally and technically) an "acted sign" or a "sign-action" rather than a "symbol" or "token."[72] This understanding of the term *sign* stands in contrast to the view of the Lord's Supper wherein the rite is viewed as solely reminding the participant of the shedding of Jesus' blood on the cross, or one of many tools that "motivate" the participant to be more faithful going forward because of the particularly bloody nature of the sacrifice Christ made on the cross.[73]

---

to a sacramental understanding of the church. Persons who have traced these histories, and who therefore have authored works on the connection between the Supper and the Church, are the subject of chapter 5.

67. Strong, *Systematic Theology*, 527.
68. Mullins, *Christian Faith in Its Doctrinal Expression*, 384.
69. Strong, *Christian Doctrine*, 273.
70. McClendon, "Baptism as a Performative Sign," 410.
71. McClendon is in concert with the larger tradition in referring to this practice in different ways. He usually calls it the Lord's Supper or simply "the Supper" in his *Systematic Theology*, but freely uses the term *eucharist* as well in those volumes. Indeed, in volume 3 he refers to the rite exclusively as "the eucharist," which is rooted in the Greek word for "offering thanks." The *Catechism of the Catholic Church*, for example, in Article 3 ("The Sacrament of the Eucharist"), Section II ("What Is This Sacrament Called?"), lists "Eucharist," "The Lord's Supper," "The memorial of the Lord's Passion and Resurrection," "Holy Communion," and "Holy Mass," among others, noting that "each name evokes certain aspects of the rite." (see *Catechism of the Catholic Church*, 1328–332.
72. McClendon, *Doctrine*, 400; cf. 375.
73. It should be noted that McClendon, in his use of sign theory, does not draw upon or claim indebtedness to Augustine, whose understanding of signs is crucial for much of

McClendon is aware that, as with baptism, Baptists have largely contended that the rite of the Lord's Supper is "merely symbolic," that it is intended to "memorialize." Although in the biblical narrative Jesus breaks the bread for the disciples at the Last Supper and says, "this is my body" (Matt 26:26), Baptists of all kinds have primarily agreed that Jesus' meaning here is "this is *a symbol of* my body." The purely symbolic interpretation has also typically applied to Baptists' interpretation of the cup.[74] Strong, for example, notes in his *Systematic Theology* under the heading "Erroneous views of the Lord's Supper" that "the Romanist view . . . rests upon a false interpretation of Scripture. In Mat. 26:26, 'this is my body' means: 'this is a symbol of my body.'"[75]

As a result of this reading, and as a corrective of the alleged view that salvation comes mechanically through partaking of Jesus' body and blood in the Eucharist,[76] Baptists and many others have said that the point of the rite and symbols of the Lord's Supper is simply to call to mind Jesus' sacrifice on the cross for the sins of humanity, and to therefore be strengthened for the journey of faith that lies before the individual believer. The confession that has guided and explained the views of many Baptists living in North America, the "Baptist Faith and Message" of the Southern Baptist Convention, says that "the Lord's Supper is a symbolic act of obedience whereby members of the church, through partaking of the bread and the fruit of the vine, memorialize the death of the Redeemer and anticipate the second coming."[77] A confession that has traditionally guided Northern

---

the Christian tradition's sacramental theology. For Augustine, a sacrament is a "visible word" (*In Joannem*, 80, 3), but elsewhere is a "sign" that pertains to divine things (*Letter to Marcellinus* 7), a sign that resembles the thing signified (*Letter to Boniface* 9). One study proposes that Augustine "discovers real union with Christ, not so much through the medium of real presence, but through the medium of the sign, and this union is not so much individual union as that of individuals among one another in Christ" (see F. van der Meer, *Sacramentum chez Saint Augustin*, in *La Maison-Dieu*, 13, 61 [no further bibliographical information available, but this is quoted by de Lubac in *Corpus Mysticum*, 14]).

74. That Baptists have typically held a "purely symbolic" view of the elements is affirmed even by Baptists attempting to recover a sacramental view of the Supper (see again Newman, "Lord's Supper," 214–15).

75. Strong, *Systematic Theology*, 543.

76. Strong also adds that the Catholic position is "erroneous" because it holds that "by a physical partaking of the elements, the communicant receives saving grace from God" (see Strong, *Systematic Theology*, 543).

77. Southern Baptist Convention, Baptist Faith and Message, 1963, in Lumpkin, *Baptist Confessions of Faith*, 396. This document is especially influenced by Herschel Hobbs.

Baptists, the New Hampshire Confession, similarly says that the Supper serves to "commemorate . . . the dying love of Christ."[78]

In a departure not only from many of his Baptist contemporaries but also from many influential ancestors, McClendon contends that by definition, as a sign, the meaning of the Supper cannot be limited to that of a rite that stands for or represents another thing. In addition to the "standing for" another thing (Christ),[79] in their pointing to Christ the elements of the Supper are active realities that point to another reality, the risen Christ whose "resurrection enables his ongoing presence in and to his community,"[80] the church.

Scripture, the baptist Vision, and the Real Presence

Of note in the quote directly above is that McClendon does not say that Christ's body is *physically* or substantively present in the bread and the cup. Indeed, McClendon here seems to follow his teacher Conner, who, again, said that a symbolic view of the elements "does not deny the spiritual omnipresence of Christ, but it does deny that Christ is present in the bread and wine of the Supper any more than he is present in any other material substance."[81] McClendon reminds the reader that Christ "promises his presence 'where two or three or gathered' in his name (Matt 18:20),"[82] but also

---

78. The New Hampshire Confession, in Lumpkin, *Baptist Confessions of Faith*, 366. This confession was adopted by the New Hampshire Baptist Convention in 1833, but after it was published in 1853 by the widely circulated *Baptist Church Manual*, "it became the most widely disseminated creedal confession of American Baptists"; it has remained influential for Baptists living in the northern United States (see Lumpkin, *Baptist Confessions of Faith*, 360–61).

79. McClendon, *Ethics*, 219.

80. McClendon, *Doctrine*, 376. We will discuss this at greater length in the "analysis" sections at the end of the chapter, but at this point the question might be asked, where is this reality located? McClendon notes that "the promise is not 'Where two or three are gathered, you will have such and such worship experiences.' He only promised to be at hand. . . . We are there, *and* he is. The congregation, to be sure, is called to be 'Christ's body' (1 Cor 12:27; Rom 12:5), and in Christian thought that powerful utterance has serious work to do. But this presence cannot be limited either to the fellowship of believers or to the signs of salvation such as baptism and preaching and eucharist; these signs, and who we come to worship, are there, but his secret presence is prior to them, more than they, more than we" (McClendon, *Doctrine*, 379).

81. Conner, *Christian Doctrine*, 287.

82. McClendon, *Doctrine*, 377.

that "his presence cannot be limited either to the signs of salvation such as baptism and preaching and eucharist; these signs, and we who come to worship, are there, but his secret presence is prior to them, more than they, more than we."[83] Thus does McClendon's account of Christ's presence carefully say that Christians are not to overprivilege the Supper as a sign of Christ's presence—he adds that "we do not produce him by some liturgical conjure"[84]—but also that Christians should not overlook Christ's presence in the Supper simply because such a view of the Supper has been "officially banished from our worship by someone's theology."[85]

McClendon articulates what he believes to be a "real" presence of Christ in the Supper which, within his theology, is rooted in the narrative of God and God's people.[86] For McClendon, the "baptist vision" names this way of reading Scripture and being church, practiced primarily by those Christians of the Reformation period who were neither Catholic nor Protestant. McClendon says that he, as a Baptist living in the twentieth century, similarly aims to understand Scripture and the story of the church in this manner:

> The baptist vision is the way the Bible is read by those who (1) accept the plain sense of Scripture as its dominant sense and recognize their continuity with the story it tells, and who (2) acknowledge that finding the point of that story leads them to

---

83. Ibid., 379. Contrast this with the *Catechism of the Catholic Church*, which says that "Christ . . . who is at the right hand of God . . . is present in many ways to his Church. . . . But he is present . . . most especially in the Eucharistic species. The mode of Christ's presence under the Eucharistic species is unique. It raises the Eucharist above all the sacraments. . . . This presence is called 'real'—by which is not intended to exclude the other types of presence as if they could not be 'real' too, but because it is presence in the fullest sense: that is to say, it is a *substantial* presence by which Christ, God and man, makes himself wholly and entirely present" (see *Catechism of the Catholic Church*, 1373–74).

84. McClendon, *Doctrine*, 378.

85. Ibid., 379.

86. Ibid., 240–41. Christ's ascension paves the way for his true presence through the Christian community's *worship, work, witness*, and perhaps most significantly in McClendon, "in the read and studied *word*." McClendon claims to move beyond traditional arguments over "substance" and "nature" that even his self-proclaimed baptist ancestors engaged in to explain Christ's presence in the Supper, turning instead to narrative, a concept central to what he calls "the baptist vision." McClendon does employ a grammar of "substance" and the Catholic doctrine of transubstantiation, however, to explain what he means by the baptist vision's "this is that" (McClendon, *Ethics*, 31–32). This will be explained below.

James McClendon

its application, and who also (3) see past and present and future linked by a "this is that" and "then is now" vision, a trope of mystical identity binding the story now to the story then, and the story then and now to God's future yet come.[87]

McClendon's claim is that baptists see themselves as participants, with the primitive church, in the story told by Scripture—"this is that, then is now"—just as the primitive church proclaimed "this is that!" on the day of Pentecost in recognition of their continuity with the prophets and the larger story of Israel.[88] The present, for these readers, is to be interpreted within the grid of the biblical narrative. "That" Sermon on the Mount is "this" word that Christians hear and respond to today. "That" Passover meal, which commemorated "that" exodus from Egypt and which was summed up in "that" Last Supper and ultimately in "that" sacrifice of Jesus—"that" is "this" eucharistic meal that Christians share together in churches around the world. The baptist vision is "the hermeneutical principle ('this is that' and 'then is now') by which Scripture interprets present practice. . . . [B]y this enacted principle the church at worship can know itself to be the church."[89]

The baptist vision can therefore be brought to bear upon what "this"—the "this" in "this is my body" and "this is my blood"—means in Scripture and in current practices of the Lord's Supper. The connection between the bread and the broken body is narratively implied by the Synoptic Gospel accounts: "this" bread broken and passed "is my body" (Matt 26:26; Mark 14:22; Luke 22:19). The Synoptics also convey the explicit claim that "this" (wine) is "my blood of the covenant, which is poured out for many" (Mark 14:24). As previously stated, however, Baptists have largely claimed that in the narrative Jesus' meaning is that "this bread *symbolizes* my body." Thus, Baptists have said that when contemporary persons "do this in remembrance" of Jesus, they participate in an eating and drinking that calls to mind the life and sacrifice of Jesus, but little more than that. The meal as a remembrance has stood over against most understandings of "the real presence," since what is remembered cannot be really present but is an object from the past. Were Jesus more than "called to mind," he would actually be in the midst of the remembering community.

---

87. McClendon, *Doctrine*, 45.
88. McClendon, *Ethics*, 31.
89. McClendon, *Doctrine*, 385.

According to the baptist vision, however, Scripture's "this is my body" applies to the present—"the remembering signs connect that great narrative to this or that believer or believing community now."[90] McClendon thus employs the term *real presence* in conjunction with Christ's presence in the Supper (though with a qualifier reminiscent of Conner): "Jesus' 'real presence' is not limited to the Supper (far less to its food and drink), but from the earliest Christian beginnings has meant a renewal of the sort of Presence that the disciples knew during the forty days (Acts 1:1–5)."[91] Christ is present in the Supper, according to McClendon, "in a way that matters" and "in such a way that *the story continues.*"[92] In making Christ present, "God acts to make [this remembering sign] effectual."[93]

For McClendon, then, that the Supper is an effectual "sign" of the church is scriptural. This is crucial for his "baptist" understanding of the Supper, as he claims "biblicism," or "humble acceptance of the authority of Scripture for both faith and practice," to be one of the defining marks of free churches.[94] In fact, McClendon spends a great deal of time and space exegeting scriptural accounts of the Supper in his *Systematic Theology*, reading the Matthean and Pauline accounts with particular emphasis. I will remark on these studies in the pages that follow, noting along the way the points at which he emphasizes the Supper's connection to the unity of the church.

---

90. Ibid., 382.

91. Ibid., 378.

92. Ibid. The mode of Christ's presence in the Supper will be examined more closely in the concluding section of this chapter.

93. Ibid., 382. Throughout McClendon's work, Christ's presence in the Supper is not greater or even different than in the other "remembering signs."

94. See McClendon, *Ethics*, 27. Faithfulness to the Christian tradition is important, but only insofar as the tradition has been faithful to the biblical narrative. Theologians and church councils are to reinterrogate the biblical narrative in ever-changing contexts, but do not exercise as much authority as does the biblical narrative, according to McClendon. The extended thoughts on the Supper offered in Scripture are therefore crucial for McClendon since Scripture, though it "does not encompass doctrine" (*Doctrine*, 288), is "uniquely fit to be the doctrinal handbook of the teaching church" (ibid., 25). As we press forward in this study, we shall also examine the understandings of Scripture and tradition put forth by de Lubac and Jenson, always with the aim of making clearer the relationship between their sacramental theologies and McClendon's work.

James McClendon

The Matthean Account of the Supper

McClendon explains in *Ethics* (volume 1 of his *Systematic Theology*, originally published in 1986), and in an essay that is the inspiration for this section of *Ethics*, that even as the rite is enacted in Scripture by the Matthean Christian community, it says something:

> Central to the rite Matthew describes are two acts of sharing by Jesus: one of bread, the other, of a cup of wine. The principal words are simply the performative acts of this sharing: "Take, eat. . . . Drink of it, all of you" (vv. 26–27). For each act a single interpretation is furnished: for the bread, "This is my body"; for the cup, "this is my blood of the covenant, shed for many unto forgiveness of sins" (v. 28). Thereby two notes are sounded, *solidarity* ("my body," "my blood," "covenant") and *redemption* ("unto forgiveness of sins").[95]

The Supper, then, is a speech act in that what is said—"notes" are "sounded" by the participants—is that "we are redeemed" and "we are one, a community." This, McClendon says, "is the rite and the emphasis that Matthew's church also has incorporated, a generation or so later, in its own passion narrative, Matthew 26."[96] He adds that the disciples in Matthew's post-resurrection account, and the later community of the author of Matthew's Gospel, would have said such a thing, "we are one," simply in gathering together their physical bodies in one place for a meal, for in that world "sharing a meal is communion (*koinonia*) with the one who either as host or as *numen* presides over the meal."[97]

McClendon also makes certain to say that Matthew carefully chooses to set Jesus' affirmation of, and covenant with, his disciples against the background of the Jewish Passover meal, the meal that celebrated God's affirmation of and covenant with Israel. In this way, Jesus' statement that "this is my body" is an affirmation of God's oneness with the disciples and their significant unity with one another, for his audience would have recalled the body of Israel and its covenant as a people with God.[98]

McClendon therefore posits that in the Matthean account of the Supper we see "the practice of establishing and maintaining Christian

---

95. McClendon, *Ethics*, 218. Cf. "Practice of Community Formation," 91.
96. McClendon, "Practice of Community Formation," 92.
97. McClendon, *Ethics*, 218. Cf. "Practice of Community Formation," 91.
98. Ibid, 219. Cf. "Practice of Community Formation," 91.

Re-membering the Body

community."[99] In the Gospels, "the point of the meal is solidarity" in the midst of a racially and culturally diverse society.[100] As Nancey Murphy writes in an introduction to McClendon's "The Practice of Community Formation," for McClendon the Supper is one of "two subpractices that effect community formation."[101] Truly, it is the case that for him the unity of Jesus' disciples, whether in the ancient era or in the contemporary era, "rests in their oneness with him. The rite pledges and performs the incorporation of the lives of the gathered disciples not only into their crucified and risen Lord, but also into one another."[102]

McClendon's Reading of 1 Corinthians

In forming his theology of the Supper McClendon works extensively with the Pauline Epistles in addition to the Gospels. He especially interacts with those portions of Paul's correspondence with the Corinthians that address the Corinthian church's practice of the Supper. As we shall see later, all important sacramental theologies incorporate these passages.

McClendon's reading of 1 Corinthians first notes that Paul, in calling Christ the "paschal lamb (1 Cor 5:7),"[103] is similar to Matthew in setting the practice of the Supper in Corinth against the backdrop of the story of Israel and its statement of thanksgiving to God for the covenant with God's people. The Christian church, then, both in the first century and in the twenty-first century, gathers together for the Supper in order to call to mind and give thanks for Christ's sacrifice and the continuing covenant between God and the church. One reason that Paul has seen it necessary to write the Corinthian church, however, is that it is divided, a fact that seems to have been most apparent in this church's practice of the Eucharist. There, the elements of the Supper, the bread and the wine, were being abused. Paul exclaims that "when you come together, it is not really to eat the Lord's Supper. For when the time comes to eat, each of you goes ahead with your own supper, and one goes hungry and another becomes drunk. What! Do you not have homes to eat and drink in? Or do you show contempt for the

---

99. Ibid., 220. Cf. "Practice of Community Formation," 86.

100. Ibid., 218. Cf. "Practice of Community Formation," 91.

101. Murphy, "Practice of Community Formation," 85. The other "subpractice" is baptism.

102. McClendon, *Ethics*, 219.

103. McClendon, *Doctrine*, 404.

church of God and humiliate those who have nothing? What do I say to you? Should I commend you? In this matter I do not commend you!" (1 Cor 11:20–22).

New Testament scholar Raymond Brown notes the possibility that within the Corinthian church, since most worship services would have taken place in the homes of the wealthy, some of the hosts and their closest friends would have a preparatory meal before what was supposed to be the bonding practice of the Lord's Supper. It seems, however, that the rich were taking advantage of their position in the Corinthian community, being selective about who would be invited to the preparatory meal and eating greedily during this time, whereas Paul clearly believes that "all Christians including the poor and slaves have to be accepted into the hospitality area of the house for the eucharist."[104] Persons were also drinking too much wine at these gatherings, thereby turning an occasion for worship and communal thanksgiving into a time of drunkenness and revelry.[105] Brown's first point is the more speculative of the two, but Paul does suggest in 1 Corinthians 11 that with each of the Corinthians "going ahead" with his own meal, the communal aspect of the celebration has been lost.

According to McClendon and many others, this is the context in which Paul states to the Corinthians that the very rite that effects unity in the church is in fact bringing to light the division in the Corinthian church— thus his statement to them that "we who are many are one body, for we all partake of the one loaf" (1 Cor 10:17). McClendon points out that when Paul writes these words to the Corinthian church, he "*reminded* them of a truth."[106] His understanding of the church's unity implies that the members of the church truly were one with each other—a body, rather than individuals—even before they consumed the elements in the rite of communion. Perhaps in his thought this is due to their having already been "baptized into one body," as Paul puts it, since another of the "remembering" (though not re-membering) signs in McClendon's framework is baptism. On this matter, however, we can only speculate.

Though in the next chapter I will more closely examine the eucharistic ecclesiology of de Lubac, a Roman Catholic who seems to have a

---

104. Brown, *Introduction to the New Testament*, 522. Brown points out that it is widely agreed upon in New Testament scholarship that this "preparatory meal" is very possibly the same as the "love feast," or agape meal, in Jude 12.

105. Ibid., 523.

106. McClendon, *Doctrine*, 401. Emphasis mine.

slightly different reading of 1 Cor 10:17, it should be noted now that many Christians, and in particular New Testament scholars, are divided on this question. A fellow Catholic of de Lubac's, Brown, says of 1 Cor 10:17 that "it is not clear whether 10:17 means that the Christian partakers form one collective body or are made participants in the one risen body of Christ."[107] Surprisingly, in contrast to de Lubac and many other Catholics, Brown does not insist, or even mention, that the passage can mean both things.[108] Indeed, due to these kinds of diversities, the reader might do well at this point to both recall and anticipate de Lubac's statement that "the Eucharist makes the church,"[109] and begin to think about whether de Lubac and McClendon are in direct conflict here. Of course, in asking these questions, one must also always keep in mind Paul's command to the Corinthian community to confess to one another, that they might not partake of the elements unworthily.

Before we conclude our extended remarks about the biblical passages, it should also be added that for McClendon, the particular sort of body that identified the Corinthian church is also crucial for Paul, hence his statement to the Corinthian church that "you are the body of Christ" (1 Cor 12:27). This reminder of the particular nature of the body that is the church comes in addition to Paul's recollection of Jesus' words at the Supper, "this is my body; this is for you" (1 Cor 11:24). Paul's point to the persons acting selfishly at the Lord's table is a simple one: if Christians are one body and therefore, as he says elsewhere, "members of one another" (Eph 4:25), then selfish behavior in any setting—and certainly at the Lord's table—is harmful to the entire body. Some theologians (including McClendon) have even followed this Pauline logic in order to claim that behavior that creates division, if the body of Christ is a "real" or "true" body, is akin to self-mutilation, even suicide.[110]

It is clear then that for McClendon the body of Christ in Scripture is *one* body. In *Doctrine* he points out his belief that "disciples are called not

---

107. Brown, *Introduction to the New Testament*, 521.

108. As we will see in chapter 3, in the theology of William Cavanaugh—whose work is heavily influenced by de Lubac—"the eucharist creates unity, it is true. But the eucharist also requires unity" (Cavanaugh, *Torture and Eucharist*, 235).

109. De Lubac, *Corpus Mysticum*, 88.

110. McClendon cites Bonhoeffer to this effect, noting that as World War II approached Bonhoeffer said in a sermon that "the members of the ecumenical church . . . cannot take up arms against Christ himself—yet this is what they do if they take up arms against one another!" (McClendon, *Ethics*, 200, citation taken from Bonhoeffer, *No Rusty Swords*, 285).

into a solitary following, but into a *body*, the church."¹¹¹ Membership in the ecclesial body is intrinsic to the Christian faith. That the church, the Christian community, in Corinth, Ephesus, and elsewhere is the "body of Christ" means that the church is a (one) living reality, more than a name for a human institution made up of like-minded or coincidentally similar individuals.

A Remembering and Re-membering Sign

McClendon's reading of Matthew, 1 Corinthians, and other portions of Scripture is, then, that the Supper is one of the "re-membering signs" through which God reconstitutes the dismembered body of Christ.¹¹² In participating in the Supper, members of the church are reminded that they are "members of one another" in the body of Christ (Eph 4:25), the body of which Christ himself was and is both "member" and "head" (Eph 4:15–17). This reading of Paul, along with Murphy's description of McClendon's reading of Matthew, prepares us for McClendon's notion of the Supper as "a re-membering sign," a description of the Supper that comes to the forefront in a chapter of *Doctrine* titled "Christian Worship: Signs of Salvation."¹¹³ There, the Supper is treated with baptism and proclamation (or preaching) as one of three practices that are the "remembering signs" of the church.¹¹⁴

For McClendon, remembering signs are secondary to, and work together with, what he calls the "historic" or "primary" signs.¹¹⁵ Historic signs are for McClendon "the crucial events in the history of redemption."¹¹⁶ Examples of historic signs include Moses' leading of the Israelites out of Egypt, Israel's exile from and return to Jerusalem, Christ's birth, and most importantly for McClendon, Christ's death, burial, and resurrection from

---

111. McClendon, *Doctrine*, 132.

112. Ibid., 402. Contemporary Baptist theologian Barry Harvey adopts this use of the term *re-membered* in his "Remembering the Body," 96–116. Another place in which this term is used relative to the Eucharist is in the work of Cavanaugh, whose *Torture and Eucharist* is explored in great detail in the next chapter.

113. McClendon, *Doctrine*, 373. It has previously been introduced by McClendon in *Doctrine*, 186–87.

114. Ibid., 386.

115. Ibid., 381. "Providential signs" constitute a third category of signs and are explained below.

116. Ibid.

the dead.[117] "Lesser signs," but signs that are nonetheless historic, are miracles. McClendon notes that "the burning bush connected with the exodus," as a sign through which God calls Moses to lead the Israelites out of Egypt, is an example of a miracle or a "lesser historic sign" in the Old Testament.[118] The burning bush that is not consumed is both miraculous and a reminder of a pivotal event in history. A "lesser sign" from the New Testament is the empty tomb on the first Easter day, a sign that points to the historic sign of Christ's resurrection.[119]

Remembering signs recall, or betoken, the great historic signs, and they do so in the context of Christian worship. As McClendon puts it, they are "subsidiary signs which cluster around each historic sign."[120] Current instances of baptism, for example, "point to" Jesus' own baptism, as well as to his death, burial, and resurrection.[121] Similarly, in its "pointing," the Lord's Supper is treated as a remembering sign "recalling the climactic moment in the story (cross and resurrection) and affirming the renewal of the pledge each in baptism makes in answer to God's proclaimed word."[122]

According to McClendon, then, as a sign the Supper "does something." We shall ask later whether McClendon ought to say more often that "God through the Supper 'does something,'" but for now it is important to emphasize that for McClendon the Supper "recalls" and also "renews," and in this sense it is for him an "effectual" sign rather than "a mere symbol."[123] The Supper draws its participants into the story of the cross and the resur-

---

117. McClendon, *Doctrine*, 386.
118. Ibid.
119. Ibid., 382.
120. Ibid., 187.
121. Ibid., 382.

122. Ibid., 386. According to McClendon, "providential signs are a third class of God's sign-acts: Neither world-historical events nor remembering repetitions, these are instances of the distinctive guidance God gives to individual lives for designated kingdom tasks." It should be sufficient at this point to say that these signs are communication from God that "guide" believers as they travel on the Christian "journey," indicating possible vocations for individuals and providing encouragement. Moreover, McClendon points out that "this three-part analysis is not hard and fast; Jesus' baptism in Jordan must belong to the first two classes, and any believer's baptism, if it becomes for another a providential sign and guide for his or her own life, belongs to both the second and the third" (McClendon, *Doctrine*, 382).

123. Indeed, since for McClendon symbols are so crucial to the makeup of signs, the term "mere symbol" is an oxymoron. Moreover, he says repeatedly that the signs of the church "are effectual" (see ibid.).

rection by pointing the participants to these signs. This is another example of McClendon's "this is that" hermeneutics. As a participant in the narrative of the church (the same narrative in which Jesus himself participates both as God and as human), one arises from the Supper renewed by an encounter with God and the narrative in which both God and the participant are vital characters. The participant is therefore empowered to go and live (and, if necessary, die) in imitation of Jesus.[124] This is in one sense a classically modern (and, some would say, "Protestant") interpretation of the Supper: the individual, in remembering and communing with the soon-to-be-crucified Jesus of Matthew's Gospel, is pulled "godward."[125]

To call this a "modern" interpretation in that sense, however, may not be fair. McClendon notes that this is what Christians have always done in the Supper: "When primitive Christians met to remember, they met to remember their Master facing his life's crisis."[126] Since the story of the ancient church is our story, contemporary Christians similarly gather around the bread and wine in order to remember Jesus and his life's work and sacrifice. Here, "remember" means to "call to mind," "recall," or even, as explained earlier by Moody, to make a past event present in a powerful way.[127] And again, though we will take a look at the scholarly work of those outside Baptist circles later in this study, this is the consensus in other Christian traditions as well. Influential Anglican theologian Dom Gregory Dix, whose work is employed to a greater extent in the next chapter, notes that while it "must have been shockingly plain to the apostles," Jesus' command to them was that they were to participate in the Supper "'for the re-calling of me.'"[128]

McClendon, however, uses the term *remembering*, or *re-membering*, in more than one way. The word is also employed in opposition to the term *dismembering*. In this sense, being "re-membered" means "reconstitution, being made part of the whole."[129] For McClendon, then, another way in which the Supper is a re-membering sign is the way in which this practice brings together the participants in the narrative of the church not only physically, but also—as we shall explore in greater detail through de Lubac

---

124. McClendon, *Ethics*, 212.
125. Dix, *Shape of the Liturgy*, 601.
126. McClendon, *Doctrine*, 405.
127. See chapter 1 above. Moody, "New Testament Significance of the Lord's Supper," 93.
128. Dix, *Shape of the Liturgy*, 58.
129. McClendon, *Doctrine*, 402.

in the next chapter—mystically.[130] That is, members are put by the sign of the Supper in the same physical space in order to partake of the bread and wine; but, to go further than this obvious sense, McClendon says, "when we come obediently together, the Risen One is there."[131] It is precisely because this gathering is brought about by the Supper that makes the Supper a "sign of salvation."[132] It is this corporate aspect of salvation that I aim to bring out below.

Sin and the Signs of Salvation

The notion of the Supper as a "sign of salvation" that re-members the church can be better understood against the backdrop of McClendon's account of sin. McClendon defines sin as "refusal" of Jesus' "way," as "reversion" to the old, inferior way of life, but finally as "rupture"—rupture of the relationship between God and humans and, in a way similar to what we will see in de Lubac, rupture of the relationships within the church, the body of Christ.[133] In refusing to follow the way of God, that is, Christians alienate themselves not only from God, but from one another. Sin, then, can be social and/or individual.[134] As a solution to this understanding of sin, McClendon proposes in this early chapter that "we encounter the Lord's Supper. In this remembering sign, the Christian company, stragglers as well as pioneers, are gathered . . . to receive as ration the sign of God's faithfulness in the body of Christ. Here the blood of sacrifice is poured to designate afresh

---

130. "Mystically" is an elusive and important term. In chapter 3, I shall spend some time unpacking what this term has meant in the Christian tradition. For now, I will simply say that positing a mystical unity among members of the body of Christ is consistent with the thought of many Christian authors—Christians believe themselves to be "truly" or "mystically" one. See 1 Cor 10:17; Eph 4:25; Eph 5:32 ("This is a great mystery, and I am applying it to Christ and his church"); Rabanus Maurus, *De Universo*, 5, c. 10 (PL 111, 131); Lombard, in 1 Cor., X. *Sentences* (PL 192, 857); Aquinas, *Summa Theologiae*, IIIa, q. 8, a. 3 and 4; de Lubac, *Splendor*, 75.

131. McClendon, *Ethics*, 378.

132. Such is the title of the chapter in which he treats the topic of the Supper (McClendon, *Doctrine*, 373).

133. Ibid., 132. For de Lubac, the Eucharist is the remedy for the sin of pride, which has shattered the image of a humanity created in the image of the triune God, meant to be "members of one another" (Eph 4:25) rather than in isolation (see de Lubac, *Catholicism*, 33). Herbert McCabe defines sin as "the disunity of people, their deep disunity" (McCabe, *God Matters*, 79).

134. McClendon, *Doctrine*, 145.

the bloodline of the redeemed. And here disciples, restored by that pledge, renew their own pledge to their Master and to one another."[135]

It is communal participation in the Supper that leads to true discipleship.[136] Since sin occurs not only when the individual but also when the community falls short of "the way," since sin "requires each generation to answer to Christ not for its ancestors' but for its own fault," it is the church as the body of Christ that is freed to follow Christ in the Supper.[137]

The Supper as a Powerful Practice

We have noted that McClendon calls the Supper a sign, and furthermore a remembering sign, and have thoroughly explained what McClendon means by these terms. And yet, in order to get at what he wants to emphasize in his account of the Supper, we must explore the rite itself not as a heady doctrine, but as something the church does, or "practices." Indeed, the term *powerful practice* is another description employed by McClendon to describe the Supper.[138] He uses this term in conjunction with the term *remembering signs*, which again are subsidiaries of the historic signs and are described by McClendon as "deliberately repetitive."[139] Understanding the repetitive nature of the remembering signs helps the reader better grasp the role played by the Supper and the other remembering signs in McClendon's work, but to say that the Supper is "repetitive" is not a sufficient account of McClendon's understanding of the Supper as a practice, for his use of this term is as complex and technical as his use of *sign*. Given that we have

---

135. Ibid., 142. McCabe follows Aquinas in saying, "we have the sacraments because of sin" (see McCabe, *God Matters*, 79).

136. McClendon, *Doctrine*, 145.

137. Ibid. I am reminded here of the corporate prayer of confession in the *Book of Common Prayer* and its "Holy Eucharist: Rite II," a prayer that eventually landed in the United Methodist Church's Book of Worship and other similar texts. It is currently recited weekly by tens of millions of Christians: "Most merciful God, *we* confess that *we* have sinned against you in thought, word, and deed, by what *we* have done, and by what *we* have left undone . . ." Here, corporate confession comes directly before the passing of the peace and the subsequent participation in the bread and wine—in continuity with Paul's statement to the church at Corinth that they should confess their sins before God and one another, so as not to partake of the Supper unworthily. In this way, too, the entirety of the liturgy is about bringing together the body of Christ. See the *Book of Common Prayer*, 360.

138. McClendon, "Practice of Community Formation," 94.

139. McClendon, *Doctrine*, 187.

heard McClendon call the Supper a practice that effects community formation, and that we also hear him call it a "powerful" practice, it is necessary at this point to unpack what is meant by the term *practice* in McClendon's work.

According to McClendon and Smith in both the earlier and later editions of *Convictions*, in order to understand what the church believes about God, one must examine and participate in the practices of the church. This claim about participation is not restricted to those wishing to understand the church and the claims of the church, but applies to any person who would endeavor to understand any community. Thus is the term *practices* defined and employed quite technically by McClendon, who appropriates a definition of practices inspired by Alasdair MacIntyre early on in the first volume of his *Systematic Theology*. For MacIntyre, a practice is "any coherent and complex form of socially established cooperative human activity through which goods internal to that form of activity are realized in the course of trying to achieve these standards of excellence which are appropriate to, and partially definitive of, that form of activity, with the result that human powers to achieve excellence, and human conceptions of the ends and goods involved, are systematically extended."[140]

Distinct in this definition of practices is their social nature. A practice such as the Lord's Supper, in the work of McClendon, is necessarily "socially established" and "cooperative." As Curtis Freeman notes, if we are guided by this definition, then the Lord's Supper is a practice "commended to the church, not individual Christians, for performance."[141] According to McClendon's framework, then, if he is consistent throughout his *Systematic Theology* in his use of the term *practice*, the Supper is necessarily social in his theology.[142]

Another important distinction to make about this definition employed by McClendon is to note that in the practice of something with others, one achieves goods internal to that practice in addition to other, seemingly

---

140. McClendon, *Ethics*, 23. Cf. MacIntyre, *After Virtue*, 187. MacIntyre's understanding of tradition was introduced in chapter 1.

141. Freeman, "'To Feed Upon by Faith,'" 202.

142. I say "if" because in *Ethics*, while McClendon goes directly from introducing a MacIntyrian notion of practices to an explication of the Supper and other practices of the church as "powerful practices," he suggests shortly thereafter that MacIntyre's notion that all human practices undergo "sequences of decline as well as progress" assumes that all practices are worthy in some sense and is therefore overly optimistic. Ultimately MacIntyre's account stands "in need of a biblical corrective" (McClendon, *Ethics*, 222).

more distant goals.¹⁴³ He notes that practices are not simply means to ends, since "not just any way of attaining these goals will do."¹⁴⁴ He therefore goes on to agree with MacIntyre that practices are worth pursuing in and of themselves. Participation in the practices of the church is necessary both for understanding the church's convictions and for becoming part of the body of the church. Reading the Scriptures, for example, and doing so in a community of believers also struggling daily through this reading and through other Christian practices, forms a people or "body" with particular beliefs and ends.¹⁴⁵ Similarly, Christians are formed by regular participation in the Supper. Indeed, this is part of what de Lubac means when he says that "the Eucharist makes the church."¹⁴⁶ It is not that de Lubac or those who follow him conceive of the Eucharist as, in McClendon's words, a "magical . . . liturgical conjure," but that participation in the eucharistic body of Christ, week after week, forms a body, a group of persons who not only *see themselves as* "members of one another," (Eph 4:25) but who *are* members of one another.¹⁴⁷

Thus for McClendon, Christian theology is inseparable from the Christian "way of life," which is constituted by Christian practices. This understanding of the relationship between theology and ethics is vitally rooted in McClendon's self-proclaimed link to the Radical Reformation, noted above. He traces his lineage as a radical Christian back to Menno Simons and aspires to write the way Menno wrote. McClendon admires the fact that in *Foundations of Christian Doctrine*, "Simons had so interwoven . . . moral theology and doctrinal theology, that the seam between the two cannot be found."¹⁴⁸ In McClendon's view, what the church *teaches* in fact directly influences what it calls persons and communities to *do*. The two are so bound together that the opposite is true as well: what the church does is also what it teaches. Thus can McClendon's title and subject matter be "ethics" in volume 1 of his *Systematic Theology*, and "doctrine" in volume 2, rather than "doctrine" in volume 1 leading to "ethics" in volume 2, since

---

143. Freeman, "'To Feed Upon by Faith,'" 202.

144. McClendon, *Ethics*, 173.

145. For example, worship (of which the "signs" are constitutive), witness, and work are listed as Christian practices by McClendon that are partially definitive of the church (see McClendon, *Doctrine*, 240–41).

146. De Lubac, *Corpus Mysticum*, 88.

147. Cavanaugh, *Torture and Eucharist*, 269.

148. McClendon, *Ethics*, 42.

for McClendon it is accurate to say that both of these layers of theology "have the same subject—the convictions of the community in relation to the triune God and to all else."[149]

There is historical precedent for placing "ethics" first, both within and outside the Christian tradition. According to MacIntyre, Aristotle thought that before he could teach his students the virtue of justice, he had to show them how to live justly through what he called friendship,[150] and McClendon undoubtedly knows of the Aristotelian influences upon the patristic figure Origen when he notes that Origen, a teacher in the Neoplatonic school, thought that "moral instruction necessarily took first place" when he trained his students at the "oldest seminary of them all."[151] McClendon describes Origen as the "greatest of ancient Bible scholars, literary critic, preacher, author of the oldest systematic theology on record," but one who, when given such students as future bishop Gregory Thaumaturgus and his siblings, "first made friends with these young men—and did it as if it were a valuable achievement on Origen's side to have such friends. Gregory felt himself a Jonathan embraced by this academic David. Then he followed the course of instruction."[152]

Understanding McClendon's notion of practices, set against the backdrop of his understanding of signs, helps us further understand the functions of the Supper in his work. In the section in which he develops the Supper into "a re-membering sign"[153] over against an individualistic Christianity, the Supper, as a "practice of the church," is by definition both deliberately repetitive and connected to the corporateness and unity of the church. Following MacIntyre, practices are therefore necessarily communal, and vitally linked—even as a guide—to the beliefs, convictions, and truth claims of the community. And for McClendon—as for de Lubac, Jenson, and a newer generation of sacramental theologians within Baptist circles—the church is a body that stands convicted that "we who are many are one body, for we all partake of the one loaf" (1 Cor 10:17).

---

149. Ibid., 43.
150. MacIntyre, *After Virtue*, 154–56.
151. McClendon, *Ethics*, 42.
152. Ibid., 41.
153. McClendon, *Doctrine*, 402.

The Supper as a Practice of Witness

In yet another description of the Supper in his work, in his *Witness* McClendon follows the late Mennonite theologian John Howard Yoder in describing "the eucharist" as one of five practices of Christian witness.[154] Yoder, who spoke of the Supper as a practice of witness in his *Body Politics* and in his essay "The New Humanity as Pulpit and Paradigm," in both of these texts likens humanity to a pulpit in order to express that, in a way similar to McClendon's "speech acts," all of human action proclaims something.[155] In participating in the five practices of witness that make up the pattern of a people called "the church"—(1) the rule of Christ (or conflict resolution or mediation), (2) the Lord's Supper, (3) baptism, (4) giving each member a role in the community, and (5) giving each member a voice in its meetings[156]—the body of Christ is not only given the Spirit and Christian habits, it also reveals "a model for how any society, not excluding the surrounding 'public' society, can also form its life more humanely."[157] In this way, Yoder says, the church is not simply "humanity," but a "new humanity."

As McClendon puts it, the new humanity is equipped with "practices that serve a double function: these were on the one hand of the essence of Christian obedience; they were on the other hand practices which could make sense to the world outside the Christian community. In other words, they were practices of *witness*."[158] The Eucharist is in this context an example of the "new humanity's" way of life. Quoting portions of Yoder throughout, McClendon says that "lost to sight in ecclesiastical struggles over what happens to bread and wine when certain words are said over them is that for New Testament disciples 'the *primary* meaning of the eucharistic gathering in the Gospels and Acts is economic.' The second practice, then, is *primeval socialism*, a commonwealth of possessions and their use. 'At the Lord's Table, those who have bread bring it, and all are fed.'"[159]

---

154. McClendon, *Witness*, 378. McClendon is quoting Yoder, "New Humanity as Pulpit and Paradigm," 44. Interestingly, McClendon refers to the rite exclusively as "the eucharist" in *Witness*, the third and most recently written volume of his systematic project.
155. Yoder, "New Humanity," 41.
156. Ibid., 44–46.
157. Ibid., 46.
158. McClendon, *Witness*, 379.
159. Ibid.

Re-membering the Body

As we move toward the next chapter, which addresses the sacramental theology of de Lubac, there are a few things to note about this quote from McClendon. First, as we shall soon see, de Lubac thought it very detrimental to the church's theology that the transubstantiation controversies had obscured some of the earlier emphases of the Eucharist. Namely, though he affirmed the doctrine of transubstantiation, he worried that in overemphasizing the doctrine against Berengar's heretical *mystici, non vere*, the church overshadowed the ancient idea that "the Eucharist makes the church."[160] In McClendon's work here, we can see some of the same concerns, though they are articulated differently. He does not hold to a doctrine of transubstantiation, but it is apparent from this and from earlier sections on the Supper that he is concerned that the ecumenical battles over "what happens to bread and wine" in the Supper have obscured the meaning of the rite for him.

This meaning, in fact, comes through in the second half of the quote. As shown earlier, unity is indeed for him part of the teaching of the Supper and therefore vitally linked to the Supper. If for McClendon the Supper is "a re-membering sign," the practice here re-constitutes the dismembered body in pointing to a particular way of life,[161] a way of life rooted not in competition for scarce goods but in sharing God's abundant gifts. Moreover, this sign, this pointing, is not only for the benefit of members of the body of Christ but for persons outside the body—it is practiced "'that the world may believe (John 17:21).'"[162] This sharing—both of the communion elements and of other goods—is rooted in the fact that, as McClendon has pointed out only a page earlier, to be Christian is to recognize that humanity was created in the image of the triune God who is in Himself perfect community.[163] None of the persons of the Trinity is a person but for the existence and reciprocity of the others. As a new humanity created in the image of this triune God—a God who is at the same time one being and three persons who are "members of one another"—Christians are called to be committed to living in solidarity with others.[164]

---

160. De Lubac, *Corpus Mysticum*, 162.

161. This way of life is, at least in *Doctrine* and *Witness*, rooted in the life of the Trinity, in "God's own unity." The Supper is illustrative of the requirements of unity more often than it is portrayed as the reason *for* unity. We will expand on this tension below through the work of Herbert McCabe.

162. McClendon, *Witness*, 378.

163. Ibid.

164. Stanley Hauerwas has pointed out (though not in relation to the Eucharist) that

Analysis of the Supper and Ecclesial Unity in McClendon's Theology

The Supper has more than one function, more than a single "point." Indeed, if one goal of this study is to show that while many have focused on the way in which the Supper not only pulls persons "godward" but also together as the body of Christ, already two of the Supper's seemingly innumerable functions have been illustrated. For McClendon another purpose of the Supper is to point to the great historic signs of the death, burial, and resurrection of Christ. This symbolic and pointing role of the Supper permeates the Christian tradition—long before Baptists, Augustine perhaps came closest to providing an exhaustive account of the symbolism in the Supper. Many have argued, however, that as a result of the free churches' emphasis on symbolism in reaction to abuses of the sacraments, "symbol became emphasized over against reality, and the practice itself atrophied."[165]

Another way to describe the Supper, as McClendon notes through Yoder, is to call it a "practice" and in so doing to emphasize its repetitive and social character. McClendon designates the Supper a "practice of witness" in volume 3 of *Systematic Theology*, where he draws upon Yoder to claim that the Supper is primarily a witness about a truly Christian economics.[166] As noted above, McClendon also claims that as a practice of witness the Supper is not only a practice but a "powerful practice," and in yet two more places he says that the Supper is one of two subpractices that are about "establishing and maintaining Christian community."[167]

---

because Christians recognize that they have been created by, and in the image of, this triune God, members of the body of Christ "ought (not) to view our bodies *as if* we were one with one another through Christ, but rather that our bodies are quite literally not our 'own' because we have been made (as well as given) a new body by the Spirit" (Hauerwas, "What Could It Mean for the Church to Be Christ's Body?" 24). Many Christian thinkers have claimed that due to the fact of creation as described in the Genesis narratives, and because we were created in the image of the Trinity, no part of the material realm—including humanity—is truly "ours" to do with what we want (see again Hauerwas, "What Could It Mean for the Church to Be Christ's Body?" 24).

165. Newman, "Lord's Supper," 219.

166. Geoffrey Wainwright's point is very similar when he says that "the eucharist provides enabling paradigms for our ethical engagement in the world: the eucharist allows us to learn, absorb, and extend the values of God's kingdom" (see Wainwright, "Eucharist and/as Ethics").

167. McClendon, "Practice of Community Formation," 85. The other "subpractice" is baptism.

Re-membering the Body

Thus does McClendon do with the practice of the Supper what the greatest theologians of the Christian tradition have done with other practices of the church—he acknowledges that it is crucial in a number of ways to persons in a number of contexts. The Supper, he says, as a practice so ancient and so powerful, "*should* have drawn to itself various meanings and purposes."[168] McClendon believes of practices—and of texts and doctrines, too—that these are not to have only one meaning, or only one sense in which they are true in order to help constitute a larger, true whole.[169] Thus can he say in summary that "the meal is about *forgiveness* ('blood shed for forgiveness of sins'); it is a meal about *solidarity* with Christ and with one another ('my body'); it is a *thanksgiving meal* ('giving thanks, he broke it'); it is a future-regarding or *eschatological* meal ('until he comes')."[170]

From a Baptist perspective, McClendon elevates the Supper to a more central position in the life of the church, partially because it has so many layers of meaning. I argue in the pages that follow, however, that after both great hindsight and foresight had allowed McClendon to name the Lord's Supper as one of the three "remembering signs" that reconstitute the church, his understanding of this practice lacks a few crucial components. Among the problems in his work on the Supper are the ways in which his account of presence meshes with the unity of the body effected by the Supper.

McClendon's Account of Presence

In McClendon's work the sense of Christ's presence in the Supper is ambiguous. To review, McClendon says that Christ is present in the Supper "in some sense,"[171] "in a way that matters,"[172] and "in such a way that *the story*

---

168. McClendon, *Ethics*, 218. Emphasis mine.

169. Stiver, *Philosophy of Religious Language*, 155. Stiver notes that saying that a text or act can have only one meaning would, in McClendon's view, subject theology to an alien perspective, to a humanly constructed epistemology.

170. McClendon, *Doctrine*, 401. Cf. McClendon, *Ethics*, 220–21, where McClendon says not only that "the point of the meal is solidarity," but that there are "two further elements of its significance." The first is "its thrust into the future" and the second is "the eucharistic or thanksgiving note." Is it telling that *Ethics*' section on the Eucharist has six paragraphs on solidarity and only one paragraph on the eschatological and eucharistic aspects?

171. McClendon, *Biography as Theology*, 77.

172. McClendon, *Doctrine*, 378.

continues."¹⁷³ Ultimately, for him "Jesus' 'real' presence is not limited to the eucharist (far less to its food and drink), but from the earliest Christian beginnings has meant a renewal of the sort of Presence that the disciples knew during the forty days."¹⁷⁴

The first claim, that Christ is present "in some sense," is not employed by McClendon when he is attempting to describe his own eucharistic theology in detail. Rather, he typically uses this description of presence when differentiating between the Catholic understanding and various Protestant understandings. McClendon claims that for most Protestants, Christ is present "in some sense" at the Eucharist.¹⁷⁵

Of the second description of Christ's presence—that Christ is present "in a way that matters"—one might ask (1) whether Christ's presence does not always "matter" for McClendon, and also (2) whether this presence is any different from God's omnipresence. I will answer the second question first. McClendon does indeed seem to privilege corporate gatherings in *Doctrine*, emphasizing that in worship Christ is "with *us* as a present friend,"¹⁷⁶ that "he promises his presence 'where two or three are gathered' in his name,"¹⁷⁷ and that "authentic church can be two of us, with him the third."¹⁷⁸ McClendon's emphasis here reconfirms what has been said previously, that for McClendon Christians are "called not into a solitary following, but into a *body*, the church."¹⁷⁹ This means that membership in the body of Christ is intrinsic to the Christian faith and practice. He therefore almost always refers to corporate gatherings when talking about Christ's presence.¹⁸⁰ This is, I believe, substantially related to the church's practice of the Eucharist.

---

173. Ibid.

174. Ibid.

175. McClendon, *Biography as Theology*, 77. Again, in McClendon's ecclesiological typology, Baptists are not Protestants in the strictest sense.

176. McClendon, *Doctrine*, 376. Emphasis mine.

177. Ibid., 377.

178. Ibid., 378.

179. Ibid., 132.

180. This is not to the exclusion of Christ's presence in times of individual devotion. See again McClendon's "providential signs," which are "instances of the distinctive guidance God gives to individual lives for designated tasks." It seems that these signs usually occur in community with other persons, but not always (see McClendon, *Doctrine*, 382–83).

McClendon's qualifier, however—that "Jesus' 'real' presence is not limited to the eucharist"—is indicative of his overarching refusal to privilege the Eucharist above other churchly practices. We shall see in the next chapter how this refusal stands in contrast to de Lubac's view that this is a sacrament that is the very heart of the church.[181] For now, we must say that McClendon's affirmation of "Jesus' 'real' presence" in other circumstances is by no means heretical; but as Dom Gregory Dix notes, one possible consequence of McClendon's approach to the Supper is that "the eucharist simply duplicates the function of non-eucharistic worship."[182] Dix's remark, meant as a criticism of what he describes as "Protestant" views of the Eucharist, is applicable to McClendon's "baptist" view as well. McClendon's view of Christ's presence stands in contrast to the Catholic tradition in which Christ's body is not only present in the church ("the body of Christ"), but in the elements themselves, the body around which the gathered church congregates. The Eucharist, again, is the very "heart of the church," according to de Lubac, and the link between the gathered body and the eucharistic body is strong.[183] To emphasize just how sharp the contrast is between the traditions of McClendon and de Lubac, let us recall for a moment the claim that from a Baptist perspective, McClendon elevates the Supper to a *more* central position in the life of the church. Now, contrast this with a statement made by Catholic theologian Herbert McCabe—yet another contemporary of McClendon, de Lubac, and Jenson—who said that any Catholic should avoid the "extreme" view which says "that Christ is present in the Eucharist is not to say that the food and drink are in themselves any different from other food and drink, it is to speak of the role which they play in a particular religious ceremony."[184] McClendon's account, however large a step into the larger Christian tradition for Baptists, still represents an "extreme" view to Catholics, according to McCabe. Indeed, this English Dominican does not even mention the "sub-Zwinglian" view wherein the bread and wine are "mere symbols" of Christ's presence.

McClendon's third description, that in the Supper Christ is present "in such a way that the story continues," is clearly linked to McClendon's understanding that the Eucharist is a practice of witness. Through the

---

181. De Lubac, *Splendor*, 77.

182. Dix, *Shape of the Liturgy*, 601. Dix is also occasionally cited by de Lubac and Jenson.

183. De Lubac, *Splendor*, 72. Cf. McCabe, *God Matters*, 116.

184. McCabe, *God Matters*, 116.

remembering signs, "the Spirit works in worship not only to bring forth exalted and memorable ritual (God's catholic gift?), and not only to inspire prophetic witness (God's protestant gift?), but also to bring forth a people taught by the Spirit to recognize God's authentic voice, a people skilled to reenact the 'old, old story' of the kingly priesthood of Christ."[185] For McClendon, the "old, old story" is that Jesus, against the backdrop of Israel and her covenant with God to be "a nation of priests,"[186] came to be a priest for all, proclaiming the good news through word and deed and sacrificing himself for the sins of humanity. This story, the story of Israel and Christ and covenant and redemption, is re-narrated in the Supper. It is also re-narrated by the people who are re-membered by the Supper, or better, by God's action in the Supper. Note that for McClendon, part of the narrative of covenant and redemption includes the sharing of all things among Christians, who have an important responsibility in managing the earth, money, and other possessions of which they are stewards. Indeed, if for McClendon, with Yoder, "'the *primary* meaning of the eucharistic gathering in the Gospels and Acts is economic,'"[187] and the Eucharist is also a sign that reconstitutes the body of Christ in the Pauline Epistles, then in the Supper the church re-narrates again and again the story that as members of Christ's body Christians are one with one another, and that this oneness extends to economic behavior as well. "Because members are one with one another," the Supper says in pointing to the unity of the church, "their food and other material goods are to be shared." This is true of first-century Christians and twenty-first-century Christians alike, according to McClendon's baptist vision. The biblical story of the economics of the first-century church is the story of our economics, because "the remembering signs connect that great narrative to this or that believer or believing community now."[188]

---

185. McClendon, *Doctrine*, 381, citing Yoder, *Priestly Kingdom*. I will argue in the final chapter that the notion "exalted and memorable ritual" is not a uniquely "catholic" gift, and more forcefully in the third chapter that for de Lubac, it is Catholic theology that chiefly inspires "prophetic witness," since for him the Eucharist makes, or produces, the church, the presence of Christ for the world. See de Lubac, *Corpus Mysticum*, 88.

186. Ibid., 368.

187. McClendon, *Witness*, 379.

188. McClendon, *Doctrine*, 382.

Re-membering the Body

Herbert McCabe and "Signs Of" versus "Signs For"

In order to shed some light upon my assertion in the paragraph above that the Supper points to the already existing unity of the church, the work of Herbert McCabe should be consulted at this point. McCabe, a Catholic theologian who like McClendon worked in the twentieth century and gleaned a great deal of insight from the philosophical work of Ludwig Wittgenstein, points out that "the most important effect of Wittgenstein on sacramental theology was to shift us from speaking of 'signs *of*' to speaking of 'signs *for*.'"[189] An example of "signs *of*" language in everyday life, McCabe says, is the phrase "a red sky at night is a sign of good weather," wherein the color of the sky points primarily to something else (good weather).[190] Simply put, "the essence of the 'signs *of*' position is that the meaning of a sign is to be found somewhere *else*, a sign stands for something and stands in for something."[191]

This is the way in which McClendon typically employs the term *sign* when he speaks of the church's remembering signs. The Lord's Supper, baptism, and proclamation recall for the church the great historic signs of the New Testament—the Last Supper, Christ's death, Christ's burial, the resurrection, and Pentecost.[192] The church is brought together to remember these events through the remembering signs, which are "signs *of*," pointers to, these great events. The remembering signs also function to remind believers of the great truths of the faith. In the section above, where we see that McClendon believes (with Yoder) that "the *primary* meaning of the Supper" is economic sharing and it is therefore a practice that reinforces primitive socialism, the Supper is a "sign *of*" Christian unity—it does not itself effect the unity of the body but points to the economic sharing that ought to take place because of a previously instantiated unity.

We can contrast this understanding of signs with the second way in which signs function for McCabe—as a "sign *for*" something. McCabe points out that according to Wittgenstein, "when we ask for the meaning of a word or other sign we are not asking 'what is it instead of,' what is the extra thing that it stands for? We are asking 'what is it for'? How do we use

---

189. McCabe, *God Matters*, 165. The reader will see below that Aquinas is also important for McCabe's understanding of signs.

190. Ibid.

191. Ibid., 166.

192. McClendon, *Doctrine*, 382.

it?"[193] He then notes that this is the way in which sacramental language functions for the church. Sacraments are signs that are employed by God in order to do something; they are instruments used *for* a particular purpose.

McCabe, a self-described Thomist, points out that for Aquinas the sacraments are in some sense *instrumenta*, comparable on a human level to the saw, for example. The saw, a tool that might serve little or no purpose in the hands of certain persons, can be used by a skilled carpenter to make a beautiful piece of furniture.[194] In the carpenter's hands, that is, it becomes an effective instrument used for the purpose of furniture-making. Similarly, for McCabe the eucharistic bread and wine function in the church as a powerful instrument *for* unity. The church's conception of Christian unity—based on Paul's belief that "we who are many are one body for we partake of the one loaf" (1 Cor 10:17)—is rooted in divine communication through signs.[195] The bread in this instance is not solely a sign *of*, a pointer to, the church's unity (though it may do that as well); it is a sign *for* unity in that it communicates God Himself and creates the unity of the body of Christ.[196] As Dix notes of the tradition's readings of 1 Corinthians 10, "there is a curious 'reversibility' about this idea as it appears in the Fathers. . . . Sometimes, as in St. Augustine, the church is the Body of Christ *because* it receives the sacrament which is His Body."[197] As I shall argue in the next chapter, this is the point that de Lubac will emphasize through his retrieval of the patristic literature.

Sacraments, then, are "a kind of instrument, though a very odd kind of instrument" (since it is primarily God who employs them).[198] They serve the double function of pointing to and actually effecting something other than themselves. These signs are divine and human for Aquinas as well, precisely "because they are signs they belong to the cultural, linguistic, social, characteristically human level of existence. They are divine, however, in his view, because God uses these signs instrumentally as his language, to communicate with us, to communicate himself to us. To say these signs are

---

193. McCabe, *God Matters*, 166.
194. Ibid.
195. Ibid., 87.
196. Ibid., 169, 171.
197. Dix, *Shape of the Liturgy*, 251.
198. McCabe, *God Matters*, 167.

divine signs just is to say that there is a level of meaning in them at which they communicate divinity."[199]

In his best moments, McClendon is similarly aware that speaking of signs as belonging to the church alone poses difficulties. As stated above, in *Convictions* and in *Doctrine* he briefly acknowledges that analyzing the "signs" or "sign-acts" of the church is not the same as analyzing the signs of any other community, since the signs or sign-acts of the church are the acts not only of humans but also of God.[200] Indeed, his claim that in the Supper "the deacons feed the flock and Christ *eo ipso* feeds the flock"[201] conveys that he differs from his teacher (Conner) and his teacher's teacher (Mullins) in that he has a higher estimation not only of the Supper, but also of the church's role in salvation.[202] When fed by the Christ and his ecclesial body in this way, one receives "as ration the sign of God's faithfulness."[203] The church is, in this vision, a gathering of recipients who come to hear God pledge his faithfulness in the Supper, but according to McClendon's concept of "double agency," here "human action and divine action converge,"[204] and together Christ and his ministers nourish the faithful.

It is critical to reinforce at this point (though it will be addressed in greater detail in the final chapter of this work) McClendon's brief mention of "double agency" since occasionally in his work on the "signs" God seems to disappear as one of the actors. When he notes, for example, that in the sign of the Supper "disciples . . . renew their own pledge to their Master and to one another,"[205] it can seem as though the gathered disciples are the ones performing the act of renewing the body, that they are the ones making the pledge (which, according to McClendon, is the best meaning of the term

---

199. Ibid., 171.

200. McClendon, *Doctrine*, 389.

201. Ibid.

202. McClendon's *eo ipso* ("by that very fact") seems to imply that he would follow de Lubac and Jenson, who, as we shall see in the next two chapters, would claim in concert with Augustine that the historical body of Jesus and the ecclesial body *together* constitute the *totus Christus*, the whole Christ. As Augustine said, "*Verbum caro factum est, et habitavit in nobis; illi carni adjungitur ecclesia, et fit Christus totus, caput et corpus*" ("the Word was made flesh, and dwelled among us; to that flesh is joined the church, and there is made the whole Christ, head and body"). Augustine, *On the Epistle of John* 1.2; cf. *Sermons* 341.1.1 and 9.1.

203. McClendon, *Doctrine*, 142.

204. Ibid., 389.

205. Ibid., 142. McCabe follows Aquinas in saying "we have the sacraments because of sin" (McCabe, *God Matters*, 79).

sacrament).²⁰⁶ In the end, it is important to recall that ultimately God is the being who is making use of the *instrumenta*, the bread and the wine.

McClendon notes of signs in chapter 4 of *Doctrine* that these are "divine actions within creation in which the presence of God shines forth in power for (creative, and especially) redemptive ends,"²⁰⁷ and then gives this brief line a great deal of weight when in chapter 9, the primary section on the remembering signs, he says that in dealing with the signs we must recall the concept of "double agency" from chapter 4.²⁰⁸ Critics might ask here whether McClendon's brief mention of double agency is sufficient. Though his is the very tradition so often accused by Baptists of trusting in the practices of humankind for salvation, Thomas Aquinas went to great lengths to emphasize that God is always the principal actor in the sacrament, and that the minister and elements are always secondary actors, or instrumental "causes" of grace. For Thomas "the instrumental cause works not by the power of its own form, but only by the motion whereby it is moved by the principal agent: so that the effect is not likened to the instrument but to the principal agent . . . it is thus that the sacraments cause grace: for they are instituted by God to be employed for the purpose of conferring grace."²⁰⁹

Christ's Presence and the Unity of the Church

McClendon's treatment of the Supper, then, is that it is preeminently a "sign *of*" God's presence and the unity of the church. He claims that this is a rite in which Christ is present in a significant way and in which participants are pointed godward and toward one another through gathering around and partaking of the communion elements. At times, it is clear that God has made these elements "effectual" in their bringing about such a gathering,²¹⁰ but more often the emphasis is placed upon the causative action of the congregation. Still, it is helpful to contrast his view with Mullins' purely symbolic understanding,²¹¹ which, when combined with an emphasis on the primacy of the individual and the identification of "soul competency"

---

206. McClendon, *Doctrine*, 388.
207. Ibid., 186.
208. Ibid., 389.
209. Aquinas, *Summa Theologiae*, III.62.1.
210. McClendon, *Doctrine*, 382.
211. Mullins, *Axioms of Religion*, 543.

as Baptists' primary contribution to religious history, meant that he never linked the unity of the church with the Supper.[212]

One of McClendon's great contributions to free church theology is that the church *must* be a unified body in order to hold fast to her convictions in a world often hostile to Christian convictions, and that the Supper, as a re-membering sign, helps effect this unity, or, in most instances in his thought, reminds Christians of this unity. The difficult vocation to which all Christians are called—that is, to have and to live out their "gutsy" convictions[213]—means for McClendon that individual Christians must be empowered by the Spirit as members of a *body*; for him, to be a Christian in solitude is an impossibility. In his work on the Decalogue, for example, it is the church that is there to ensure that its members live up to the radical expectations of the people called "the way." He calls this practice "watch-care,"[214] and such care is impossible without the support of a community with commonly held convictions and practices. For McClendon, the body of Christ, which is strengthened by and defined by the practice of the re-membering signs, is uniquely equipped for this care. Again, however, we must note that when understanding the Supper as a sign *for*, as an instrument, it is most often ambiguous whether it is God or humanity who is the essential actor. Is it the church that receives the Supper as "ration" and is "reconstituted" by it, or the church that through the Supper proclaims a certain economic model to the world?[215]

Conclusion

There is, of course, the question of emphasis at play in evaluating McClendon's understanding of the Supper and its relationship to the church's unity. We have repeated the claim that this "intrinsic church" is for McClendon

---

212. Ibid., 45–58. I am indebted to Barry Harvey for pointing out that since McClendon's teacher, W. T. Conner, was taught by Mullins, and we have outlined aspects of the eucharistic theologies of Mullins, Conner, and (in much greater detail) McClendon, we can see in this chapter that in two generations of Baptist theologians we have moved from a purely symbolic and individualist interpretation of the Supper to one that acknowledges Christ's presence and emphasizes the corporate nature of the rite. As we shall see in chapter 5, this is perhaps a natural progression toward the sacramental views of those influenced by McClendon.

213. McClendon, *Ethics*, 31.

214. Ibid., 7, 49.

215. McClendon, *Doctrine* 142, 402; McClendon, *Witness*, 379.

reconstituted by the practice of the Supper.²¹⁶ Yet, in a *Systematic Theology* exceeding twelve hundred pages, McClendon limits his work on ecclesial unity rooted in the Supper to only a few paragraphs in *Ethics* and *Doctrine*. Furthermore, though one could argue that the relatively few sentences on "the eucharist" in *Witness* must be read in light of the passages in *Ethics* and *Doctrine*, McClendon's treatment of the Supper there is thinnest of all.²¹⁷ While others have adopted McClendon's use of the Supper as "a re-membering sign" in order to emphasize a vital connection between the Supper and the unity of the church,²¹⁸ McClendon himself never nails down the relationship between the Supper and the church's unity in his ecclesiology. He never refers to the Supper as a "sacrament" in his major works, using the term only when surveying the decisions of church councils, presenting the position of another theologian, or engaging the Catholic Church's appropriation of sacramental language.²¹⁹ It is possible that this is a strategic or pastoral decision by McClendon, since he does note that "there can be but small objection to the language of mystery and sacrament, provided the original sense is retained,"²²⁰ but one must (*a*) wonder what McClendon thinks the "small objection" would be, and (*b*) note that a "small objection" is an objection nonetheless. It should also be noted that he says in two places that in the Supper we have "a rite, not magical nor even (in many

---

216. Ibid., 402.

217. It should be noted that in *Witness*, his final major work, McClendon refers to the rite solely as "eucharist." The Eucharist, however, is only mentioned on three occasions.

218. Harvey, for example, adopts the term *re-membered* in his *Can These Bones Live?* and in an article for the *Baptist Sacramentalism* volume titled "Remembering the Body: Baptism, Eucharist, and the Politics of Disestablishment," but clearly and consistently uses "sign *for*" language. For Harvey, largely through its own fault the church has been "dismembered" in part by the state, which, in exchange for religious toleration, reduced the role of religion to caring for "souls" while claiming the bodies of persons for the purposes of the state (Harvey, "Re-membering the Body," 96–97). As we shall see in the final chapter, Elizabeth Newman, while using different terminology, recognizes a deep connection between acknowledging "some sense of a real presence" and the unity of the church (Newman, "Might Baptists Accept a Theory of the Real Presence?" 217). Newman—and Harvey, for that matter—knew McClendon well and, as we shall see, coauthored a controversial document with him in which (among other things) the preeminent Baptist understanding of the Eucharist was examined and criticized.

219. For McClendon's examples of others using the term *sacrament*, see McClendon, *Biography as Theology*, 77; McClendon, *Ethics* 35, 55, 58, 266; McClendon, *Doctrine*, 113, 339, 386; McClendon, *Witness*, 346.

220. His understanding of this "original sense" is that "in Latin lands, a *sacramentum* was a pledge or sacred promise" (McClendon, *Doctrine*, 388).

usual senses of the term) 'sacramental'—but moral and ethical first of all; that is, aimed at the shaping of the common life of Christian community."[221]

On the other hand, it is possible that as his career progressed, McClendon came to what we might call a more "Catholic" understanding of this important practice. For example, he refers to the rite exclusively as "the eucharist" in the final volume of his *Systematic Theology*, and though he co-edited it with others, his *Baptist Roots* volume retrieves sources affirming a weekly observance of the rite. There, in addition to Grantham, McClendon also retrieves the work of Benedictine-turned-Anabaptist Michael Sattler, who deeply influenced the Schleitheim Confession. Sattler believed that "the Lord's Supper shall be held, as often as the brothers meet."[222]

Finally, as we shall explain more fully in the final chapter, late in his career a mature McClendon attaches his name to a document penned by Baptists who not only call for a more frequent observance, but who employ 1 Cor 10 in order to say that "the bread is a sign of Christ's body and the cup is a sign of the new covenant in his blood. As we remember Jesus in communion through the bread of fellowship and the cup of life, the Lord himself is with us declaring that we who are many are one body. In the Lord's Supper the Spirit thus signifies and seals the covenant that makes us one with Christ and one with one another."[223]

Since at least the second century—and according to a particular understanding of Acts 2:42 and Acts 20:7, perhaps since the first century—the church has typically participated in the eucharistic meal when meeting for worship.[224] To use McClendon's language from *Convictions*, the Eucharist has historically been a regular speech act of the Christian community and therefore partially definitive of that community. The church is the community that *characteristically* participates in the Eucharist. Moreover, according to McClendon (and contrary to popular belief), the earliest of the free churches also participated in the Supper on a weekly basis.[225]

---

221. See McClendon, *Ethics*, 219–20. Cf. "Practice of Community Formation," 86–87. Again, in the note directly above, McClendon notes elsewhere that in the ancients, the word *sacramentum* means "pledge."

222. Sattler, "On Congregational Order," 49.

223. Broadway et al., "Re-Envisioning Baptist Identity," 220.

224. Chadwick, *Early Church*, 32, 261.

225. He attempts to show this in the free church theologians he chooses to retrieve and publish in his *Baptist Roots* (see again Grantham, *Christianismus Primitivus*, 98–108; Sattler, "On Congregational Order," 49).

If weekly participation in the Eucharist is one of the things that makes the church the church, then we might ask for McClendon, with Calvin and Luther, whether a community that does not regularly practice the Eucharist belongs to the body of Christ.[226] Put another way (to return to the language of convictions introduced in chapter 1): if to understand the convictions of a community one must understand the speech acts or sign-acts of that community,[227] and the Eucharist is uniquely a sign-act of the church, then the Eucharist must be a regular practice of the church.

After a career of emphasizing the organic character of Christian theology and Christian action, McClendon in his very latest work seemed to be moving toward a theology that grasped the importance of the Eucharist and the unity effected by the practice. It should come as no surprise, then, that as interim pastor of a divided Baptist church in California, McClendon urged the congregation to move from quarterly observance of this practice to monthly observance.[228] Without a doubt, McClendon believed that the church bound together is not an unfree church, but rather the opposite—hence his use of *imago Dei* as a source for the unity of the church.[229] The biblical and Christian narratives' insistence that humans are "created in the image of God" means for McClendon not that each individual is ultimately autonomous, but that humanity is created in the image of the triune God, the mutually indwelling *hypostases*. Humans are made for communion with one another.

As the reader will see in the next chapter, the sacramental theology of Henri de Lubac emphasizes that the symbolism of the unity of the church and the unity actually present due to the rite of the Eucharist must be held together.[230] De Lubac will also say that the social aspect of the Supper has too often been overlooked. Catholic teachings about what "happens" to the elements in the Supper are true but have been emphasized at the expense of the social aspect of the Supper, which is again for him "the heart of the church." It would seem that McClendon cannot agree with the very last of these claims, especially since, in line with other baptists, preach-

226. "The church is wherever the gospel is preached and the sacraments duly administered" (Calvin, *Institutes of the Christian Religion*, IV.27.44).

227. McClendon, *Convictions*, 106.

228. See McClendon, *Making Gospel Sense to a Troubled Church*, xix.

229. McClendon, *Doctrine*, 448. See also *Witness*, 378.

230. De Lubac, *Corpus Mysticum*, 171. As the next chapter will show, de Lubac emphasizes that the latter is the most important aspect, that the Eucharist, as a sacrament, produces the church's unity.

ing has assumed a "sacramental" role in McClendon's theology as the more frequently enacted remembering sign. The Supper is not the heart of the church for McClendon, though for him it is truly one of the signs of the church's salvation. If for de Lubac the church, through the Supper, is made an extension of Christ in time, for McClendon the Supper at the very least extends the church's story into time, and at the very best it reconstitutes the local church.

3

Henri de Lubac

The Eucharist Makes the Church

Introduction

THUS FAR I HAVE argued that James McClendon's understanding of the Supper as "a re-membering sign" of the Church is particularly groundbreaking among Baptist theologians living and working in North America in the latter half of the twentieth century. He believes that in the Supper, Christians are drawn not only godward but together as the body of Christ. While "something happens" in the sign of the Eucharist, however, McClendon stops short of calling the rite "sacramental."[1]

As I noted in chapter 2, in making the claim that "something happens" in the Supper, McClendon can appear to be something of a "radical" from the perspective of most Baptists, even if he stops short of using the language of sacrament. Since I argued through Herbert McCabe in the last section of that chapter, however, that from the perspective of truly sacramental theologies McClendon's view remains an extreme one in the opposite sense, in order to provide the reader with an example of a truly sacramental theology and a corrective to McClendon, the thought of Catholic theologian Henri de Lubac will be introduced here. A contemporary of McClendon, de Lubac will make for a fine interlocutor not only because he and McClendon lived and worked in the same era and because the Catholic tradition in which he

---

1. Again, for McClendon the Supper "is a rite, not magical nor even (in many usual senses of the term) 'sacramental'—but moral and ethical first of all; a rite aimed at the shaping of the common life of Christian community" (see McClendon, *Ethics*, 219; McClendon, "Practice of Community Formation," 86–87).

participated has traditionally been held in contrast to McClendon's "baptist" tradition,[2] but ultimately because (1) for de Lubac the Eucharist is a sacrament—which means for him that it "represents [Christ], in the full and ancient meaning of the term; it really makes him present,"[3] and (2) for de Lubac the Eucharist is the very heart of the Church,[4] while for McClendon it is one of three signs (of seemingly equal centrality) through which the Church is gathered.[5] De Lubac's work, I will argue, indicates precisely what is at stake in having a sacramental understanding of the Eucharist, and importantly, his sacramentalism is rooted in a close reading of Scripture and the Christian tradition.

In line with others before him, de Lubac takes the idea of the Eucharist as a sign that, as McClendon says, "reconstitutes the church," and yet he extends this to say that it is the Eucharist—and in a sense the Eucharist *alone*—that "*makes* the Church."[6] While this might sound extreme to Protestant and Baptist ears—even to those who will concede to McClendon that in the Supper we have one of the Church's three remembering (and re-membering) signs—in this chapter I will argue that de Lubac comes to this conclusion in part because his Catholic ecclesiology better takes advantage of the early tradition's vast array of resources, an early tradition that emphasized that the Eucharist effects the unity necessary for living the radically Christian existence for which McClendon calls. The Eucharist, as de Lubac argues through a careful reading of Scripture and a wide array of figures from the Christian tradition, is historically crucial not only for understanding, but indeed for effecting, the unity of the ecclesial body of Christ.[7] Just as we explored McClendon's understanding of the Eucharist

---

2. Again, according to McClendon himself, Catholic, Protestant, and "baptist" ecclesiologies represent three different ecclesiological "types" (McClendon, *Doctrine*, 341).

3. De Lubac, *Catholicism*, 76.

4. De Lubac, *Splendor*, 74. The *Catechism of the Catholic Church* claims that, even among the sacraments, "the mode of Christ's presence under the Eucharistic species is unique. It raises the Eucharist above all the other sacraments" (*Catechism of the Catholic Church*, 1374).

5. McClendon, *Doctrine*, 402. The other two are baptism and preaching.

6. De Lubac, *Corpus Mysticum*, 88. Again, for McClendon, baptism, proclamation, and the Supper stand on equal footing as the remembering signs—with the Lord's Supper certainly practiced less frequently than the other two—while for de Lubac the Eucharist is the very heart of the Church, unique in the way it makes Christ present, and is practiced weekly (De Lubac, *Splendor*, 74).

7. As I will show in the following section, like McClendon, de Lubac frequently employs biblical exegesis in his theological works. This is yet another reason these two

through the lenses of the New Testament authors, so also shall we read the New Testament with de Lubac.

Scripture, Tradition, and Eucharist in de Lubac's Sacramental Theology

In his *Corpus Mysticum*, de Lubac provides the reader with a very focused study of the history of two words—*corpus* (body) and *mysticum* (mystical)—and shows in this, his second major work, how the evolution of only two terms has major implications for ecclesiology.[8] This is a classic example of the way in which de Lubac examines the Christian tradition and the various uses of terminology within the Church's discourse. Part of a movement described by many as the *nouvelle theologie*,[9] de Lubac was one of a handful of twentieth-century theologians, most of whom were both French and Catholic, who saw that in a period in which the Church was coming under attack both as an institution and as an idea, "the renewal of Christian vitality is linked at least partially to a renewed exploration of the periods and of the works where the Christian tradition is expressed with a particular intensity."[10] Thus, while it is important to note that he vigorously disputed both the notion that what he was doing was "new" and that persons who were (derisively) labeled the *nouvelle theologie* were a tightly organized

---

thinkers make for good conversation partners.

8. De Lubac, *Corpus Mysticum*, xix.

9. Sources conflict as to when the term was coined and who coined the term, but all agree that the label *nouvelle theologie* was derisive in its original context. Hans Urs von Balthasar, an influential historian who was both student and close friend of de Lubac, says that the Dominican "Father Garrigou-Lagrange spearheaded the catchword 'Nouvelle theologie' (1946) against de Lubac and friends, the Pope picked it up, at first with hesitation; *L'Osservatore Romano* repeated it" (von Balthasar, *Theology of Henri de Lubac*, 17). Marcellino D'Ambrosio, however, claims that "the term was actually coined by Msgr. Pietro Parente in his 1942 *L'Osservatore Romano* article attacking M. D. Chenu, O.P. and Louis Charlier, O.P. of Saulchoir," two theologians often grouped with de Lubac as *ressourcement* theologians (D'Ambrosio, "Ressourcement Theology, Aggiornamento, and the Hermeneutics of Tradition," 530–55). Opponents of these theologians charged that the movement was anti-Thomist because it sought to correct, in part, what A. N. Williams calls "a monolithic neo-Thomism which had become as remote from contemporary concerns and the needs of the twentieth-century church as it was arguably distant from the spirit of Thomas himself." Thus, these thinkers, some of whom were Jesuits but two of whom were Dominicans, set out to retrieve and interpret anew a variety of patristic and medieval sources (see Williams, "Future of the Past, 349).

10. De Lubac, *Mémoire*, 94.

movement, their return to other particularly vital periods in the Christian tradition in order to inspire their work was a common and revolutionary theme in twentieth-century theology. As Marcellino d'Ambrosio puts it, de Lubac and others believed "that 1) theology had to speak to the Church's present situation and that 2) the key to theology's relevance to the present lay in the creative recovery of its past."[11] It is with good reason, then, that others, not so derisively, have labeled the methods of de Lubac and others "*ressourcement* theology"[12]—that is, a method of doing theology that is "a creative hermeneutical exercise in which the 'sources' of the Christian faith were 'reinterrogated' with new questions, the burning questions of a century in travail."[13] This cadre of thinkers called "*ressourcement*" theologians or articulators of the *nouvelle theologie*—however close or distant they were personally—worked together in beginning the production of a massive collection of works called *Sources chrétiennes*, an ongoing series of patristic translations with commentary that are gathered together based largely upon the assumption that in order for the Church and theology to speak effectively to the concerns of the twentieth century, the Church and its teachers must draw upon their own vital, living tradition.[14]

It is crucial for de Lubac, then, that the Eucharist's vital link to the unity of the Church is firmly rooted in the Christian tradition. He and other *ressourcement* theologians also repeatedly make the point, however, that if concepts are rooted in and permeate the earliest works in the Church's history, then they are almost always rooted in Scripture. This is an important point for Baptist readers who would investigate de Lubac's sacramental theology (especially Baptists who follow McClendon when he claims that the Bible is "uniquely fit" to be "the doctrinal manual of the church"[15]): de Lubac's understanding of the patristic tradition is that the Fathers were interpreting Scripture when doing theology.[16] Though it is often

11. D'Ambrosio, "Ressourcement Theology, Aggiornamento, and the Hermeneutics of Tradition," 532.

12. Ibid.

13. Ibid.

14. For an explanation of the background behind the launching of this series, see Daley, "*Nouvelle Théologie* and the Patristic Revival," 362–82.

15. McClendon, *Doctrine*, 45.

16. De Lubac, *Splendor*, 11–12. It should be noted that de Lubac's reading of the Christian tradition is not uncritical. As *Corpus Mysticum* reveals, de Lubac reads all patristic and medieval theologians against the standard of Scripture and the larger tradition. Moreover, he does not hesitate to correct even Augustine or Aquinas when he believes they have erred. For example, de Lubac claims that Augustine makes some serious

an overlooked aspect of his work because of his famously in-depth studies of patristic and medieval figures, de Lubac's knowledge of the history of biblical exegesis plays an especially important role in his writings.[17] As even a cursory reading of his first work, *Catholicism*, reveals, de Lubac's theology is saturated in Scripture;[18] in one place a young de Lubac likens the Old and New Testaments to "two fruitful breasts at which her [the Church's] children draw a nourishment which surpasses wine."[19] Often called "mother" by de Lubac,[20] the Church cannot be the nourishing, protecting Church without the Eucharist, but neither can the Church be the Church without Scripture. D'Ambrosio notes that de Lubac's most voluminous work of all, *Exégèse Médiévale*, was a study of the interpretation of Scripture.[21] Bryan Hollon goes further than D'Ambrosio, claiming that this emphasis is not only in one book but permeates de Lubac's entire career. According to Hollon, "although de Lubac is best known for his works on the social nature of *Catholicism*, the relationship between nature and grace, and the Eucharistic nature of the church, de Lubac wrote more pages on the history of biblical exegesis than on any other single issue."[22]

De Lubac's engagement with the history of biblical exegesis taught him that when practicing what modern and postmodern academics term "theology," the church fathers were exegeting Scripture for the Church.[23] As a result of this reading, he advocated a continuation of this way of practicing theology,[24] believing that just as in the eras of the early and the medieval Church, Scripture must guide the Church as it addresses and seeks to be the body of Christ for the world in "the present situation."[25] The statement "the

---

errors on the nature of the soul (see de Lubac, *Mystery of the Supernatural*, 22).

17. Susan K. Wood shows how de Lubac especially advocates spiritual or figural exegesis as seen in patristic literature and its relationship to the Church (see Wood, *Spiritual Exegesis and the Church in the Theology of Henri de Lubac*).

18. Daley, "*Nouvelle Théologie* and the Patristic Revival," 376.

19. De Lubac, *Catholicism*, 210.

20. This description of the Church permeates *Catholicism*, written early in his career, as well as the post-conciliar work *The Motherhood of the Church*. It borrows from traditions both Catholic and Protestant, from Augustine and Cyprian but also from Calvin.

21. D'Ambrosio, "Ressourcement Theology, Aggiornamento, and the Hermeneutics of Tradition," 542, n. 50.

22. Hollon, "Ontology, Exegesis, and Culture," 4.

23. De Lubac, *Catholicism*, 41.

24. See, for example, de Lubac, *Scripture in the Tradition*, 67–68.

25. De Lubac, *Catholicism*, 305. Cf. D'Ambrosio, "Ressourcement Theology,

Eucharist makes the Church" as it arises in *Corpus Mysticum*, for example, is connected to St. Paul's words to the Corinthians that "we who are many are one body, for we all partake of the one loaf" (1 Cor 10:17), and this is also true of the manner in which the phrase is placed within the later work *The Splendor of the Church*.[26] Moreover, in the latter part of his career, de Lubac also claims through a reading of the Synoptic Gospels that it was not the preaching of the disciples that created the Church, nor even Jesus' "you are my rock" statement to Peter, but that "the Church . . . was conceived, so to speak, in the institution of the Eucharist" at the Last Supper.[27]

Interpretation of these passages of Scripture and of the power of the Eucharist flowers anew through the centuries, but the acknowledgment that the claim is at its core scriptural is crucial, for de Lubac believes that "nothing solid can be achieved in theology without tested materials, with which the long history of Christian reflection supplies us. All research must be first of all a revival through Tradition. All renewal presupposes continuity, even in the face of new situations."[28] De Lubac shows in *Corpus Mysticum* that St. Augustine, for example, "never created anything from the start. Not only are all his doctrinal principles contained in Scripture, but the essential elements can also be found ready-made among his predecessors, and chiefly St. Cyprian, St. Hilary, St. Gregory of Nyssa, St. John Chrysostom, or in a contemporary like St. Cyril of Alexandria."[29]

These are important words to read for Protestants and Baptists who believe the sacramentalism of the patristics and even contemporary Catholics to be unbiblical (and, as we have seen in chapter 2 through McClendon and will continue to see in chapter 4 through Jenson, they do). The Scriptures, along with other texts of the Church, are believed by Catholic theologians—and especially those from within the *ressourcement* group—to be the materials that have proven to withstand challenges posed to the Church from within and without. And yet, in calling them "tested," de Lubac does not mean to imply that the Scriptures' usefulness is finished, nor that their

---

Aggiornamento, and the Hermeneutics of Tradition," 532.

26. De Lubac, *Corpus Mysticum*, 88. One sentence before he turns this increasingly famous phrase, de Lubac cites a Chrysostom sermon on 1 Corinthians 10. Cf. de Lubac, *Splendor*, 78ff.

27. De Lubac, *Motherhood of the Church*, 19. Cf. "The Priesthood According to Scripture and Tradition: An Interview with Father Henri de Lubac Conducted by Gwendolyne Jarczyk," in *Motherhood of the Church*, 337–63. De Lubac cites Luke 22:20 here.

28. De Lubac, *Drama of Atheist Humanism*.

29. De Lubac, *Corpus Mysticum*, 176.

meaning has been fully discovered or exhausted. Rather, Scripture continues to offer fresh insights to the contemporary Church. Persons who live and teach and write in future eras will continue to interpret Scripture for the Church. He says in *The Splendor of the Church* that "however great the number and value of theological tasks completed, there will be no closed circuit of doctrine which puts an end to discussion and reflexion alike and discourages the raising of new questions. Such an Utopia fits in neither with the nature of revealed truth nor that of the human intelligence; the experience of history is incompatible with it."[30]

What has de Lubac on Scripture and tradition to do with de Lubac on the eucharistic unity of the Church? In order to answer this question, take, for example, de Lubac's understanding that "in the thought of St. Paul faithfully expounded in the Fathers,"[31] salvation is found not only in being joined to God, but in so being joined to God being joined to one another.[32] This understanding, which de Lubac calls "the horizontal view" of salvation,[33] is according to him both scriptural and a word that the contemporary Church needs to hear. Moreover, de Lubac contends that Paul had "the horizontal view" of salvation in mind when he said that "we who are many are one body, for we all partake of the one loaf" (1 Cor 10:17). "The loaf," here, is an allusion to the Eucharist, and the Eucharist "makes the Church."[34] Here we see a Eucharist that is essential to the unity of the Church, not completely unlike McClendon's understanding that Paul saw the Supper as "a re-membering sign," a sign that "reconstitutes the church."[35]

De Lubac's claim that the Bible's words to first-century Christians and later churches are also words for the Church of the twentieth century should remind the reader of McClendon's "baptist vision" as well. Scripture's call to "that church" for ecclesial unity is for de Lubac also a call to "this church," the contemporary Church.[36] And yet, some would contest that the two read Scripture very differently. While de Lubac reads Scripture through the lens of contemporary culture, as stated above, he seems to always read Scripture

30. De Lubac, *Splendor*, 19.
31. De Lubac, *Catholicism*, 44.
32. Ibid., 82.
33. Ibid., 41.
34. De Lubac, *Corpus Mysticum*, 88. Again, a mere half sentence before he utters these words, de Lubac cites a sermon of Chrysostom's on 1 Corinthians 10.
35. McClendon, *Doctrine*, 402.
36. Ibid., 45.

through the eyes of a large sampling of the Christian tradition. Meanwhile, though Steven Harmon's important book *Towards Baptist Catholicity*, introduced in great detail at the beginning of chapter 5, names McClendon as one of only two major Baptist theologians from the twentieth century to engage the breadth of the tradition,[37] some might object that McClendon's "this is that" hermeneutics is an exemplar of typical Baptist theology in that it focuses on the eras in which Scripture was written and the present, but very little of the tradition in between (or, at least, very little of the tradition between the first century and the Reformation). As one example, the reader might note that de Lubac's examination of a large portion of materials written between the ninth and eleventh centuries is crucial to his eucharistic theology, while in McClendon's sign theory he does not draw upon or claim indebtedness to Augustine, whose understanding of signs is crucial for much of the Christian tradition's sacramental theology. For Augustine, a sacrament is a "visible word,"[38] but elsewhere is a "sign" that pertains to divine things,[39] a sign that resembles the thing signified.[40] This is perhaps the most important understanding of signs to emerge in the first millennium of the life of the Church, and yet McClendon never mentions Augustine when explaining the meaning of signs.[41]

The Eucharist Makes the Church

As a result of his careful attention to Scripture, then, it comes as no surprise that the famous statement that "the Eucharist makes the Church"[42] was first

---

37. Harmon, *Towards Baptist Catholicity*, 5. Of course, whether the number "two" does justice to Baptist theology from the twentieth century depends on what one believes qualifies a theologian as "major."

38. Augustine, *In Joannem*, 80, 3. See F. van der Meer, *Sacramentum chez Saint Augustin*, 13, 61. Quoted by de Lubac in *Corpus Mysticum*, 14.

39. Augustine, *Letter to Marcellinus*, 7 (see again, de Lubac, *Corpus Mysticum*, 14).

40. Augustine, *Letter to Boniface*, 9 (in de Lubac, *Corpus Mysticum*, 14).

41. This is a complicated discussion, but often one wonders if McClendon is drawing on a figure without mentioning him or her. We noted in chapter 2, for example, that when proclaiming that in the Church's "signs" we have not only human but Divine action, McClendon uses the phrase "double agency" to describe this dual activity. One wonders if he is not leaning upon Aquinas as Paul Fiddes is when he uses the term "double agency" and cites Aquinas at length. See Fiddes, "*Ex Opere Operato*," 228.

42. De Lubac, *Corpus Mysticum*, 88; de Lubac, *Splendor*, 78. Michael Mason's 1953 translation of *Splendor* uses the language of production: "the Church produces the Eucharist, but the Eucharist also produces the Church." "Produces," we will see, is a verb

written by de Lubac in the midst of a close examination of Scripture and the Christian tradition in *Corpus Mysticum*. This book was written shortly after his first work, *Catholicism*, which sets the orientation for all subsequent works in his career, its individual chapters all flowering into different books.[43] In *Catholicism* he places a great deal of emphasis upon the social nature of the Christian church's salvation, arguing along the way that "sacraments make the Church"[44] and then that "the Eucharist is . . . especially the sacrament of unity."[45] He later makes an extended argument in *Corpus Mysticum* that "the mindset of the Church in the first millennium and on through much of the eleventh, twelfth, and thirteenth centuries" was that the Eucharist makes the Church.[46]

It was only after this period of the Middle Ages that the complementary idea that the Eucharist is made *by* the Church "took root." This shift, de Lubac argues, was due to an evolution in the way in which the components of the threefold body of Christ—the historical body of Jesus of Nazareth, the eucharistic body (the *corpus mysticum*), and the Church (the *corpus verum*)—were discussed. The evolution ultimately contributed to the eleventh-century transubstantiation controversies inspired by Berengar's views on the substantial nature of the communion elements.[47]

Though from the first century to the eleventh century the Eucharist was preeminently known as the "mystical body" and the Church preeminently as the "true body," nevertheless controversy arose when in the eleventh century Berengar of Tours, bishop of Angers, France, and the teacher of many future bishops of the Church, followed John Scotus Eriugena in making the claim that in the Eucharist Christ was "mystically, not truly" present (*"mystice, non vere"*). He made public this view of the Eucharist in

---

that will be carried forward by a future generation of theologians impacted by de Lubac, especially William Cavanaugh. It should also be noted here that de Lubac had already said in *Catholicism*, following Pseudo-Haymo, "sacramenta faciunt ecclesiam," or "sacraments make the Church" (see de Lubac, *Catholicism*, 87).

43. Von Balthasar, *Theology of Henri de Lubac*, 10.

44. De Lubac, *Catholicism*, 87.

45. Ibid., 89.

46. De Lubac, *Corpus Mysticum*, 88. *Corpus Mysticum*'s writing also preceded the destructive and utterly divisive Second World War by only a few months, though its publication was delayed until 1944 because of the difficult conditions in France during the war. Thus was the theme of unity very important to de Lubac (de Lubac, *Corpus Mysticum*, ix).

47. Ibid., 114.

1047, unsuccessfully defended the doctrine at Church councils in Rome and Vercelli in 1050, and was condemned by the council at Vercelli and imprisoned by the king of France in 1050, having been deemed a danger to young persons studying for the priesthood because of his teaching and because of his quick mind.[48] Doctrinally speaking, the Christian church, following Radbertus, countered "*mystici, non vere*" with the claim that in the elements Christ was "truly" present, and further that Christ was therefore not "mystically" present. The latter portion of this claim constitutes the mistake, de Lubac says, thus causing the Church to overshadow itself as the real or "true" body of Christ by emphasizing that the true body was located in the eucharistic elements.[49]

Due to a misreading of these claims de Lubac was accused of arguing against the doctrine of transubstantiation in the wake of the publication of *Corpus Mysticum*.[50] Contrary to this accusation, de Lubac deeply affirms transubstantiation, but carefully makes the case that while there are two mysteries in those works of the ancients that focus upon the Eucharist, "the first of these two mysteries, the Real Presence, stands out less boldly" than the mystery of the Church which is generated by the Eucharist's power.[51] In spite of this, de Lubac claims, in the later stages of the medieval era "eucharistic theology became more and more a form of apologetic and organized itself increasingly round a defence of the 'real presence.' Apology for dogma succeeded the understanding of faith."[52] This constituted a mistake in emphasis in de Lubac's eyes, for since the medieval teachers were "fixated on the truth of presence," they forgot that the Eucharist's link to the unity of the Church is central.[53] De Lubac does not deny the "real presence" of Christ in the elements, but rather shows that, as Cavanaugh puts it in his

---

48. McCue, "Doctrine of Transubstantiation from Berengar of Tours through Trent," 386; cf. Knowles, *Evolution of Medieval Thought*, 88–89.

49. De Lubac, *Corpus Mysticum*, 162, 167, 248–51. I am reminded at this point of the instance in which McClendon employs Yoder in order to say that "almost lost to sight in ecclesiastical struggles over what happens to bread and wine when certain words are said over them is that for New Testament disciples 'the *primary* meaning of the eucharistic gathering in the Gospels and Acts is economic'" (McClendon, *Witness*, 379). While de Lubac would no doubt disagree with the last part of this claim, he would certainly concur that the controversies obscured the most important aspect of the Eucharist.

50. Cavanaugh, *Torture and Eucharist*, 213.

51. De Lubac, *Catholicism*, 100.

52. De Lubac, *Corpus Mysticum*, 220.

53. Ibid., 221.

appropriation of de Lubac's work, "the best way to emphasize 'eucharistic realism' [is] precisely through an 'ecclesial realism' which sees Christ's presence as dynamic, working toward the edification of the church."[54]

It also important to note that, for de Lubac, these two claims—that the Eucharist makes the Church and the Church makes the Eucharist—are not mutually exclusive. Indeed, de Lubac goes to great lengths in order to emphasize that "it was principally to that end that her [the Church's] priesthood was instituted. 'Do this in memory of me.'"[55] Thus the Church as the body that gathers the congregants to partake of the body and blood of Christ is not precluded by the idea that the Church is formed through communal participation in the Eucharist. The ideas are dependent upon one another in the eyes of de Lubac, and in retrieving both of them he reminds readers that it is the Eucharist that resides at the center of an ecclesiology of unity: "The Church and the Eucharist are formed by one another day by day: the idea of the Church and the idea of the Eucharist must promote one another mutually and each be rendered more profound by the other."[56] This follows a similar statement in *Catholicism*, where he has already said that

> the Church is . . . the assembly which results from the reuniting of all peoples. . . . Yet in the second place it is she on the contrary who summons them. She is baptized and she baptizes. The one metaphor of the Bride conjures up two contrary visions, both founded on Scripture and both frequently portrayed: the wretched being on whom the Word took pity and whom He came to save from prostitution at the Incarnation; on the other hand, the new Jerusalem, the bride of the Lamb coming out of heaven from God.[57]

De Lubac, then, places himself in line with Tertullian, Origen, Cyprian, Basil, and Augustine when he says that "the Church is a mother . . . [who] draws to her those who are to be her children," just as primarily as she is the feminine figure who is wooed by her one, true love.[58] The Church is the gatherer as well as the result of the gathering.[59] In relationship to the Eucharist, this means that the Church is indeed the one who continually calls persons together in order to participate in the Eucharist—"the ministry of

---

54. Cavanaugh, *Torture and Eucharist*, 213.
55. De Lubac, *Splendor*, 92.
56. De Lubac, *Corpus Mysticum*, 260. See also *Splendor*, 92.
57. De Lubac, *Catholicism*, 68–69.
58. De Lubac, *Motherhood of the Church*, 48–51.
59. De Lubac, *Catholicism*, 48. See also de Lubac, *Motherhood of the Church*, 49.

the Twelve was in fact instituted in order to 'make' the Eucharist"[60]—even if the Church is the one made by the Eucharist. John Milbank notes that for de Lubac the Church is both receptive (and therefore, he suggests, Marian) and productive (Petrine): "at the heart of its shaping activity it also has to do with a receptive giving birth again to Christ in the Eucharist, from whence (according to de Lubac) flows the body of the Church."[61] As stated in chapter 2, Dom Gregory Dix, an Anglican theologian sometimes cited by de Lubac, agrees that the Church is both the cause and the result of the Eucharist, and confirms de Lubac's point that this is often rooted in the portions of patristic literature that draw upon 1 Corinthians 10–11. Dix's research of patristic literature reveals that "there is a curious 'reversibility' about this idea as it appears in the Fathers. Sometimes (and perhaps this is on the whole commoner in pre-Nicene writers) the sacrament becomes the Body of Christ *because* it is offered by the church which is the Body of Christ. Sometimes, as in St. Augustine, the church is the Body of Christ *because* it receives the sacrament which is His Body. Both ideas are true, and both go back to St. Paul in 1 Cor. for their starting-point."[62]

John Zizioulas, an Eastern Orthodox figure who cites de Lubac's eucharistic theology as extremely influential in his own work and who is placed in conversation with de Lubac in Paul McPartlan's *The Eucharist Makes the Church*, notes that in the Eucharist the Church is both institution and event, since Christ instituted the Eucharist at the Last Supper as "the structure of the Kingdom," which would continue to gather the Church out of dispersion into one body and thereby provide a framework for the life of the Church through history. Moreover, Zizioulas points out that the fact of the body of Christ is never guaranteed by the past or by any formal institution, but only comes in *epiclesis*, in the renewed pleading of the faithful that the Holy Spirit enact the Kingdom in their midst.[63] While the Eucharist, that is, "can only be genuine in the Church,"[64] the Church eats "sacramentally" and is transformed into the body of Christ only when it partakes of the elements in faith.[65]

---

60. De Lubac, "Priesthood," in *Motherhood of the Church*, 337–63.
61. Milbank, *Suspended Middle*, 105.
62. Dix, *Shape of the Liturgy*, 251.
63. Zizioulas, *Being as Communion*, 204–8.
64. Von Balthasar, *Theology of Henri de Lubac*, 108.
65. Hemming, "Transubstantiating Our Selves," 419, 424.

De Lubac sincerely believed that this idea of the Church as the gatherer, while both important and true, had become overly emphasized in the late medieval, modern, and postmodern eras at the expense of its counterpart.[66] McPartlan notes that "while [de Lubac] says that the Church and the Eucharist stand 'as cause to each other,' it is clearly the second half of the principle that he regards as having been more neglected."[67] As we saw with McClendon and Yoder in chapter 2, de Lubac's concern that the transubstantiation controversies obscured a major theological thrust of the Eucharist is not a purely theoretical one. Rather, for him the concern is that what was obscured was the idea that the Eucharist makes the Church. For de Lubac, that is, it is important to acknowledge that in saying that "something happens" in the Eucharist, one not only affirms that the bread and wine are transubstantiated into the body and blood of Christ, but that through Christ's presence in the Eucharist members of the Church are united with God and, importantly, with one another, effecting the body of Christ.[68] In chapter 2 we explained in great detail that this is part of what James McClendon means when he, in a move very unusual for Baptists, called the Supper "a re-membering sign," a sign that reminds the congregation that they are called to unity, and in so doing effects their unity.[69] McClendon and de Lubac both want to emphasize, then, that in the Eucharist it is not only the elements employed in the rite that are changed (if they are changed at all for McClendon), but also those persons who participate in the rite. Long before the twentieth century, this was put forward in William of St. Thierry, who said that "to eat the body of Christ is to become the body of Christ,"[70] and also (with an emphasis on the community) by Gerhoh: "by eating the body of Christ they became the body of Christ."[71]

---

66. De Lubac, *Corpus Mysticum*, 88.

67. McPartlan, *Eucharist Makes the Church*, xv.

68. De Lubac, *Corpus Mysticum*, 88. He later adds that "the Eucharist is far more than a symbol because it is most truly that sacrament by which the Church is bound together in this age" (de Lubac, *Corpus Mysticum*, 253).

69. McClendon, *Doctrine*, 402.

70. William of St. Thierry, in Migne, *Patrologia Latina* (hereafter cited as *PL*) 184, 403. Cf. de Lubac, *Corpus Mysticum*, 82. William was an important figure in the twelfth century.

71. Gerhoh, *In Psalmum* 9 (*PL* 193, 780 D). Cf. De Lubac, *Corpus Mysticum*, 82. Gerhoh was one of the most important German theologians of the twelfth century. This provost of Reichersburg was held in particularly high esteem by Pope Eugene III (1145–53).

Re-membering the Body

De Lubac, then, takes further McClendon's idea to emphasize again the Eucharist[72]—de Lubac believed that the Church should return to, or better emphasize, the practice of the Eucharist as the basis of its unity in order to better articulate the unique unity of the Church as an alternative to nineteenth- and twentieth-century humanism.[73] For de Lubac, following the work of St. Leo, the Church is not just any unified body, not "merely a body," but uniquely and "truly" the body of Christ as a result of its participation in the eucharistic body of Christ.[74] This retrieval of the Eucharist as that great sacrament that unifies the Church as the body of Christ shaped much of the Catholic Church's Second Vatican Council and the documents that emerged from the Council. In fact, even though it has been noted that de Lubac continued to be held in suspicion throughout his life by many in the hierarchy of the Church, and especially among the most influential members of the Society of Jesus,[75] it should also be pointed out that he had many supporters in the hierarchy of the Church. Indeed, the *Catechism of the Catholic Church* now directly states that "the Eucharist makes the Church."[76] As we shall see in the pages to come, de Lubac was very influential in the life and development of Benedict XVI. In summary, de Lubac's work eventually influenced much of late twentieth-century Catholic theology and, later, as we shall see in chapters 4 and 5, spread even more broadly through Protestant and Baptist circles.[77]

72. Again, since Baptists only practice the Supper a few times a year, we cannot overstate the importance of McClendon's call to a divided Baptist church to start participating in this "re-membering sign" at least monthly (see McClendon, *Making Gospel Sense*, xix).

73. De Lubac, *Corpus Mysticum*, 104. See also *Splendor*, 106.

74. St. Leo, *Sermo* 4, c. 1 (*PL*, 54, 149 A). For de Lubac, the Church is also "mystically" the body, but as we shall see below, that term has been misunderstood: "the Church, the body of Christ, is a mystery and, against the flat notion of it conceived in the Enlightenment and repeated by a few followers of liberal Protestantism, it should be maintained that a mystery is what continues to remain obscure, hidden, and 'mystical,' even once it has been described, signified, and 'revealed'" (de Lubac, *Corpus Mysticum*, 251).

75. Von Balthasar, *Theology of Henri de Lubac*, 19.

76. *Catechism of the Catholic Church*, par. 1396.

77. Von Balthasar, *Theology of Henri de Lubac*, 20. Von Balthasar concisely narrates de Lubac's life and theological and ecclesiastical biography. Importantly, de Lubac spent a period of over five years in exile from the Church due to a particular reading of his understanding of the relationship between the natural and supernatural realms articulated in *Surnaturel*. The readings of this book, along with some of his other works (including *Corpus Mysticum*, according to von Balthasar), caused him to be deprived of permission to teach, expelled from Lyons, and censored by the Catholic Church. Though there is not sufficient space to treat it fully here, the reversal of de Lubac's reputation within the

Henri de Lubac

The Threefold Body

Though de Lubac blames the loss of the connection between the Eucharist and the unity of the Church in part upon the transubstantiation controversies, he recognizes that a shift in terminology that took place earlier in the Middle Ages set the stage for the controversies and also played a large role in the loss of the Church-Eucharist link. *Corpus Mysticum* is a close study of this shift,[78] tracing the evolution of the ways in which the term *corpus* ("body") was employed in relation to the Church and the Eucharist. De Lubac carefully shows that for the ancients, the *corpus verum* ("true body") was the Church and the *corpus mysticum* ("mystical body") was more often the Eucharist, but that gradually an inversion occurred wherein the Church came to be referred to as the mystical body and the Eucharist became the central location of the "true body" of Christ.[79] "In antiquity," he says "if, in an explanation of the Eucharist, we encounter the unqualified phrase 'the body of Christ,' it is often not the Eucharist but the Church which is meant by the term."[80] Moreover, the Eucharist, not the Church, is Christ's "mystical body" during this time, and this expression survives as a description of the Eucharist until at least 1165. The Church is referred to by Paul as "the body"

---

hierarchy of the Church was only gradually accomplished, perhaps completed by Pope John XXIII's nomination of de Lubac as a "consultor for the preparatory theological commission of the Council" (19). For further information on de Lubac's influence on Vatican II, see von Balthasar, "Achievement of Henri de Lubac," 42; Ratzinger, foreword to de Lubac, *Catholicism*, 12; Rowland, *Culture and the Thomist Tradition*; Milbank, *Suspended Middle*, 7; D'Ambrosio, "Ressourcement Theology, Aggiornamento, and the Hermeneutics of Tradition," 533; Chantraine, "Cardinal Henri de Lubac (1896–1991)," 297–303.

78. De Lubac, *Corpus Mysticum*, xxi.

79. Ibid., 9. The following pages trace de Lubac's interpretation of the way in which the shift occurred, but there is more than one version. Dix traces the shift, and apparently after seeing hints of it in de Lubac's *Catholicism* (see Dix, *Shape of the Liturgy*, 244–51). Sarah Beckwith highlights some different figures, but agrees that "the ecclesiastical use of the term 'corpus mysticum' originally referred to the consecrated host, not to the church or Christian society. However, in the mid-twelfth century its meaning changes. . . . The 'corpus mysticum' becomes the phrase which expresses the doctrine that the church is the organized body of Christian society united in the sacrament of the altar" (Beckwith, *Christ's Body*, 31). Another important study that looks closely at this shift and its political implications—and is called a "classic" by Cavanaugh—is Ernst Kantorowicz's *The King's Two Bodies*. Among those who employ de Lubac's examination of the shift for their constructive theological projects are Cavanaugh, *Torture and Eucharist*; de Certeau, *Mystic Fable*, 82–84; Marion, *God Without Being*, 176–81; Hauerwas and Wood, "How the Church Became Invisible," 61–93.

80. De Lubac, *Corpus Mysticum*, 13.

and the "the body of Christ" throughout Ephesians and 1 Corinthians;[81] it is considered the "true and perfect body of Christ" by Origen[82] (in comparison with the risen, crucified body of Christ);[83] and it is called the "full body of Christ" by Augustine.[84] Paschasius Radbertus, deeply involved in ninth-century debates regarding how to best speak of "the threefold body of Christ"—the ascended body of Christ, the eucharistic body of Christ, and the Church as the body of Christ—also attaches the adjective *mystical* preeminently to the Eucharist.[85]

Writing later in his career, however, de Lubac notes in his *Church: Paradox and Mystery* that the Pauline Epistles also apply the word *mystery* to the Church, the word that is also used to describe Christ.[86] Even in *Corpus Mysticum*, de Lubac is careful to note that Christ is called the "mystical head" of the Church,[87] and that the Church's *unity* (as opposed to the Church itself) is described as "mystical" in Leo, Hilary, and Augustine. Moreover, the Church in heaven, or "the communion of saints," is described as "mystical" by Theodoret and Augustine. The Church on earth that is the body of Christ, however, is not described as the "mystical body" in the ancients or the High Middle Ages.[88]

According to de Lubac, in the ninth century a contemporary of Radbertus', Rabanus Maurus, referred solely to the Eucharist as the *corpus mysticum* but said that the Church is "mystically" the body of Christ, bringing in an adverbial usage of the term.[89] After a time in which, in response to Berengar, the Church virtually ceased using the adjective *mystical* in

---

81. See, for example, Eph 1:22–23; 2:16; 3:6; 4:12, 16; 5:23, 30. For the most explicit reference in Paul, see 1 Cor 12:27. Cf. de Lubac, *Corpus Mysticum*, 4.

82. Origen, *In Joannem*, X.20. Cf. de Lubac, *Corpus Mysticum*, 5.

83. Dix, *Shape of the Liturgy*, 246. Dix translates Origen to say that the Church is "the real (*alethinon*) and more perfect (*teleioteron*) Body of Christ."

84. St. Augustine, *In Psalmum 68*, S. 1, n. 11. De Lubac, *Corpus Mysticum*, 14. The *totus Christus*, or the whole Christ, is for Augustine Christ with the Church. This will be very important in the next chapter as we explore the relationship between the work of de Lubac and Jenson, who draws heavily upon Augustine's concept of the *totus Christus*.

85. Radbertus, *PL* 123, 1284–86. Cf. de Lubac, *Corpus Mysticum*, 29–30.

86. De Lubac, *Splendor*, 54. He refers here to Eph 5:32, which, after a section examining the unity of husband and wife, says, "This is a great mystery, and I am applying it to Christ and the Church."

87. Ibid., 74.

88. De Lubac, *Corpus Mysticum*, 6. De Lubac adds, without qualification, that if we do find this description in these eras, "it is always by the hand of later editors."

89. Ibid., 101.

reference to both the Eucharist and the Church, preferring simply *corpus Christi* for both,[90] this usage echoes through the Church again "two or three centuries later" in the works of Lanfranc and Gregory of Bergamo, who do not call the Church the mystical body but nonetheless use the adverbial *mystically* with reference to the Church instead of the Eucharist.[91] A transition slowly occurs, and in the influential *Sentences* of Peter Lombard,[92] written in the middle of the twelfth century, the term *mystical flesh* is used to describe the Church.[93] After that, de Lubac claims, "mystical flesh" as a referent of the Church comes into "general use . . . [at] the dawn of the thirteenth century" with Simon of Tournai[94] and later in that century with St. Thomas Aquinas, who repeatedly refers to the Church as the mystical body in the *Summa Theologiae*, especially in the eighth question of the Third Part.[95] In the meantime (though not noted by de Lubac), the Fourth Lateran Council of 1215 was emphasizing that the Eucharist was the "true" body of Christ in an attempt to undermine Berengar's symbolist views:

> There is one universal church of the faithful outside of which absolutely none is saved, and in which Jesus Christ is himself at once both priest and sacrifice. His body and blood are truly contained in the sacrament of the altar in the forms of the bread and the wine, the bread being transubstantiated into the body by divine power. . . . And no one can perform this sacrament except a priest ritually ordained according to the [authority of] the keys of the church.[96]

Though the Church is the ark of salvation according to the Fourth Lateran Council, it is the sacrament of the Eucharist that contains the "true" body of Christ over against Berengar's *"mystice, non vere."* According to de Lubac, however, this is because the decline of the importance of the Church as the body of Christ had already begun in the ninth century with the trend of attaching mystical language to the Church, when such language had previously been attached to the Eucharist. Conceiving of the Eucharist and the

90. Ibid., 101–6.
91. Ibid., 101.
92. Ibid., 105.
93. Ibid.. 102.
94. Ibid., 107.
95. Ibid., 113.
96. *Concilium Laterensae*, IV, ch. 1, Mansi, vol. 22, col. 982, quoted in Beckwith, *Christ's Body*, 31.

Re-membering the Body

body of the historical Jesus as the "true" or "real" bodies and the Church as something more vague had already made inroads. In fact, de Lubac says that "the reaction against Berengar had only served to strengthen a movement that had been initiated in the time of Paschasius Radbertus, and that was increasingly identifying the first two of the three 'bodies' [the historical body of Jesus of Nazareth and the eucharistic body] and, on the other hand, detaching them from the third [the Church]."[97] This *caesura* (primarily a temporal one) which had previously distinguished the historical body of Jesus from the coupled eucharistic and churchly bodies no longer existed in the minds of most Christians. Instead, the gap was "relocated," posited now between the bodies of Jesus of Nazareth and the Eucharist on the one hand and the Church on the other. De Lubac notes that in antiquity, "of the three terms that had to be ordered in relation to one another . . . the caesura was placed between the first and the second, whereas later it came to be placed between the second and the third."[98] Rather than being paired with the Eucharist, which "mystically" linked the contemporary Church to the historical body (hence the sense that the Eucharist "made" the Church),[99] the Church as the mystical body of Christ was now beginning to stand alone. This stands in stark contrast to patristic thought, where, as Cavanaugh puts it (using, in places, language similar to that of McClendon),

> the church and the Eucharist form the liturgical pair of visible community (*corpus verum*) and invisible action or mystery (*corpus mysticum*) which together re-present and re-member Christ's historical body. The gap is a temporal one. The link between past event and present church is formed by the invisible action of the sacrament. The "mystical," then, is that which "insures the unity between the two times" and brings the Christ event into present historical time in the church body, the *corpus verum*.[100]

97. De Lubac, *Corpus Mysticum*, 162.
98. Ibid.
99. Cavanaugh, *Torture and Eucharist*, 214.
100. Ibid., 212. As I will show in the final section of this chapter, Cavanaugh appropriates de Lubac's historical research on the threefold body for his own constructive work. Here, five years after McClendon calls the Supper "a re-membering sign" that "reconstitutes the church" (using the term *re-membering* in opposition to the term *dismembering*), Cavanaugh conceives of the Eucharist as a practice that "re-members" Chilean Christians who were created to be "members of one another" but who were dismembered by the state's practice of torture, a practice that was imposed on a few persons and yet instilled fear in many others, supporting the regime's goal of producing "fearful and isolated bodies, bodies docile to the purposes of the regime" (see McClendon, *Doctrine*,

Henri de Lubac

"It took a long time," de Lubac says, but eventually using the term *corpus mysticum* in order to describe the Church "takes root" in the fourteenth century,[101] undoubtedly helped along by Lombard, Aquinas, and by Boniface VIII's "famous bull *Unam Sanctum* (18th November 1302), which speaks of 'One holy Church . . . which represents one mystical body, of which the head is Christ, just as the head of Christ is God.'"[102] By "takes root," de Lubac means that the term became entrenched in the language of the Church as a referent to the ecclesial body, and he illustrates this by pointing out that at the First Vatican Council (late in the nineteenth century), "the Church was defined from the outset as the mystical body."[103] Thus does he maintain, in summary, that "from the thirteenth century onwards, whether understood correctly or incorrectly, it [this usage] never fell into decline"[104]—even though "the Fathers were not familiar with the term."[105]

De Lubac compacts *Corpus Mysticum*'s argument later in *The Splendor of the Church*. As a way of summarizing for the reader what we have just said in this section, I quote in full his introduction to the ancient Eucharist-Church connection from that text:

> In Christian antiquity we do often come across a "spiritual body" or "great body" of Christ; or again a "complete body," a "universal" or "common" body, a "true and perfect" body, of which Christ is the "mystical head" and Christians the "mystical members." We come across the assembly of the blessed as in a "mystical Church," or again the "mystery of the body of Christ," or the "mystical union" of the faithful within the body of Christ. Yet nonetheless it is only toward the midpoint of the Middle Ages—in the second half of the twelfth century—that this body of Christ which is the Church begins itself to be qualified by the adjective "mystical."

402; Cavanaugh, *Torture and Eucharist*, 206).

101. De Lubac, *Corpus Mysticum*, 114.

102. Ibid., 3. Cavanaugh notes that it is important to remember that the pope was specifically addressing Philip the Fair here, noting that the Church, not the state, is in some sense the body of Christ. Cavanaugh's critique, however, is that in conceiving of the Church as the mystical rather than the true body, Boniface has already internalized the meaning of participation in the Eucharist and given control of Church members' bodies over to Philip and the state (see Cavanaugh, *Torture and Eucharist*, 214).

103. De Lubac, *Corpus Mysticum*, 117. It would seem that recognition of the link has returned since paragraph 1396 of the *Catechism of the Catholic Church*, no doubt due to de Lubac's influence, bluntly states that "the Eucharist makes the Church."

104. Ibid., *Corpus Mysticum*, 117.

105. Ibid., 3.

> Previously, this description was confined to the Eucharist. But from that point onward it was to be the Church that was so called and thus distinguished from both the Eucharist and Christ in his earthly life or his heavenly glory.[106]

The Inversion and Individualism

Cavanaugh notes in his *Torture and Eucharist* that "what concerned de Lubac about the inversion of *verum* and *mysticum* was its tendency to reduce the Eucharist to a mere spectacle for the laity."[107] In a study of the relevant terms (*corpus, corpus Christi, corpus mysticum*) that mentions neither de Lubac nor Cavanaugh, Sarah Beckwith, professor of English and religion at Duke University, also claims that due to the shift, especially for the laity "the emphasis was increasingly on watching Christ's body rather than being incorporated into it."[108] Dix comments on the shift, apparently having been made aware of it by the brief mention of it in *Catholicism*. Speaking of life in late medieval England, he says of the inversion's relation to individualism that

> though popular belief and devotion were not affected directly by these wire-drawn subtleties, yet the absorption of theological teachers in this particular aspect of eucharistic doctrine did in the end greatly encourage the characteristic bias of medieval eucharistic piety towards an individualistic and subjective devotion. The clergy trained under such influences were not likely to teach their people a balanced doctrine of the eucharist.
>
> In the later fourteenth and fifteenth centuries popular eucharistic devotion becomes more and more one-sided, treating the sacrament less and less as the source of unity and of the corporate life of the church (and through this of the spiritual life of the individual soul), and more and more only as a focus of purely personal adoration of our Lord therein present to the individual. The infrequency of lay communions which was still general in this period . . . was no doubt partly responsible for this trend. Deprived of frequent communion . . . private adoration was all that was left to the unlettered layfolk.[109]

106. De Lubac, *Splendor*, 74.

107. Cavanaugh, *Torture and Eucharist*, 213.

108. Beckwith, *Christ's Body*, 36.

109. Dix, *Shape of the Liturgy*, 249; cf. 618. Dix cites *Catholicisme*, 64–67 and 307 on the previous page, noting that de Lubac alludes to the eleventh- and twelfth-century

Henri de Lubac

Dix goes on to point out that "private adoration" was soon replaced in the Reformation and the Catholic Counter-Reformation by "personal reception of the sacrament,"[110] which he maintains in the end was "nothing less than the atomizing of the Body of Christ . . . [given] formal and official encouragement."[111] What previously had been an emphasis—that it is the ecclesial body that is changed (even created) through the Eucharist—became virtually ignored. Moreover, Dix argues that even when held in corporate settings, the Eucharist increasingly came to be about what an individual was "thinking" and "feeling," and the gathering of the parishioners was a mere vehicle for attaining an opportunity for individual self-examination, while the corporate, or bodily, aspect of worship was moved to the periphery.[112]

I would add here a word about these authors' discoveries as they relate to the overarching concerns of McClendon. While he only once raises the point that the transubstantiation controversies obscured the corporate aspect of the Supper, as was noted in chapter 2 he employs a MacIntyrian definition of practices to emphasize that they are inherently social, and he describes the Supper preeminently as a practice. Indeed, in *Ethics* he moves directly from introducing a MacIntyrian notion of practices to an explication of the Supper and other practices of the Church as "powerful practices."[113] This is for McClendon a sign that is intended to unify the Church, to "reconstitute the church,"[114] and this study has contended throughout that Baptists—or better, "baptists"—should take more seriously this aspect of the Supper.

It is lamentable, then, in the eyes of de Lubac and McClendon (as well as Dix, Cavanaugh, and others who take note of the alteration in the meaning of the Eucharist) that the controversies distracted the Church from a fulsome understanding of the Eucharist, but de Lubac in particular spends a great deal of space contending that this marginalization of the connection between the Eucharist and the Church's unity led to an overemphasis upon

---

theologians mentioned earlier in this study.

110. Ibid., 249.

111. Ibid., 250. Although Basil the Great had in 372 encouraged private communions, this was during a time of persecution and seems to be an exception during the patristic era (see Basil, *Epistle 93*, in Quaesten, *Patrology*, 3:233).

112. Dix, *Shape of the Liturgy*, 599ff.

113. See McClendon, *Ethics*, 222.

114. McClendon, *Doctrine*, 402.

the individual. Von Balthasar notes that de Lubac saw this as a classic example of the catastrophes that result when, "for reasons of apologetics, polemics, or an apparent logic, one abandons a total, catholic standpoint for the sake of a particular standpoint, an *anti*-position."[115] When the Church, that is, felt the pressure to ensure that the bread and wine "really" or "truly" became the body and blood of Christ over against those who did not make such an affirmation, its ardent articulation of a doctrine of the real presence forgot other truths, and especially the doctrine that the Church itself really becomes the body of Christ in the rite. Thus, in de Lubac's opinion, "orthodoxy was perhaps saved, but in return doctrine was surely impoverished,"[116] and this poverty led to an endless supply of "individualistic aberrations of theology."[117] Parishioners became "more easily oriented towards an overly individualistic devotion, and sometimes proved poorly defended against certain sentimental excesses."[118]

De Lubac's concerns are very close to Dix's here, and von Balthasar believes that this tendency toward individualism is the central thesis of *Corpus Mysticum*, that the Church's "giving up of a genuinely theological symbolic thinking in the case of the Eucharist . . . was the occasion for a one-sided emphasis upon the real presence and thus for the disintegration of the Church-Eucharist mystery."[119] He even goes so far as to claim that *Corpus Mysticum*'s primary point of departure is that the accent of eucharistic theology had been displaced from the social aspect to that of the real presence, so that "individualistic piety [won] a handhold."[120] Whether or not this is the central thesis of *Corpus Mysticum*—and some believe that von Balthasar overstates this point[121]—individualism as it relates to the Eucharist is certainly troubling to de Lubac, as shown above. This concern is shared by authorities across the spectrum of the Church universal.[122]

115. Von Balthasar, "Achievement of Henri de Lubac," 10.

116. De Lubac, *Corpus Mysticum*, 251.

117. Ibid., 266–67.

118. De Lubac, *Corpus Mysticum*, 259.

119. Von Balthasar, "Achievement of Henri de Lubac," 10.

120. De Lubac, *Corpus Mysticum*, xii. Cf. von Balthasar, *Theology of Henri de Lubac*, 32.

121. Laurence Paul Hemming and Susan Frank Parsons, editors of the English translation of *Corpus Mysticum*, state in the introduction to this new translation that von Balthasar overstates his case and that "much more than individualism alone is at issue in the book you have before you" (de Lubac, *Corpus Mysticum*, xii).

122. See again Dix, *Shape of the Liturgy*, 618.

De Lubac notes that "from the moment when it became the mystical body, the ecclesial body was already detaching itself from the Eucharist."[123] This mindset stands in stark contrast to the picture he paints of the patristic era in *Catholicism*, wherein ancient Christians saw in the Eucharist not so much an opportunity to privately approach Christ, but to become part of God's corporate body. He notes that "when, with St. Augustine, they [our forebears] heard Christ say to them: 'I am your food, but instead of my being changed into you, it is you who shall be transformed into me,' they unhesitatingly understood that by their reception of the Eucharist they would be incorporated the more in the Church."[124] As seen here and later in *Corpus Mysticum*, de Lubac believes that in the Eucharist Christ "transforms into himself those whom he nourishes with his substance."[125] Similarly, Joseph Cardinal Ratzinger (now Pope Benedict XVI), who penned the foreword to the 1988 English translation of de Lubac's *Catholicism* and cited the book as very influential in his own work and faith, notes that in Augustine's eucharistic thought "it is truly the one, identical Lord whom we receive in the Eucharist, or better, the Lord who receives us and assumes us into himself."[126] In being assumed into the Divine, persons are necessarily changed; the communicant who participates in faith cannot help being altered. Indeed, in one sense, for de Lubac full participants are no longer even individual persons, but members of one another and thereby the "true" body of Christ, "a singular and not to be confused with an aggregate."[127] This is the remedy for the sin of pride, which has shattered the image of a humanity created in the image of the triune God, meant to be "members of one another" (Eph 4:25) rather than in isolation.[128]

The Church is this single reality for de Lubac as a result of the Eucharist, and in partaking of the Eucharist the ecclesial body becomes as truly

---

123. De Lubac, *Corpus Mysticum*, 246.

124. De Lubac, *Catholicism*, 99. De Lubac does not say where Augustine says this, but the quote is an allusion to *Confessions*, 7.10.16, and actually, Augustine says there that Jesus says, "I am the food of strong men, grow and you shall feed upon me; nor shall you convert me, like to food of your flesh, into you, but you shall be converted into me."

125. De Lubac, *Corpus Mysticum*, 178. In addition to recovering the Church-Eucharist link, if in the Eucharist the Church is consuming Christ's "substance," this is another point in de Lubac's work in which it is evident that he has no intentions of undermining the doctrine of transubstantiation.

126. Ratzinger, "Eucharist, Communion, and Solidarity."

127. De Lubac, *Catholicism*, 48.

128. Ibid., 33.

the body of Christ as the eucharistic elements.[129] In Michael Mason's 1953 English translation of *The Splendor of the Church*, de Lubac's famous claim is rendered "the Eucharist produces the Church."[130] Even on the first page of *Corpus Mysticum*, we find that "the Eucharist corresponds to the Church as cause to effect, as means to end, as sign to reality."[131] Thus, as McPartlan puts it, "de Lubac's aim was to reinstate *the Church* as the 'marvel,' and to understand the Eucharist as 'the mystical principle, permanently active' to realise it. The Church makes the Eucharist, but she does so because 'in the strict sense . . . the Eucharist makes the Church.'"[132]

These are the "concrete" implications of the thesis that the Church was in the eyes of the ancients the *corpus verum* before the foci of eucharistic theology changed.[133] In both *Corpus Mysticum* and a crucial chapter on the sacraments in *The Splendor of the Church*, de Lubac notes that long before an allegedly Enlightenment-driven individualism pervaded the Church,[134] in overemphasizing the idea that the Church makes the Eucharist into the *corpus verum*,[135] the Church forgot that she was to focus upon not only the miracle of the elements being transubstantiated, but also (and most centrally) upon her own change, her being pulled godward and together as the body of Christ. Thus, at the opening of *Catholicism*, de Lubac can say that the *Church* is a sacrament—indeed, she is the sacrament that holds all the other sacraments, because she, more than any other aspect of creation,

---

129. De Lubac, *Corpus Mysticum*, 88. De Lubac adds that even the Fathers of Vatican I complained that *mystical* as an adjective for the body of the Church was too vague (de Lubac, *Corpus Mysticum*, 117).

130. De Lubac, *Splendor*, 78. As we shall see in the final section of the chapter, this is the language Cavanaugh has come to adopt.

131. De Lubac, *Corpus Mysticum*, 13.

132. McPartlan, *Eucharist Makes the Church*, 79. McPartlan cites de Lubac, *Corpus Mysticum*, 88.

133. De Lubac, *Corpus Mysticum*, 248.

134. Indeed, while de Lubac is skeptical of Enlightenment conceptions of knowledge, he notes in several places that "the individualist aberrations of recent centuries were due not so much to some special conception, to the use of some special philosophical mode or system, but to a general development of individualism. They are just one aspect of it among a hundred others. We are dealing with a universal phenomenon which, moreover, defies definition in a single formula, just as it cannot be condemned without reservation or limited to certain dates, although it appears to coincide with the dissolution of medieval Christianity" (de Lubac, *Catholicism*, 308–9).

135. De Lubac, *Corpus Mysticum*, 259.

"represents [Christ], in the full and ancient meaning of the term; she really makes him present."[136]

The Humanity of the Church

As we shall see in greater detail in the next chapter through the work of Robert Jenson, to say that the body of Christ is enacted in, or produced by, the eucharistic performance is in itself a large claim. Accordingly, theologians down through the centuries have understood that to confuse the liturgically enacted body of Christ, constituted by sinners, with the sinless body of the historical Jesus of Nazareth would be to commit an egregious error. For de Lubac, that is, we cannot discuss the "real presence" of Christ in the Church or the Eucharist without similarly acknowledging what, in some sense, amounts to an absence of Christ. The body of Christ that is produced in the eucharistic performance does not exhaust the fullness of Christ's body, which is at the same time seated at the right hand of the Father in heaven.

In order to help him illustrate the way in which the second person of the Trinity is to be understood in relation to the Church, de Lubac borrows heavily from Paul, who speaks of the Church as the body of Christ not only throughout 1 Corinthians, but also in Ephesians, where in de Lubac's eyes we find "a single organism of Jesus Christ and his Church, signifying at the same time the subjection of the members to the head."[137] Though de Lubac makes claims like "as God is our father, the Church is our mother,"[138] and "the Spirit has reposed in her [the Church] a unique power of divinization,"[139] for him the Church is not to be conflated with the second person of the Trinity. She is, for Paul, the "body of Christ" (1 Cor 12:27)—and therefore in some sense truly an extension of Christ's presence into the world, into time[140]—but is also "at once human and divine,"

---

136. De Lubac, *Catholicism*, 76.

137. De Lubac, *Church*, 24. He is working with Eph 4:14–16 where the Church, the body of Christ, "grows up into Him who is the head."

138. Ibid., 24.

139. Ibid., 7.

140. Ibid., 35. Cf. *Catholicism*, 76. The proper elevation of the Church above ordinary human institutions on the one hand, but avoiding an idolatrous understanding of the Church on the other hand, is a major topic of the next chapter, where I examine the very high view of the Church affirmed by Jenson.

Re-membering the Body

a paradox.[141] Preserving these doctrines was actually yet another function of the ancient conceptions of the threefold body, de Lubac says: the ancient Eucharist-Church link and the posited caesura between these bodies and the historical body of Jesus, it turns out, had served in antiquity also as an indication of the distinctions between the human and the Divine that Christians must preserve.[142]

How the Church can in some sense, like Christ, be both human and divine is indeed mysterious. Thus does de Lubac suggest that "mystical" be preserved as a description of the Church in addition to remaining a description of the Eucharist.[143] He notes that even "St. Paul applies to her this same word 'mystery' that he had first used of Christ."[144] As stated above, it is not that speaking of the Church as mystical is heretical by any means, but that the mystery of the Church should not come at the expense of her reality, should not make her superfluous or merely optional for the individual. Long before de Lubac, Augustine said, "*Verbum caro factum est, et habitavit in nobis; illi carni adjungitur ecclesia, et fit Christus totus, caput et corpus*" ("The Word was made flesh, and dwelled among us; to that flesh is joined the Church, and there is made the whole Christ, head and body").[145] Christ and his Church together, that is, form the *totus Christus*—"the whole Christ." This, I argue, in concert with von Balthasar's claim, is the true importance of de Lubac's historical survey of the threefold body. I believe that Baptists can especially benefit from taking this de Lubacian point very seriously since, as shown above, they have bought into what he calls a "flat notion" of the Church inspired by the Enlightenment.[146] This is something I have already argued in chapters 1 and 2, but I shall revisit this claim yet again in chapter 5 through the "Baptist Sacramentalists" who interact with both McClendon and de Lubac.

---

141. De Lubac, *Church*, 2.

142. De Lubac, *Corpus Mysticum*, 92–93.

143. De Lubac, *Splendor*, 27–28.

144. De Lubac, *Church*, 54.

145. Augustine, *On the Epistle of John*, 1.2. Augustine was certain to point out that it was not that Christ would be incomplete without the Church, but rather that Christ did not wish to be complete without us or without a Church (cf. *Sermons* 341.1.1 and 9.1). This theme is drawn upon by Jenson. We will discuss this understanding of Christ and the Church as the *totus Christus* at greater length in the next chapter.

146. De Lubac, *Corpus Mysticum*, 251.

Re-sourcing De Lubac and the "Productive" Eucharist in Recent Contexts

In *Corpus Mysticum* and *The Splendor of the Church* it is clear that that the practice of Eucharist does not function merely as one Church practice among a slew of equals, but rather it is said to effect or make or produce the Church.[147] Unlike McClendon's work, which does not elevate the practice of the Supper over and above other churchly "signs" (however "sacramental" it seems to be among Baptist theologians working in the twentieth century), for de Lubac this practice is the very center of the Church.[148] In the pages that follow I will argue that the same description of the Eucharist—as the "center" or the "heart" of the Church—is characteristic of the work of persons who have employed de Lubac's work on the Eucharist.

Laurence Paul Hemming

Catholic theologian Laurence Paul Hemming echoes de Lubac's call for the centrality of the Eucharist as the great sacrament of unity. Hemming, coeditor of the recently released English translation of de Lubac's *Corpus Mysticum*, suggests an image that helpfully illustrates the re-creation of the body of Christ in the eucharistic performance. He adopts the term *transubstantiation*, so long associated with the essential change of the bread and wine into the body and blood of Jesus Christ during the eucharistic institution, and employs the term to describe the change that also occurs in the ecclesial body during the Eucharist.

As outlined above, the controversy as to whether the bread and the wine are transubstantiated in the Eucharist has served as one battleground between Protestants and Catholics for hundreds of years, and again is one of the controversies that de Lubac believes has obscured the true meaning of the Eucharist. Yet Hemming diverges from the usual appropriation of the term *transubstantiation*, employing it to describe the way in which persons

---

147. Indeed, this last way of putting it is found in chapter four of *Splendor*, a chapter titled "The Heart of the Church" (de Lubac, *Splendor*, 74).

148. In McClendon's framework, the Supper is not *the* remembering sign (in the sense that remembering signs are signs that reconstitute a dismembered Church), but is with baptism and preaching one of three remembering signs (see McClendon, *Doctrine*, 187). In *Catholicism*, which again was published prior to *Corpus Mysticum*, de Lubac does not say that "the Eucharist makes the Church," but that "sacraments make the Church," following Pseudo-Haymo (de Lubac, *Catholicism*, 87 n. 15).

are changed into the body of Christ through the rite. Hemming proposes that "knowing *that truth of faith* [that 'what is substantially bread and wine is by the power of God alone transubstantiated into the body and blood of his Son'], we can by perfect eating of the sacrament be ourselves transformed into what it is we eat, a transubstantiation of its own kind."[149] In eating the body of Christ, Hemming reasons, Christians become the body of Christ, "members of one another" (Eph 4:25). The Eucharist, here, makes the Church, and Hemming is certain to cite de Lubac's famous line in his essay.[150] One passage Hemming does not cite, however, is the following one on the verbs used by the ancients:

> The verbs *"to be changed," "to pass," "to be transferred," "to be transfigured"*—in anticipation of *"to be transubstantiated"*—indicate, and sometimes in the writing of the same author, both the change undergone by the bread and wine, and—as with the verb *"to be transferred"*—our being brought into the body of Christ. The verb *"to confect," "to be confected"* in some sense provides the technical term for the "confection" of the Eucharist, is also commonly used for the "confection" of the Church in this mystery: "one body is confected, which is both Christ and the Church."[151]

Joseph Ratzinger

Ratzinger employs the language of *assumption* instead of Hemming's language of *transubstantiation*, but his point is very similar to Hemming's when he says that "it is truly the one, identical Lord whom we receive in the Eucharist, or better, the Lord who receives us and assumes us into himself."[152] For Ratzinger the Eucharist is "the place where the Church is generated," and "just as in the taking of nourishment the body assimilates foreign matter to itself, and is thereby enabled to live, in the same way my 'I' is 'assimilated' to that of Jesus, it is made similar to him in an exchange that increasingly breaks through the lines of division. This same event takes

---

149. Hemming, "Transubstantiating Our Selves," 436.

150. Ibid., 437.

151. De Lubac, *Corpus Mysticum*, 83. He cites here Rabanus Maurus, *De clericorum institutione* (*PL*, 107, 318 A); Thomas Waldensis, *Doctinale fidei catholicae* 2, c. 16 (1757 ed., vol. 1, 319); Augustine, *In psalmum 88*, s. 1, n. 24 (*PL*, 37, 1129); Paschasius, (*PL*, 120, 54 A, 209 D).

152. Ratzinger, "Ecclesiology of the Constitution *Lumen Gentium*," 253.

place in the case of all who communicate; they are all assimilated to this 'bread' and thus are made one among themselves—*one* body."[153]

The man who would go on to become Benedict XVI acknowledges being heavily influenced by de Lubac—especially in the years directly after the Second Vatican Council[154]—and this influence is evident in the quote above. De Lubac, through his own work and through the work of the dozens of authors who have employed him, has helped the Church remember that, as *Lumen Gentium* states, "sharing in the body and blood of Christ has no other effect than to accomplish our transformation into that which receive."[155] While in all other meals, food is converted by the human body to serve its purposes (to repair muscle tissue, to strengthen bones, to ward off viruses and help prevent other diseases), in the Eucharist it is the human body, created in the image of the triune God, that is altered in order to become what it consumes—the body of Christ.

William T. Cavanaugh

More than any other theologian, Cavanaugh has appropriated de Lubac's work on the centrality of the Eucharist for the purposes of constructing a political theology. He proposes that the Eucharist, the center of the Church,[156] is productive in the sense that it builds up a body empowered to resist the impulses that have gripped the world around it. Following the image of the "two cities" in St. Augustine's *City of God*, "the world" for Cavanaugh is that city which stands in contrast to the Church in that it is consumed with obtaining "power over bodies, and not just individual bodies but social bodies as well."[157] Both the Church and the world, that is, have practices that habituate persons and incorporate persons into themselves. In a sense, Cavanaugh reasons, all bodies seek to habituate persons in order to support what they believe are very good "causes"—the masses need to be organized and disciplined in order to help a country (or any other kind of body) to develop.[158]

153. Ratzinger, *Called to Communion*, 37.

154. Gaillardetz, *Church in the Making*, 128.

155. *Lumen Gentium*, 1561. In *The Companion to the Catechism of the Catholic Church*, 564.

156. Cavanaugh, *Theopolitical Imagination*, 113.

157. Cavanaugh, *Torture and Eucharist*, 2; cf. Cavanaugh, *Theopolitical Imagination*, 7.

158. Cavanaugh, *Torture and Eucharist*, 25.

For Cavanaugh, then, nation-states are particularly acute examples of social structures concerned to control persons through disciplines and habituation. Citizens' allegiance to the Church, another body that "disciplines its citizens," would threaten the state's stronghold. Cavanaugh believes that this body of Christ is the only body with the strength to overcome all other bodies. He therefore sets up an interesting contrast when he says that "the production of the nation-state depends especially on people imagining themselves as contemporaries not with the apostles and the saints, but with all other presently living French (or Chileans or English)."[159]

In *Torture and Eucharist*, Cavanaugh focuses on the situation of the Church in Chile, and particularly "the Catholic Church there, before and during the military dictatorship of General Augusto Pinochet Ugarte, 1973–90."[160] Written not long after he lived there in the latter years of the regime, Cavanaugh contrasts the Eucharist—which (as in de Lubac) "makes the Church"—as a productive practice of the Church, with torture as one of the "productive" practices of Pinochet's regime. This is an era in which, according to Cavanaugh, "Chile was driven indoors. Behind some doors, champagne corks popped; behind others, there was only an anxious silence. In the streets, military patrols sped by on their hungry search for enemies. Those labeled as enemies faced a terrible dilemma. They could stay at home and await capture, or they could attempt to flee, a choice which would take them out into the streets ruled by the regime."[161]

Persons who voiced their disagreement with the policies of this regime, including Catholic priests, were routinely beaten, tortured, and killed.[162] Cavanaugh focuses on torture in the text as a "results-oriented" practice and social strategy that creates fearful and isolated bodies disciplined to serve the purposes of the state.[163] It is not only that torture isolates individuals, thereby making them fearful, but also that torture itself has as its aim "the very creation of individuals," isolating persons' bodies so as to dismantle social, or collective, rivals of the nation-state,[164] and also

---

159. Ibid., 223.
160. Ibid., 2.
161. Ibid., 205.
162. Ibid., 81.
163. Ibid., 2.
164. Ibid., 3.

producing pain so incommunicable that victims cannot and will not even attempt to discuss it with others at a later date.[165]

Producing, through physical torture, a confession of treason against Pinochet's Chile is just one example of the state's dismantling of a rival body, of creating individuals.[166] The loss of the sense of time through indefinite incarceration of persons is another tactic employed by nation-states to destroy bodies. This practice—which, although imposed on only a few persons, instilled fear in many—also helped the regime produce "fearful and isolated bodies, bodies docile to the purposes of the regime."[167] Pinochet's Chile understood, as many other nation-states have recognized down through the centuries, that "the key . . . is individualization. Torture breaks down collective links and makes of its victims isolated monads. Victims then reproduce the same dynamic in society itself, with the net result that social bodies which would rival the state are disintegrated and disappeared."[168] Indeed, the torture applied by the state is for Cavanaugh "much more than an attack on individuals; it is rather an assault on social bodies."[169]

True resistance to this kind of body, Cavanaugh claims, requires "the reappearance of social bodies capable of countering the atomizing performance of the state."[170] Like the state, these social bodies must have practices that produce particular kinds of persons, and it is in this sense that the Eucharist is, like torture, a "productive practice"—or, as McClendon might put it, a "powerful practice."[171]

---

165. Ibid., 34–35.

166. Cavanaugh, *Torture and Eucharist*, 1. Cavanaugh cites specific times and places in which such torture took place under Pinochet's rule in Chile. He notes, for example, the torture chamber "at Villa Grimaldi on Jose Arrieta Avenue" in the capital city of Santiago.

167. Ibid. Clearly some practices engaged in by the state to discipline and obtain information from its citizens are more onerous than others. Cavanaugh notes that he wants to avoid applying the label "torture" to too many of the state's "disciplining" practices in order to avoid thinning down the definition of torture (see *Torture and Eucharist*, 21).

168. Ibid., 34.

169. Ibid., 22.

170. Ibid., 4. "Atomizing," we recall, is the language used by Dix when he refers to the increase in focusing upon individual piety in the Eucharist at the expense of the communal emphasis. See again Dix, *Shape of the Liturgy*, 250.

171. McClendon, "Practice of Community Formation," 85, 94. Moreover, he shares with Cavanaugh a MacIntyrian understanding of practices insofar as practices form communities, form bodies.

Re-membering the Body

The similarities between torture and Eucharist end here, Cavanaugh is quick to add, for while in the Eucharist the Church recalls the torture and death of Christ, the rite "produces" a social body, the Church, which is called to resist forces that impose torture and even death upon their constituents as a way of instilling in them a sense of "discipline"[172]—thus his claim that "the Eucharist is the Church's 'counter-politics' to the politics of torture."[173] There are more than simply "symbolic connections between the ritual and what happened in the 'real world,'" he says. There is an "actual and potential impact of the Eucharist on the dictatorship."[174]

The Eucharist "produces" a body, then, in that the Church is not the body of Christ unless it is continually participating in this practice, one that "makes the Church" in assimilating, mass after mass, the Church into the body of Christ, in a sense becoming that which she eats.[175] For Cavanaugh, "the point of saying that the Eucharist makes the church the body of Christ" is to emphasize that the body of Christ "must be constantly received anew in the Eucharistic action."[176] The Church is construed by Cavanaugh as a faithful body when she knows her power lies beyond herself, when she is dependent upon her continual reception of Christ.[177]

Just as in the contrast of the Eucharist and torture, Cavanaugh makes it clear that the ecclesial body of Christ that is made by partaking of the eucharistic body of Christ also stands over against the state through its resistance to violence, and thus gives witness to the oppressor and to others that there are alternatives to violence. While torture creates victims (and victims who are sacrificed for the good of the state alone), the Eucharist forms a body of witnesses.[178] These witnesses may die for the gospel, yet they believe that physical death is not the end of life but actually serves to launch that life for which humans were truly made—the beatific vision.[179]

---

172. Cavanaugh, *Torture and Eucharist*, 4, 14.
173. Ibid., 205.
174. Ibid.
175. Ibid., 269.
176. Ibid.
177. Ibid.
178. Ibid., 232.
179. Cavanaugh, *Theopolitical Imagination*, 14–15. Also, see where, in analyzing Paul's letters to the Corinthians, Cavanaugh says it is a biblical truth that "the Eucharist can kill you." Such death is not entirely negative, for in this death is a foretaste of the kingdom (Cavanaugh, *Torture and Eucharist*, 236).

Henri de Lubac

The Eucharist also stands opposed to torture in that it effects a body, and therefore overcomes isolation. Isolation—even the kind produced by an act as horrific as torture—is overcome in the Eucharist by the building of a community that resists a fallen world and the attempts of governments to tame it.[180] In the Eucharist, persons have become unified in such a way that "'if one member suffers, all suffer together with it; if one member is honored, all rejoice together with it' (1 Cor 12:26)." Cavanaugh notes that for Paul, this oneness is not "a feel-good hymn," but in fact comes on the heels of "a reprimand issued to the [first-century Corinthian church] community for its misconduct."[181] As we discussed through McClendon, the Corinthian church has not discerned the body of Christ in her selfish behavior regarding the meal, and to live according to the ways of the world and at the same time participate in the Eucharist "is to assault the unity of the church."[182] "The eucharist creates unity, it is true," says Cavanaugh, "but the eucharist also *requires* unity."[183]

For Cavanaugh, then, "coexistence" is to be the characteristic experience in this body—and coexistence is in this context much different than the "voluntary fellowship of like-minded individuals" examined in chapter 2 of this study. Persons have been "transubstantiated" into a body, to use Hemming's language; in being made "members of one another" (Eph 4:25) through their faithful participation in the Eucharist, they have been made to image the persons of the triune God, locked in a perichoretic embrace. Marked by these members' common resistance to worldly power—though these members have varying gifts and live in a wide array of cultural contexts[184]—in the ecclesial body difference is desired, and it is difference that is beneficial to the body.[185] Citing Eph 4:11–13, Cavanaugh notes that "in the Eucharist, one is fellow citizen of another," but the differences as well as the similarities among members lead to this "unity in faith."[186]

Cavanaugh frequently points out, however, that without a historical retrieval such as the one de Lubac has offered to the Church, an understanding of a Eucharist so powerful is impossible. Calling the Church the

---

180. Cavanaugh, *Torture and Eucharist*, 206.
181. Ibid., 235.
182. Ibid.
183. Ibid.
184. Cavanaugh, *Theopolitical Imagination*, 120.
185. Cavanaugh, *Torture and Eucharist*, 149.
186. Cavanaugh, *Theopolitical Imagination*, 121.

"mystical body" does not in and of itself constitute heresy, he says with de Lubac, but if by "mystical body" the Church means to call itself a body less real than the transubstantiated bread, or a body confined to a spiritual realm and separated from and irrelevant to the material realm, then the Church has been unduly reduced.[187] He wants to avoid any emphasis of the reality of Christ's presence in the Eucharist that comes *at the expense of* the Church as the true body. Such an overemphasis can, in effect, utterly secularize the churches that lay beyond the bread and the wine, leaving them to think that God is "really" present elsewhere, and that the Church is a coincidental gathering of individuals who share this belief.[188]

Like de Lubac's claims, Cavanaugh's strong language about the reality of the Church can be easily misconstrued as a slight to the eucharistic body of Christ. Cavanaugh, however, also carefully affirms the doctrine of transubstantiation while avoiding an overemphasis on the elements; for him the "Eucharist makes real the presence of Christ both in the elements and in the body of believers. The church becomes the very body of Christ."[189] Cavanaugh's vision is one of both the consecrated host and the gathering of the faithful becoming the body of Christ in the eucharistic performance. As in de Lubac's work on the threefold body of Christ, the eucharistic body mystically unites, or "re-members" (to use McClendon's language), the Church contemporary and all the communion of saints to the historical, resurrected person of Jesus. Thus does the Eucharist function in de Lubac and Cavanaugh as Scripture functions in McClendon's baptist vision—relating the Christian story now unites the narrator and the audience to Jesus and his followers in the first century. "This" Eucharist is "that" Last Supper, in a sense, and yet in the Eucharist the Church as the *corpus verum* is called and empowered to engage in other practices in order to be an extension of Christ in the world—practices that are "eucharistic" in the sense that the Eucharist makes them possible by uniting the Church as a body capable of engaging in such practices.[190]

---

187. Cavanaugh, *Torture and Eucharist*, 269. Specifically, Cavanaugh has in mind the work of Jacques Maritain as reducing the Church in this sense. As my colleague Jason Whitt has shown in his own doctoral work, "Cavanaugh argues that the very ecclesiology of the Chilean church, dependent as it was upon Maritain's distinction of planes and the church only functioning as the inspiration of temporal society, meant that when it was confronted with the torture of citizens at the hands of the government, the church had no way to respond" (Whitt, "Transforming Views of Baptist Ecclesiology," 247).

188. Cavanaugh, *Torture and Eucharist*, 214.

189. Ibid., 205.

190. Ibid.

Cavanaugh's work, then, concretizes de Lubac's claim in a sense—the Eucharist "makes the Church into Christ's Body,"[191] or "generates a body, the Body of Christ" and does so "by gathering [persons] in the local assembly."[192] These persons enact a story in local congregations across the globe, a particular but universal story that is "about the origin and destiny of the whole world."[193] This destiny, Cavanaugh claims through Augustine, is for all persons to be members of one another, "one body" in eternal worship of the one triune God.[194] "All persons" includes for Cavanaugh not only all persons living today, but also those from all generations. In this act of recollection, then, especially "those in heaven who have gone before us and toward whom we now strain forward (Phil 3:13)" are gathered into one body with the contemporary Church.[195] Understood in this way, Cavanaugh says, the Eucharist is the "decentred centre" of the entire Church, gathering persons not only from disparate geographic spaces but from all eras—the entire "communion of saints." Through this practice the Church becomes at the same time local and everywhere: "her periphery extends to 'the very ends of the earth' (Rev 1:18), a periphery that in any case can never be far from the midpoint."[196] Cavanaugh retrieves twelfth-century Frenchman Alain of Lille on this point: in the Eucharist the Church has a center that is everywhere, and the Church therefore has no circumference.[197]

The Eucharist is the center of the Church in at least two other senses for Cavanaugh. The rite is treated as the chief discipline of the Church, and as a result, any discipline of the Church "can only make sense as a Eucharistic discipline."[198] The meal is taken every time the Church meets for worship—"day by day, week by week, the church is gathered around the Eucharist, but then disperses, only to be gathered again at the next Eucharist."[199] Moreover, this weekly event is a center in that it both recalls

191. Cavanaugh, *Theopolitical Imagination*, 88.

192. Ibid., 83.

193. Ibid., 113.

194. Ibid., 14–15.

195. Ibid., 5. Cavanaugh notes in at least three places that persons who are "non-members" of the body are at least prospective members. He employs Augustine in saying that this too is a body that can be said to be "mystically" the body of Christ, in the sense that is potentially the body of Christ.

196. Cavanaugh, *Theopolitical Imagination*, 114.

197. Ibid., 50.

198. Cavanaugh, *Torture and Eucharist*, 221.

199. Ibid., 270.

the earthly life and death of the "historical body" of Jesus—in a sense, the "first coming" of Jesus—and has eschatological implications in its looking forward to the return of Christ, the "second coming," which will relieve all earthly suffering. (Again we hear echoes of McClendon's narrative theology and ecclesiology, where the Church of the twenty-first century is the first-century Church, and the Church then as now strains forward to the return of Christ:[200] "Then is now, this is that.") Along with the Church, the Eucharist is the embodied Christ between the two "comings" of Christ. As it is put in the 1982 Lima Report on baptism, Eucharist, and ministry (issued by the World Council of Churches' Faith and Order Commission, in which the Catholic Church fully participates): "The Holy Spirit through the Eucharist gives a foretaste of the Kingdom of God: the Church receives the life of a new creation and the assurance of the Lord's return."[201] Cavanaugh similarly emphasizes that the present life of the Church and her Eucharist constitute a temporary arrangement between the two comings of Christ.

That the Church participates in the Eucharist each time she meets, and that she looks forward to the parousia each time she participates in the Eucharist, does not mean that the Church is a completely "inward-facing" body. The eschatological dimensions of the rite, that is, are not intended to imply that the Church is a body fleeing the trials of an earthly existence in favor of a completely heavenly one. Rather, eucharistic practice as the "heart of the Church" grounds every other discipline in which the Church engages. It not only makes real the body of Christ, but in recalling the sacrifice of Christ and many of Christ's followers down through the centuries, the Eucharist teaches sacrifice, unity, abiding, and faithfulness in the midst of any and all circumstances—with the hope that one day Christ's unity will reign. The Eucharist in this sense organizes the life of the Church, as a foretaste of the heavenly kingdom. For Cavanaugh, disciplines are eucharistic only if they are sacrificial—teaching us to "die to ourselves"—but also only if they are abiding, bringing about unity, pointing to Christ's return, and so on. It is also in this sense that the Eucharist, as de Lubac put it, is "the heart of the Church."[202]

Because Cavanaugh believes that the Church is not a body fleeing the trials of an earthly existence, and because I began the section on Cavanaugh by stating his claim that in an environment such as the one in Chile in

---

200. McClendon, *Doctrine*, 45.
201. World Council of Churches, *Baptism, Eucharist, and Ministry*.
202. De Lubac, *Splendor*, 76.

the 1970s there could be an "actual and potential impact of the Eucharist on the dictatorship,"[203] let us examine some of the examples of this impact. In the early years just after the coup and government takeover led by Pinochet, the Church was unable to resist the state because, in understanding itself as a body purely "mystical," it understood its role to be one of caring for the soul while ceding control of the body to the state. As Cavanaugh puts it, "it was assumed that [Chilean] society constituted an organic whole in which it was the church's duty to act as conscience or soul, exhorting the body, the state, to act for the common good."[204] Cavanaugh contends that this amounts to the disappearance of the Church itself as a visible, social body able to resist publicly the fragmentation produced primarily by the practice of torture. This ecclesiology made the Church initially incapable of responding to the regime.

Only gradually did a shift take place. It started, Cavanaugh believes, "when people began to knock at the Cardinal's [Silva] door."[205] The cardinal and some Chilean bishops and priests helped form a "Committee of Cooperation for Peace in Chile" to help the unemployed, the families of those in prison, or persons fleeing the police. Still, this committee was reluctant to challenge the state publicly. Only in 1976, after Pinochet forced Cardinal Silva to disband that committee, did Silva form the Vicariate of Solidarity, giving visibility to the Church as a social body. By 1980, seven bishops excommunicated anyone having anything to do with torture. In December 1983, the whole episcopal conference followed.

This ecclesial movement did not necessarily involve all the bishops, and it was interrupted from time to time by threats issued by the state. There were many Christians who feared resisting the state—including bishops and priests—and of course there were mistakes made by the Church along the way. As Cavanaugh says, "there was no neat march from less prophetic to more prophetic."[206] And yet, the Church became visible and prophetic nonetheless.

Cavanaugh is very clear that in returning to the early medieval understanding of the Church and the Eucharist he is not seeking to "rebuild the Old Christendom on the ruins of the New," but he argues that if the Church is to resist a totalitarian state (or any other coercive force), she must see

---

203. Cavanaugh, *Torture and Eucharist*, 205.
204. Ibid., 74.
205. Ibid., 87.
206. Ibid., 119.

herself as a social body with her "own disciplinary resources—Eucharist, penance, virtue, works of mercy, martyrdom . . . which produce actions, practices, habits that are visible in the world."[207] In short, the Church, the "true body" of Christ, must be a contrast society with its own distinctive counter-politics. This is where the Church's faithfulness to be a eucharistic community is crucial—participation in the eucharistic body of Christ produces the body of Christ, the *corpus verum*, which alone has the resources to resist the powers of the world. As McClendon taught us earlier, the ability of the ecclesial body to enact such resistance comes about through our corporate participation in powerful practices.

Conclusion

The sacramental theology of Henri de Lubac picks up the conversation on the Eucharist and the unity of the Church where McClendon stops short. Where McClendon is hesitant to apply the term *sacrament* to the Supper (though he does apply it to other rites), de Lubac uses the term freely in relation to the Eucharist and emphasizes the way in which the Eucharist not only unites the participants with God but also knits the participants to one another. Cavanaugh takes these emphases in de Lubac and adopts them for his projects in the arena of political theology.

As shown above, theologians and laypersons from other traditions have appropriated the work of de Lubac. As I will suggest in the final chapter, there is evidence that both the nod toward sacramentalism offered by McClendon and the thoroughly sacramental thought of de Lubac and contemporary Catholics influenced by de Lubac are proving to be valuable resources for Baptist theologians concerned for ecclesial unity. I hope to show there that Baptists cannot ignore these authors' work on the Eucharist if they want to enter into fruitful discussions about ecclesial unity.

The next chapter, however, focuses upon Protestant theologian Robert Jenson, whose extensive work in biblical and patristic theology has given him the resources to make arguments about the Eucharist and the Church that are similar to de Lubac's, yet even more radically ecclesiocentric. Jenson is a Lutheran and therefore a representative of what McClendon would call the "protestant type" of ecclesiology, but unlike many Protestant theologians, his own understanding of the Church as the "true" body of Christ is so extensive that, in fact, he is often accused of going too far

207. Ibid., 197.

in emphasizing the divine nature of the Church—and, as we shall see, by interpreters of de Lubac's work at that! Jenson contests this critique of his work quite ably, and he relies upon an emphasis on the sacraments in order to do so. He is therefore extremely important to this study's conversation about the Eucharist and the unity of the Church.

4

Robert Jenson and the Gathered Body of Christ

Introduction

IN CHAPTER 2, I argued that although McClendon sees a link between the Supper and the unity of the Church, rarely does he use the term *sacrament* in his work, nor does he indicate that the Supper is the center or the "heart" of the Church.[1] On the other hand, it is clear from chapter 3 that to say that de Lubac employs the term *sacrament* freely is an understatement. For him, the Eucharist is the very heart of the Church's unity in that it both symbolizes and effects the unity of the ecclesial body of Christ.[2] In this chapter, I shall show that Robert Jenson is one Protestant who uses the term *sacrament* as naturally as de Lubac.[3] In Jenson's work, however, all of the sacra-

---

1. Although, as noted in chapters 2 and 3, because he does understand the Supper as *one of* the three major remembering signs, theologian and pastor McClendon called for Baptist congregations to move from only quarterly participation in the Supper to monthly participation (see McClendon, *Making Gospel Sense to a Troubled Church*, xix).

2. De Lubac, *Splendor*, 176.

3. While Jenson states that he is a Lutheran in the sense that he believes "the Reformation needed to happen," he notes that the issue of whether the Supper is a sacrament "situates some denominational Protestants on the Catholic side," and it will become increasingly clear as the chapter progresses that he is one such Protestant (Jenson, *Unbaptized God*, 12, 127). Of his denomination as a whole, he says that regarding the Eucharist, "Lutheranism has been more Catholic than most other Protestants and more Protestant than are normal Catholics" (Jenson, *Unbaptized God*, 30–31). As we shall see below, however, esteemed de Lubac commentator Susan K. Wood believes that "Lutherans must concede more to his theology than must Roman Catholics" (Wood, "Robert Jenson's Ecclesiology from a Roman Catholic Perspective," 187).

ments—and not just the Eucharist—are the "center" of the Church, those things that the Church gathers around in order to hear the gospel and learn to be the Church.[4] For Jenson, "when the gospel gathers people, they do not merely verbalize. They eat and drink, they wash some of their number or anoint them with oil, they touch in a variety of symbolic ways, they sit and they stand and kneel, they make parades, they make cross-signs with their fingers, they do all sorts of body-things. These performances, insofar as they occur in the course of telling and hearing the gospel, are what the church-language calls 'sacraments' and 'sacramentals.'"[5] The Eucharist is one of these sacraments—a sacrament through which God effects the Church's unity ("we become one body and blood of Christ and members of one another")[6]—as are baptism, marriage, and an indefinite number of other sacraments.[7]

---

4. Jenson, *Visible Words*, 35. Moreover, wherever the sacraments are "visible words," they are "communication-events of the gospel," and for Jenson "gospel" means the "cheering message" that "there has lived a man wholly for others, all the way to death; and he has risen, so that his self-giving will finally triumph" (see Jenson, *Story and Promise*, 2).

5. Jenson, *Story and Promise*, 165.

6. Jenson, *Systematic Theology*, 2:212. Jenson takes seriously the notion that there is no unity with God that does not entail unity with the Church. The description cited above, for example, is drawn from the introductory remarks of a chapter titled "The Great Communion," a title intended to describe both the Church and the practice of the Supper, which only takes place in the unique community called "the Church."

7. Jenson points out with Paul that Christians are "baptized into one body" (1 Cor 12:13), thereby being made one with one another, even "members of one another" (Eph 4:25). Pointless, then, are arguments over whether the Church's unity is brought about through the Eucharist or baptism or through some other means (Jenson, *Systematic Theology*, 1:204; 2:183). Neither in de Lubac is it as if one has to "decide" between the unity created by baptism, Eucharist, or another sacrament, but de Lubac's emphasis on the Eucharist in particular—it is "especially the sacrament of unity" (de Lubac, *Catholicism*, 89)—is consistent with the Catholic tradition that so influenced him and (as we have proven by now) has been influenced by him. The *Catechism of the Catholic Church* reads that "the mode of Christ's presence under the Eucharistic species is unique. It raises the Eucharist above all the sacraments..." (see *Catechism of the Catholic Church*, 1374). This emphasis is consistent with de Lubac's work and represents a hierarchy unlike that in Jenson, for whom there is no "list of," but rather an indefinite number of, sacraments (Jenson, *Visible Words*, 11). Jenson indicates that some have argued that the most important sacrament is the one with which Jesus founded the Church: "whether Christ founded the church by being baptized, or by choosing the apostles, or by celebrating the last supper, or by, as the risen one, breathing the Spirit on his disciples or mandating the mission..." But for Jenson, "it is the Son's whole life, from his conception by the Holy Spirit to his Ascension, that in fact founds the church" (Jenson, *Systematic Theology*, 2:183).

Re-membering the Body

In line with McClendon's three types of ecclesiologies—which distinguish between Catholics and Protestants, Catholics and baptists, and, perhaps most significantly for our purposes, Protestants and baptists—I will treat Jenson's sacramental theology separately here.[8] Jenson will also function as a helpful interlocutor because like McClendon and de Lubac, he is a twentieth-century theologian who sees a deep connection between the Eucharist and the unity of the Church. Moreover, like his Baptist and Catholic counterparts in this study, Jenson's understanding of the Eucharist is formed by his close attention to Scripture, paired with a deep respect for the Christian tradition as the interpretation of Scripture.[9] Indeed, in his *Systematic Theology*, Jenson notes that he relies upon de Lubac's retrieval of the Church's traditional method of exegesis.[10] Finally, as we shall see below, Jenson will serve as a helpful discussion partner for McClendon and de Lubac because in contrast with McClendon (but in concert with de Lubac) he uses the language of sacrament quite freely, and in contrast with de Lubac (but in concert with McClendon) he is familiar with the types of questions and critiques being posed by persons who are averse to the language and practices of "sacramentalists."[11]

---

8. Jenson is not just any "Protestant" figure but has been called "North America's leading Lutheran theologian" by Alistair McGrath, editor of Blackwell's *Christian Theology Reader* (see McGrath, *Christian Theology Reader*, 382).

9. Alasdair MacIntyre's definition of tradition as an "historically extended, socially embodied argument," explained in chapter 1, is important here (MacIntyre, *After Virtue*, 222ff.). Scripture will be introduced below as the normative story of God and God's people, while the Christian tradition, or "Christian theology," will be portrayed as the Church's ongoing discussion about God and God's people. Jenson claims that "there should be continuous argument in the church" in order to determine the rightness of any claim or movement. If, finally, the tradition strays from the norm, which is the biblical narrative—as Jenson believes it did with "the commands 'sell indulgences' and 'mediate transcendentally,'" for example—then it is not to be heeded, but challenged (Jenson, *Systematic Theology*, 1:57 ff.).

10. Jenson, *Systematic Theology*, 1:81, n. 54.

11. See again, for example, his acknowledgment that to ask the question, "'would God really let his body be pushed about on the Supper's table' so that the Church could be the body of Christ?" is to wade into strange waters for many Protestants (Jenson, *Visible Words*, 33, 37). Or, perhaps better, see his note that many might ask, "Why is it not enough privately to think and feel Christ's presence and to know that others in their privacies do the same?" (Jenson, *Systematic Theology*, 2:214).

Scripture, Tradition, and the Body of Christ

Jenson believes that his sacramental theology and ecclesiology are rooted in Scripture and the best of the Christian tradition. Scripture is the telling of the gospel by which all other tellings must be judged,[12] and, as Jenson puts it, "the Christian sacraments, as 'visible words' of the gospel, seem so profoundly and primitively and obviously biblical that I have no special way to argue for them."[13] Regarding baptism, for example, Jenson notes that "the Scriptures say 'Baptize,'" and so the Church has, since the time of the disciples and the earliest leaders of the institutionalized Church, baptized persons who sought to become members of the Church.[14] As for the Eucharist or "the Supper,"[15] Jenson underscores that Jesus offered the disciples the new Passover meal on the eve of his crucifixion, saying, "do this in remembrance of me."[16] A generation later the Apostle Paul took it for granted that the practicing Church regularly participates in the thanksgiving meal, citing Jesus' words above and adding "as often as you eat this bread and drink this cup, you proclaim the Lord's death until he comes" (1 Cor 11:26).[17] Finally, regarding the postbiblical tradition, Jenson points out that across the generations the most influential theologians of their respective eras—giants such as Chrysostom, Aquinas, and Luther—assume the correctness of the practice of the Eucharist and (importantly) explain its unitive effect as a result of their readings of Scripture.[18]

12. Jenson, *Systematic Theology*, 1:26–27.

13. Jenson, *Visible Words*, 5.

14. Ibid., 9.

15. This is McClendon's preferred language (aside from his very latest works), but Jenson also uses this term frequently. Jenson changes his terminology more often than de Lubac and McClendon, shifting easily between "the Supper," "communion," and "Eucharist."

16. Jenson, *Story and Promise*, 168. "Do what? The account is plain: share a loaf and a loving-cup of wine, and give thanks to God. If we do these things, we obey the command."

17. Jenson, *Visible Words*, 71.

18. See again Jenson, "Church and the Sacraments," 215, 222. On the authority of tradition, like de Lubac, Jenson aligns himself with Aquinas on the matter, arguing that the role of the tradition is to "preserve the biblical understanding" of God and God's relationship with God's people (Jenson, *Systematic Theology*, 1:220), since the biblical narration of the life of God and God's people is the telling of the Gospel "from which all other tellings draw," the telling by which all other narratives of God are to be judged. Scripture is "one part of the tradition," he says, but is ultimately "the norm of the tradition as a whole," the "*norma normans non normata*, the norm with no norm over it, although other norms establish it in this position, and . . . are necessary to its function in it" (for

The Body of Christ: Comparing Jenson to de Lubac

To claim that Scripture and the Christian tradition play a central role in the development of Jenson's sacramental theology and ecclesiology—as I have just done—is not specific enough.[19] It is the Pauline Epistles and the unfolding therein of the concept of the body of Christ that seem to drive Jenson's thinking on these matters.[20] Jenson's work here is extensive and closely related to the emphases of de Lubac—it even seems to allude (though vaguely) to a few of the Jesuit's findings when talking about the unique link between the ecclesial and eucharistic bodies[21]—but his situating of the term *body* as it is employed in the New Testament also sets him apart from de Lubac and makes unique his exegesis related to the Church and the Eucharist. I shall explain this in the pages that immediately follow.

---

two versions of this quote, see Jenson, *Visible Words*, 9, and Jenson, *Systematic Theology*, 1:26–27). In spite of this high view of Scripture, many free church readers are uncomfortable with Jenson's understanding of tradition, saying he cedes too much authority in matters of doctrine. To such readers, Jenson would say that "canon, creed, and episcopate were but parts of a single norm of faith, discovered in response to a single historical crisis; if one of the three is alienable, how are the other two not? It was precisely in their interaction that they were to guard the apostolicity of the church's teaching; what justifies separating one as dispensable?" (Jenson, *Systematic Theology*, 2:239). Jenson's point is that the Church (or "tradition") and Scripture are closely linked in terms of their authority. To do away with one of them (for our purposes, tradition) would threaten the existence of the others. After all, the Church is the very authority that, by the power of the Holy Spirit, established what it would consider to be Scripture going forward (Jenson, *Systematic Theology*, 1:26–27). Robert Louis Wilken is one example of a patristics scholar who admires Jenson's rootedness in Scripture and the earliest church fathers. See Wilken, "Is Pentecost a Peer of Easter?" 177.

19. Though it is a departure from the way in which I organized the previous chapters, sacramental theology and ecclesiology are intentionally introduced together here as the "body of Christ"—primarily as a way of proceeding in concert with Jenson. Jenson himself notes that while "all *loci* of theology are interconnected as nodes of an intricate web, these two make a systematic couple as most possible pairings would not" (Jenson, "Church and the Sacraments," 207).

20. It should be noted here that, like many of the best theologians, Jenson's body of work is so extensive that one could say this about many aspects of his work on Scripture. It could be claimed without much dispute at all, for example, that Jenson's unusually extensive work on Israel and the Old Testament seems to drive his understanding of Jesus and the New Testament.

21. Jenson, *Systematic Theology*, 2:220. Namely, he alludes to de Lubac's finding that for the patristics, the "true" body of Christ was the Church prior to this description being applied to the Eucharist.

The Ecclesial Body

Jenson asserts that in the New Testament "the only body of Christ to which Paul actually refers is not an entity in heaven but the Eucharist's loaf and cup and the church assembled around them."[22] In works that are undisputedly written by Paul, the apostle calls the Church "the body of Christ," and this description is found elsewhere in Pauline materials.[23] Jenson is quick to add, however, that in order to understand the ancient view of the Church it is not enough to simply know that the title "body of Christ" is given to the Church. Rather, one must know what this title means, and Jenson believes that from the time of the eucharistic controversies that swirled around Berengar, persons have mistakenly assumed that they understand the term.[24]

Just as de Lubac, then, Jenson mines the New Testament in order to show the sense of "body" in ancient Christian literature (and especially in Pauline literature).[25] He concludes that for Paul, "someone's 'body' is simply the person him or herself insofar as this person is *available* to other persons and to him or herself, insofar as the person is an *object* for other persons and him or herself."[26] He adds that Paul is interrogated by the Roman soldiers only as he is bodily available to be interrogated,[27] and that "the organism

---

22. Jenson, *Systematic Theology*, 1:204.

23. See 1 Cor 12:27; Rom 12:5; Eph 1:22-23; 4:12. Indeed, in all of Scripture, only the Pauline materials apply the title "body of Christ" to the Church.

24. Jenson, *Systematic Theology*, 1:205. Just as we did in McClendon and de Lubac, then, we encounter in Jenson the view that in the Church's reaction to Berengar her vision was clouded by the controversy.

25. This is not to say that Jenson is doing exactly the same kind of *ressourcement* that de Lubac is performing. Though the two are strikingly similar in terms of their understanding of the Church "retrieving" the best of the tradition in order to be an effective and relevant Church now, while Jenson involves a number of disciplines and perspectives on the term *body* and focuses primarily upon the way it is used in the New Testament, de Lubac exegetes the New Testament, patristic, and medieval literature and often overwhelms the reader by the sheer number of examples of certain uses of the term *corpus* (see, for example, de Lubac, *Corpus Mysticum*, 4-5, 13-14). Perhaps the closest de Lubac comes to doing what Jenson does with the term *body* is to say that as body, the Church is "a single organism of Jesus Christ and his Church, signifying at the same time the subjection of the members to the head" (de Lubac, *Church*, 24).

26. Jenson, *Systematic Theology*, 1:205. Or elsewhere, "in Paul's language, a person's embodiment is his or her *availability* to other persons and thereupon to her or himself" (Jenson, *Systematic Theology*, 2:213).

27. Jenson, *Systematic Theology*, 1:205.

that was Jesus' availability—that was his body—until he was killed would have as a corpse continued to be an availability of this person."[28] Bodies are, in Scripture, availabilities that give other persons a certain amount of freedom to act upon them.[29]

For Jenson, then, the Church is a body in that it is *available*. Specifically, "The church, according to Paul, is the risen body of Christ,"[30] the very manner in which Christ is available to and for the world. This is not an analogy, according to Jenson—"In the complex of these passages there is no way to construe 'body' as a simile or other trope that does not make mush of Paul's arguments"[31]—but a very real way of referring to the Church as Christ's concrete availability, the means through which Christ is encountered. Jenson points out by way of Orthodox theologian Geoffrey Preston that "the relation of the Church to Christ is not 'like' that of a man's body to the man himself. It *is* that of Christ's body to the Lord himself."[32] In Jenson's own words, "the risen Christ as a complete living human being has a body and the church is this body."[33] This body is "available to be found, to be responded to, to be grasped."[34] Jenson carefully (but boldly) says, then, that "Christ is personally the second identity of God, and the *totus Christus* is Christ with the church."[35]

---

28. Ibid., 206.

29. Jenson, "You Wonder Where the Body Went," in *Essays in the Theology of Culture*, 221. I will return to this last idea, as free church readers are ordinarily the first to ask why Christ needs to be bodily available in the first place.

30. Jenson, *Systematic Theology*, 1:205.

31. Ibid. As I pointed out in chapter 3, employing de Lubac's retrieval of the threefold body, Cavanaugh says that "body" is not an "image" at all, but a reality. Referring to the title "body of Christ" as one among many "images" of the Church seems to Cavanaugh to over-spiritualize, and therefore unduly reduce the role of, the Church (Cavanaugh, *Torture and Eucharist*, 170).

32. Jenson, *Systematic Theology*, 2:212, citing Preston, *Faces of the Church*, 89. Emphasis mine.

33. Jenson, "Church and the Sacraments," 209. Elsewhere (and again more boldly): "God is a person; and that means he is Spirit and Body" (Jenson, *Visible Words*, 25).

34. Jenson, "Church and the Sacraments," 210.

35. Jenson, *Systematic Theology*, 2:167. Christ and his Church together form the *totus Christus* ("the whole Christ"). To retrieve a quote used in chapter 3, Augustine said, "*Verbum caro factum est, et habitavit in nobis; illi carni adjungitur ecclesia, et fit Christus totus, caput et corpus*" ("The Word was made flesh, and dwelled among us; to that flesh is joined the Church, and there is made the whole Christ, head and body") (Augustine, *On the Epistle of John*, 1.2). Elsewhere, however, Augustine says that it was not that Christ would be incomplete without the Church, but that Christ did not wish to be complete

Though this is an ancient claim, the idea that "the *totus Christus* is Christ with the church" comes as a shocking one to most Protestants as well as members of free churches.[36] Does it follow necessarily from this claim that the Son, the second person of the Trinity, is not wholly the Son without the Church? Jenson seems to think so. This view is apparent when he claims that Paul's understanding is that "we are the body of Christ . . . in that we have been 'baptized into' it. And what we have been baptized into is simply 'Christ.'"[37] Elsewhere, when speaking of God as "the triune community," the Church is called "the body of the second person of that community."[38] This is no less bold than de Lubac, who said that the Church "not only carries on [Christ's] work, but she is his very continuation, in a sense far more real than in which it can be said that any human institution is its founder's continuation."[39]

The comparison between de Lubac and Jenson—or at least between their respective traditions—on the divine nature of the Church bears further investigation. In a piece written in honor of Jenson, Lubacian scholar Susan K. Wood argues that in Jenson the Church is "a prolongation of the incarnation"—in a way very similar to the traditional Anglican claim that the Church is an extension of the incarnation into history,[40] but perhaps in

---

without the Church (cf. *Sermons* 341.1.1 and 9.1).

36. Jenson laments that "Protestants have sometimes proclaimed with satisfaction or even glee, 'in the Kingdom there will be no church,' thereby in fact blaspheming" (Jenson, *Systematic Theology*, 2:171).

37. Jenson, *Systematic Theology*, 1:204. See 1 Cor 12:13.

38. Jenson, "Church and the Sacraments," 217. It is interesting that in one place, when speaking of the triune life as a model for the way the Church is to live in the world, he calls the Church "the Son's *created* body, with all creation as it is made through and for the Son, the church's petition and praise represent before the Father the petition and praise of all creation" (Jenson, *Systematic Theology*, 2:227, emphasis mine). Elsewhere, calling the Church the *totus Christus* seems to entail even a status as a preexistent reality (Jenson, *Systematic Theology*, 1:151). Jenson fully understands the implications of this language, noting that this is one place in which we encounter "the great offense of Christian discourse about God" (Jenson, *Visible Words*, 25).

39. De Lubac, *Catholicism*, 29.

40. Though in contemporary theology John Milbank and the school of Radical Orthodoxy are often credited with this phrase, it is a classically Anglican expression that predates Milbank and, moreover, is also found extensively in the sixteenth-century Anabaptist Pilgram Marpeck's thought. For Anglicans' application of this phrase to the Church, see Curran, "J. Deotis Roberts and the Roman Catholic Tradition," in Battle, *Quest for Liberation and Reconciliation*, 90. For an intriguing example of the similarity of the thought of Anabaptist Pilgram Marpeck and the Radical Orthodoxy movement, see

a manner exceeding the Roman Catholic Church's claims about the status of the ecclesial body.[41] Wood believes this to be an important difference between the ecclesiologies of de Lubac and Jenson, claiming that here the Lutheran, not the Catholic, identifies Christ with the Church in a dangerous manner and "tends to place the church on the same plane as the other three persons" of the Trinity.[42] The difference, Wood believes, lies in de Lubac's use of the term *sacrament*. For de Lubac, she says, "the church is here below the sacrament of Jesus Christ, as Jesus Christ himself is for us, in his humanity, the sacrament of God."[43] At this point in de Lubac's work, as in the documents of the Second Vatican Council, "the church is likened to the incarnate word; it is not equated to the incarnate word. The concept of the church as the sacrament of Christ avoids too close an identification between Christ and the church. The concept of sacrament is able to express the unity between the sign and the referent of that sign at the same time that it maintains the distinction between sign and referent."[44]

Jenson never uses the exact words that Wood employs to describe his view of the Church—"a prolongation of the incarnation"—but Wood and Michael Scott Horton both believe that this is Jenson's direction, and Horton argues that he takes this path as a direct result of his following John Milbank's Thomistic interpretation of de Lubac's view that the supernatural (in this case, God) does not destroy the natural (in this case, the Church), but perfects it. The natural can indeed mediate grace.[45] Horton retrieves Lutheran theologian Mark C. Mattes' critique of Jenson. Mattes has said

---

Blough, "Church as Sign or Sacrament."

41. Wood, "Robert Jenson's Ecclesiology from a Roman Catholic Perspective," 182.

42. Ibid., 180. Wood's use of the term *other* is curious here. She seems to accidentally place the Church on equal footing with Father, Son, and Spirit here, though we can see from the rest of her article that this is the opposite of her intent.

43. Ibid., 183.

44. Ibid.

45. Horton, *People and Place*, 167. Wood, a Catholic introduced in chapter 3, says that in Jenson's ecclesiology the Church is an extension of the incarnation into history. Fellow Lutheran Mark C. Mattes says that, if this is indeed Jenson's direction, it is problematic, arguing that Jenson's conflation of Christ and the Church "ignores the truth that before God, we are fundamentally passive—solely receivers. . . . The moral life that accords with such passivity is active service to the neighbor, and the appropriate metaphor for the Christian life is 'descent' in charity toward others. . . . In a radical departure from the Lutheran affirmation that the church is an assembly of people shaped by the gospel's message and sacraments, Jenson believes that God expresses his identity to the world as a creature, the body of the church" (cited in Horton, *People and Place*, 168).

that "besides erasing the distinction between Christ and the church, this interpretation loses the Reformation's insistence that grace redeems and restores nature rather than adding something to it or elevating it to a supernatural status. Humanity is absorbed into deity, and the church is the site of this new being."[46]

Protestants and Catholics alike, then, share Horton's concern. It turns out that Jenson's description of the Church is too lofty not only for Baptists, but surprisingly for most contemporary Catholics! According to Wood, "his treatment of the church elevates it beyond creaturely status [and] in this elevation Jenson not only resonates with Roman Catholic ecclesiology, he exceeds it . . . [T]he church risks becoming a prolongation of the incarnation in a way that *Lumen Gentium* attempted to avoid."[47] Again, for Wood, in *Lumen Gentium* "the church is likened to the incarnate word; it is not equated with the incarnate word," and it is the concept of sacrament that prevents "too close an identification."[48] Indeed, Wood's reading has some merit—the Church is defined as sacrament in the very first paragraph of *Lumen Gentium*.

Jenson must have anticipated this critique, however, for in his systematic works he takes time to show that it is crucial to recognize the Church as the body of the Son, and yet she is not the body of the Son *biologically*.[49] He follows the book of Ephesians on this point and the comments on Ephesians of his favorite theologian, Jonathan Edwards.[50] Edwards points out that while for Paul "Christ is the head of the church, the body of which he is the Savior" (Eph 5:23), he compares the relationship between Christ

---

46. Horton, *People and Place*, 167.

47. Wood, "Robert Jenson's Ecclesiology from a Roman Catholic Perspective," 182. Yves Congar says that the Second Vatican Council was very careful not to identify the Church too closely with Christ, noting that the cardinals knew well that "at the very moment when for the first time in history the Church defined, or rather declared and described itself, it wanted to avoid an ecclesiocentrism of such a sort that would end by transferring to a very human reality an interest and ultimately the worship due to God and his Christ" (Congar, *Un people messianique*, 73).

48. Wood, "Robert Jenson's Ecclesiology from a Roman Catholic Perspective," 182.

49. And yet, he says that "for Paul, a spiritual body, whatever that may be, is as much or more a body as is a biological body" (Jenson, *Systematic Theology*, 2:205).

50. Praise for Edwards is found throughout Jenson's work, most poignantly in the fact that as a mature theologian he penned a book on Edwards titled *America's Theologian*. In his *Systematic Theology*, Jenson bluntly calls Edwards "the eighteenth century's only at once fully Christian and robustly constructive theologian" (Jenson, *Systematic Theology*, 1:119).

and the Church to that of husband and wife. The way in which husband and wife are one "is a mystery," according to the apostle (making it obvious that he is speaking of something more than sexual "oneness," which is sometimes emphasized), and he goes on to say that he is "applying" this mystery to Christ and the Church (Eph 5:32). According to Edwards, for Paul, entering into the life of the triune God through the Church is akin to entering a new family through marriage: "There was, [as] it were, an eternal society or family in the Godhead, in the Trinity of persons. It seems to be God's design to admit the church into the divine family as his son's wife."[51]

Jenson believes that if we are to allow with Edwards that the Church is the body of the Christ who is one with the Father and the Spirit, then it follows necessarily that the Church is in fact "the body of God."[52] To say this is not to say that the Church has somehow earned entrance into the Trinity, or that it is on equal footing with Father, Son, and Spirit. Neither is the Church to be characterized as sinless. Rather, as Jenson says through *Lumen Gentium*, the Church, "during its pilgrimage on earth, is 'still in its members liable to sin'"; she is "'clasping sinners in her bosom,' she is at once holy and always in need of purification."[53]

Thus it is solely in her unity with Christ (which comes only through faith) that the Church presumes to be the body of God. This is not unlike de Lubac's retrieval of Augustine's comments on Eph 5:25–27. When noting that Augustine claims that "the Church has neither spot nor wrinkle," de Lubac (who, in a way similar to Jenson, likes to refer to the ecclesial body

---

51. Edwards, *Miscellanies*, 704, quoted in Jenson, *Systematic Theology*, 2:19. Jenson notes in volume 1 of *Systematic Theology* that *Miscellanies* is unpublished (Jenson, *Systematic Theology*, 1:119). Perhaps Jenson's use of this quotation by Edwards prompts Susan K. Wood to say that "Jenson identifies the church as the fourth dramatic person in the biblical narrative, the first three being the persons of the Trinity" (Wood, "Robert Jenson's Ecclesiology from a Roman Catholic Perspective," 180).

52. Jenson states that "God does in fact have a body, the body born of Mary and risen into the church and its sacraments. When the disciples turned to the object Jesus, or when we turn to the object loaf and cup or bath or gathered community, we have precisely the body of God for our object" (Jenson, *Systematic Theology*, 1:229). It is appropriate that this quote comes in the closing pages of volume 1 of *Systematic Theology*, subtitled *The Triune God*, and just prior to volume 2, subtitled *The Works of God*. See also a book Jenson coedited with Carl E. Braaten, in which Jenson writes that "Christ, we said earlier, is the body of God. It is into the embodiment of the gospel, that is, into the objective life of the church, that Christ is bodily risen. It is the embodiment of the gospel that is the the 'body of Christ' and so the body of God" (Braaten and Jenson, *Christian Dogmatics*, 1:177).

53. Jenson, *Unbaptized God*, 102.

Robert Jenson and the Gathered Body of Christ

not only as the body of Christ but as "the body of the Lord") is sure to say that this does not mean that "she is already thus, but rather that she is in preparation to become thus."[54]

Jenson, too, wants to walk this fine line, affirming (he believes) a vision in which the Church is the body of Christ, even "the body of God,"[55] but is not identical with the second person of the Trinity. "We may not," he says, "so identify the risen Christ with the church as to be unable to refer distinctly to the one and then to the other."[56] Jenson employs a large number of the Christian tradition's resources while trying to achieve a balanced view of the Church, and his understanding, like de Lubac's, is that these sources root their claims in Scripture. Indeed, however disparate the above theologians may seem—from Augustine and Edwards to de Lubac, Wood, and Horton—Paul does indeed claim in Ephesians that the Church is one with Christ as wives are one with their husbands, and yet in many other places that the Church is the body of Christ. One section of Jenson's *Systematic Theology* sums up his understanding of what this means, and it is worth quoting at length:

> It is time for theology . . . to let what Paul meant by "body" teach us also what to mean by "body" . . . We must learn to say: the entity rightly called the body of Christ is whatever object it is that is Christ's availability to us as subjects; by the promise of Christ, this object is the bread and cup and the gathering around them. *There is where creatures can locate him, to respond to his word to them.*
>
> No metaphor or ontological evasion should be intended. Sacrament and church are *truly* Christ's body for us, because Christ himself takes these same things for the object as which he is available to himself . . . The subject that the risen Christ is, is the subject who comes to word in the gospel. The object—the body—that the risen Christ is, is the body in the world to which this word calls

---

54. Augustine, *Retract.*, bk. 2, ch. 18. De Lubac says that when Paul speaks of the Church in this way, he speaks not of the Church Militant but of the Church as the Bride (de Lubac, *Splendor*, 119). Regarding the Church as the body of the Lord, de Lubac retrieves William of St. Thierry and Gilbert of Nogent on the matter, and notes that "we still like to use this title" when referring to the ecclesial body (see de Lubac, *Catholicism*, 388; *Corpus Mysticum*, 79).

55. Jenson, *Systematic Theology*, 1:229.

56. Jenson, *Systematic Theology*, 2:213. Again, Horton critiques: "Radicalizing the Lutheran interpretation of the *communicatio idiomatum*, Jenson seems to be saying that in his ascended state, even Jesus' human body need not have the properties that render it genuinely human" (Horton, *People and Place*, 167).

our intention, the church around her sacraments. He needs no other body to be a risen man, body and soul.[57]

The final sentence of this quote may remind readers of Teresa of Avila's celebrated claim: "Christ has no body now on earth but yours, no hands but yours, no feet but yours; yours are the eyes through which is to look out Christ's compassion to the world; yours are the feet with which he is to go about doing good; yours are the hands with which he is to bless now." Jenson goes further than Teresa here.[58] He does not say that "Christ has no body now *on earth*," but that Christ "*needs* no other body" than the Church. As examples like this mount, Susan K. Wood's assessment of the relationship between the ecclesiologies of Jenson and de Lubac (and other Catholic writing) gains momentum.

The Eucharistic Body

In establishing what it means for the Church to be the body of Christ, the long quotation above also makes it clear that the Church is this available body as a result of its participation in the Eucharist.[59] That is, for Jenson it is through participation in the eucharistic body of Christ that persons become the ecclesial body. As stated above, "the entity rightly called the body of Christ is whatever object it is that is Christ's availability to us," and "this object is the bread and cup and the gathering around them."[60] This is scriptural, according to Jenson: "the body that is the church, and the sacramental bodies around which it gathers, are said in Scripture to be the body of the living Christ . . . and the ensemble of all these is in fact his body."[61]

It is clear here that for Jenson, the Eucharist is a sacrament and not "merely a symbol" (to use the language of the "sub-Zwinglian" free church theologians cited in chapter 2).[62] And yet some Protestant churches, espe-

---

57. Jenson, *Systematic Theology*, 1:205–6. "Truly," but on these two defining pages he never uses the word "physically."

58. And is therefore again going further than someone we characterize as "Catholic"!

59. Jenson, *Systematic Theology*, 1:205.

60. Ibid.

61. Jenson, *Visible Words*, 35.

62. See Harmon, *Towards a Baptist Catholicity*, 13. Most free church theologians do not believe that the Supper is a sacrament, but it is debatable whether the same can be said about Protestant thinkers. In chapter 1, it is shown that the purely symbolic view was limited primarily to persons in the radical wing of the Reformation early on, and by

cially those in the free church tradition, have often been described as holding to a purely symbolic role for the Supper. Recall again the words of (the Anglican and therefore Protestant) Dix, who said that "the only meaning which protestants could assign to the eucharist which did not contradict its own basic principle of 'justification by faith alone' is that the service is a very specially solemn reminder to all who attend it with faith of the passion and atonement of Christ, and so it is a valuable means of eliciting devout feelings of gratitude, love, confidence, and union with Him in those who make use of His ordinance."[63] Contrary to Dix's statement, Jenson is a Protestant who believes that the Eucharist is a sacrament, which means he believes that God conveys grace through the Eucharist. He says that "it is a disastrous mistake to distinguish analysis of Christian sacraments as communication from analysis of them as events of God's real presence and action."[64] How "disastrous"? He offers the following analogy:

> Consider, for trivial example, the abolition of the 4th of July firecracker. Merely that it was slightly dangerous could not have sufficed to ban it; equally useless and far more dangerous items proliferate in our commerce: snowmobiles, martinis, hunting weapons, much marriage counseling, etc. We gave up on the firecracker because it was "only" the ceremonial embodiment of our patriotic sentiments, and social technologists persuaded us we could be just as patriotic without it. But the whole 4th of July died with it. Read the nineteenth-century newspapers of your town or city: its rich ceremonial life was that almost of another culture.[65]

Just as he believes the "4th of July" has all but disappeared, Jenson believes that without a sacramental understanding of the Church's practices we would witness and participate in nothing less than the disappearance of the visible Church. There are sacraments, and sacraments, says Jenson

---

subsequent Baptists and Anabaptists. Luther, instructive here both as the linchpin of the Protestant Reformation and because he founded the denomination of which Jenson is a member, held both that the Church was wherever the word was preached and the sacraments duly administered, and that in the sacrament of the Supper, Christ was in, under, and around the elements—truly present.

63. Dix, *Shape of the Liturgy*, 601. Again, the well-known Dix is cited by McClendon, de Lubac, and Jenson, and is perhaps most frequently employed today in Protestant circles by Geoffrey Wainwright, a British Methodist who is professor of systematic theology at Duke University Divinity School and past president of the World Council of Churches.

64. Jenson, *Visible Words*, 5.

65. Ibid., 17.

by way of the Council of Trent, "contain the grace they signify."[66] They are words, spoken or acted,[67] that are "gospel-communication."[68]

Jenson makes these claims though he is well aware that many Protestants want nothing to do with the term *sacraments*. To groups who doubt their existence, he says, "I would have little argument to present: I could only say 'Go and *watch* the church for a while.' Church groups that themselves claim not to have sacraments are only indulging a semantic prejudice."[69] Yet Jenson believes this indulgence will "create vacuums that will be filled somehow, perhaps most inappropriately to the gospel."[70]

What are these vaccuums? How will they be filled? McClendon might answer that we see evidence of Jenson's claims in the fact that in most free church worship, since the Supper is practiced only annually at worst and monthly at best,[71] the sermon and its preacher have taken on a more central role in modern and contemporary worship services. For the earliest churches the Eucharist, held at least weekly, was almost always "preceded by a service of the word, with readings, preaching and intercessory prayer, concluded by the exchange of a holy kiss, as a 'seal' of their prayers and an expression of unity."[72] Thus has proclamation of the word through preaching, along with the Eucharist, been an important feature in Christian worship services since the inception of the faith.

And yet, if the Eucharist is "the heart of the Church" and therefore the climax of the liturgy for de Lubac (and to a lesser extent Jenson), it is the sermon that has become the "heart" of most free churches' worship services.

---

66. Jenson, *Systematic Theology*, 2:123.

67. Jenson, *Visible Words*, 10.

68. Ibid., 11. Moreover, as I have endeavored to show and will continue to endeavor to show in this chapter, "gospel-communication" involves more than the communication of ideas; gospel-communication—whether through preaching, baptism, the Supper, or other forms of communication—is the communication of Christ himself.

69. Jenson, *Visible Words*, 5.

70. Ibid.

71. While working at Judson College in central Alabama, for example, I have learned from the African-American students here that National Baptists in this region consistently have a service of the Lord's Supper on a monthly basis. Though McClendon devotes a large section of his *Systematic Theology* to African-American evangelicals and their strong sense of community, he does not link this sense of oneness to their participating in the Lord's Supper more frequently than their Caucasian brothers and sisters. Again, however, it is important that the reader recall that as interim pastor he urged his own congregations to participate in the Supper at least monthly.

72. Bradshaw, *New Westminster Dictionary of Liturgy and Worship*, 172.

Robert Jenson and the Gathered Body of Christ

On Sunday mornings in many self-proclaimed "evangelical" churches, after the congregation sings two or three hymns and says—or (more often) listens to—two or three fervent prayers, the sermon occupies most of the last half of the worship service. This is an emphasis that, according to Anglican theologian David Broughton (D. B.) Knox, is foreign to Christianity from the Apostle Paul until well after Martin Luther.[73]

As noted in chapter 2 of this study, McClendon is one free church theologian and pastor who has called members of the body of Christ to a more frequent celebration of the Supper—even as a remedy for disunity in a "troubled" Baptist church in California that he served as pastor.[74] By making this move in a Baptist church in North America constituted primarily of Caucasian members,[75] McClendon could be called a "radical."[76]

Of course, it has often been pointed out that the increasing centrality of the sermon in Protestant and free church worship was part of a long overdue corrective to the alleged mentality that participation in the Eucharist was a mechanical, human work in which the believer could attain a purely spiritual salvation.[77] Indeed, as early as the fourth century preach-

---

73. Knox, "Nature of Worship." Knox is an Anglican priest, theology teacher, and has been principal of Moore College in Australia for twenty-eight years. Critics of his statement here may cite Acts 20:7–11, where Eutyches falls out of a third-story window and dies because he fell asleep during one of Paul's very lengthy teaching (preaching?) sessions. It is disputed, however, whether Paul is preaching or even teaching within the context of a worship service. Moreover, this passage does not indicate that this was a normal practice for the apostle.

74. McClendon, *Making Gospel Sense to a Troubled Church*, xix. We are reminded in *Doctrine* that the Supper is a "sign of salvation" over against sin, which McClendon defines as "refusal" of Jesus' "way," as "reversion" to the old, inferior way of life, and finally as "rupture"—rupture of the relationship between God and humans and, in a way similar to what we will see in de Lubac, rupture of the relationships within the Church, the body of Christ (McClendon, *Doctrine*, 132).

75. Again, National Baptists and other Baptist groups constituted primarily by African-Americans have largely retained the practice of observing the Lord's Supper on a monthly basis.

76. Again, McClendon calls himself a radical Christian in *Biography as Theology*, saying, "I am a *radical* Christian. 'Christian'—that pays tribute to Augustine and Edwards, to Schleiermacher and Barth, and to all who challenge pat solutions, proximate loyalties, as idolatrous. 'Radical'—that affirms my solidarity with experience-saturated believers: with Anabaptists so little known, with revivalists and pietists, with Pentecostalists and communal celebrants of many sorts" (McClendon, *Biography as Theology*, 69–70). One of my primary teachers, Ralph C. Wood, often points out that radical comes from the word *radix*, which means "base" or "root." Radicals are "rooted," not folks without roots.

77. For a balanced reading of this reaction, see Haymes, "Towards a Sacramental

ers complained that churchgoers came only for the Eucharist and resisted any preaching having to do with moral reformation.[78] Moreover, one might argue that though most Protestants and members of free churches are not gathering around the eucharistic elements on a weekly basis, the hearing of most sermons is an act done primarily in community.[79]

On the other hand, not being explicitly reminded of the Church's unity—or better, "re-membered" to one another (again, the key difference being McCabe's distinction between signs *of* and signs *for*)—on a weekly basis in the practice of the Supper generates another vacuum of which Jenson takes note: the privatization of Christianity coupled with believers' inability to articulate reasons for, or even affirm, the unity of the Church. This inability is manifested by those students who frequently ask Jenson, "Why is it not enough privately to think and feel Christ's presence and to know that others in their privacies do the same?"[80] Such a question can be answered in many ways. One answer—that it *is* "enough privately to think and feel Christ's presence"—is in Jenson's eyes the result of a modern and unbiblical notion of voluntarism as articulated by John Locke, Thomas Hobbes, John Adams, and James Madison, among others.[81] That is, without this specifically Christian rite in which Christians are pulled both godward and made one with one another, the Church is but a human society that one can "volunteer" to be a member of one minute and then "unvolunteer" the next, just as one could volunteer or unvolunteer were she or he a member of the local chamber of commerce or country club.[82]

This privatization is dangerous on many levels, according to Jenson, who believes that if we get our beliefs wrong "we cannot help but get our

---

Understanding of Preaching," 262–63. Also, see Knox, "Nature of Worship," where he balances this claim with the point that "to put trust for salvation in rites which had no other support than church tradition was idolatry, and the depriving of the true God of His due honour. Yet medieval worship consisted in almost nothing else than this. For this reason, the reading of the Bible and its exposition in the sermon are essential and central elements in public worship. For unless the people hear the Scriptures in their own language and understand the meaning, their faith cannot be rightly directed to the true promises of God."

78. Bradshaw, *New Westminster Dictionary of Liturgy and Worship*, 173.

79. With the advent of televangelism, this claim might be difficult to uphold.

80. Jenson, *Systematic Theology*, 2:214.

81. Jenson, "Kingdom of America's God," in *Essays in the Theology of Culture*, 60.

82. In chapter 3, I employ William Cavanaugh in order to demonstrate the many differences between the unity of the Church and that of other institutions. There I especially focus upon what Cavanaugh believes to be the false unity engendered by the nation-state.

lives wrong."[83] Thus when Jenson affirms that since the dawn of Christianity "freedom is not escape from the body, but the resurrection of the body,"[84] he is claiming that when one's faith becomes an essentially private and voluntary affair, it is not simply a very thin conception of the Church that results, but rather nothing less than a mentality that could result in Christians marginalizing other people. For example, he claims that when "religion becomes a private affair, we no longer pray 'O Lord, succor the poor'; we pray instead 'O Lord, make us feel better toward the poor.'"[85] His point: the Church has allowed a foreign understanding of freedom—namely, the Western and relatively new notion that freedom is primarily a private individual's right to "life, liberty and the pursuit of happiness"—to influence the uniquely Christian understanding of freedom: "being able to drink from one cup with the rich and the poor, the healthy and the alarmingly diseased . . . , having to forgive and be forgiven."[86]

In order to be freed to serve others, then, it is crucial that the ecclesial body gather around the eucharistic body. Indeed, the Eucharist, along with baptism, is an intrinsic part of the Church—the gathering is the body of Christ only as it regularly gathers around the eucharistic body.[87] Jenson points out that many say that this is a "historically contingent fact"—that had the gospel first arisen in medieval Germany, for example, perhaps the eucharistic elements would be beer and bratwurst.[88] Yet even if this were the case, Jenson points out, the central act of proclaiming Christian unity would still be a meal. This is important, since "in all cultures, eating together is an expression of fellowship; in oriental cultures, it creates permanent brotherhood; and in Israel, because of the table prayers, it creates brotherhood before God. Jesus' chosen brothers before God were the outsiders."[89] Indeed, for Jenson, second to sexual intercourse, eating together is one of the most intimate acts in which two persons can share.[90] Thus, when in the

---

83. Hauerwas, "Only Theology Overcomes Ethics," 255. Hauerwas is the one who says Jenson "believes" this.

84. Jenson, "Kingdom of America's God," in *Essays in the Theology of Culture*, 64.

85. Ibid.

86. Jenson, *On Thinking the Human*, 44.

87. Eucharist and baptism "would be dropped only if the gospel itself were dropped" (Jenson, *Story and Promise*, 167–68).

88. Jenson, *Visible Words*, 63.

89. Jenson, *Story and Promise*, 39.

90. Jenson, *Visible Words*, 62; cf. Jenson, *Systematic Theology*, 2:92.

first century Jesus wanted to tell society's "bottom-feeders" that they, too, "mattered," he told them so not only by speaking words of compassion to them, but through a "visible word"—by eating with them. Jesus "did not merely proclaim to the poor, the publicans, and the sinners that in God's future they would be new men, he treated them then and there as the new men they would be. His message had nothing in it of 'pie in the sky by and by.' This is the point of one of the most pervasive recollections about Jesus' actions: that he 'ate with publicans and sinners.'"[91]

This "bonding" is one sense in which Jenson's thought represents sacramentalism in its purest form. In a way that other meals (all of which effect a bond, in some sense) cannot, the Eucharist conveys grace in that it binds persons to one another. As with de Lubac, the Eucharist is an Augustinian "visible word" that not only symbolizes grace, but in so doing imparts grace—namely, through it God molds persons into a body and empowers this body to "live to the praise" of this Lord.[92] Jenson cites Lutheran reformer Martin Chemnitz to this end:

> In the Supper . . . we all receive one and the same Body of Christ. . . . And because in this way the members of the church are joined together to one Body of Christ, they are also joined with one another and become one Body whose head is Christ. So also, when in the Supper we receive the body and blood of Christ, we are intimately joined with Christ himself . . . and through Christ we are united to the Father. . . . Thus we are made fellows (*koinonoi*) with the Father, the Son, and the Holy Spirit. All these result from the . . . communion (*koinonia*) of the body and the blood of the Lord.[93]

Jenson assumes, then, that the Supper is a sacrament that conveys grace, a rite that gives unto the believer nothing less than Christ in giving her or him the body of Christ. It is a miracle that Christ is present in the eucharistic elements, but a "reliable miracle," since "the ministry of the church was credited with authorization to petition the presence with absolute assurance that it would occur."[94]

For Jenson, then, the Church is not a "voluntary association" but the very body of Christ, and is so in large part because it partakes of a unique

---

91. Jenson, *Visible Words*, 63.
92. Jenson, *Triune Identity*, 33.
93. Jenson, *Systematic Theology*, 2:221.
94. Jenson, "You Wonder Where the Body Went," in *Essays in the Theology of Culture*, 218.

kind of meal. The Church *is* the body of Christ for the world and for her members in that she is "constituted a community by the verbal and 'visible' presence *to* her of that same body of Christ. The body of Christ is at once his sacramental presence within the church's assembly, to make that assembly a community, and is the church-community herself for the world and her members."[95]

This is perhaps the closest Jenson comes to affirming de Lubac's claim that "the Eucharist makes the Church." The meal exists to create a community. Indeed, in a comment on 1 Cor 10:17, he says, "that believers are one body because we eat of the one loaf belongs to the substance of our believing."[96] The eucharistic celebration is a pivotal component in the unity of the body[97] in that it continually creates a community that for Jenson is the body of the risen Christ, the body of the living Christ.[98] If this meal is the one given to the Church in Scripture that has been handed down through the tradition for two thousand years, then according to Jenson there is no substitute for it—it is the way in which God has chosen to effect and re-present the Church's unity.

Why "Body"? (A Question from Modernity)

Raised earlier, Jenson's question, "Why is it not enough privately to think and feel Christ's presence and to know that others in their privacies do the

95. Jenson, *Systematic Theology*, 2:168.
96. Jenson, *Unbaptized God*, 2.
97. Jenson, *Systematic Theology*, 1:204–6.
98. Jenson, *Visible Words*, 35. As for Jenson's relationship to McClendon at this point, it is noted in chapter 2 how the language of Jenson is subtly, but importantly, different. In the baptist's version of the "Supper as sign," he only once acknowledges that talking about the Church's "signs" just as we talk about other communities' signs is problematic, saying that the signs or sign-acts of the Church are the acts not only of humans but also of God. McClendon more typically opts for the explanation that he employs early on in his *Convictions*—that for all communities and persons there are "speech acts that are especially revealing of convictions," acts that proclaim and indicate what a community or person persistently believes, and he preeminently treats the "signs" of the Church in much the same way as he treats the signs of, for example, the community called "lawyers." Indeed, for McClendon the best way to interpret the term *sacrament* (a term he largely avoids) is "pledge," and in the Supper "disciples . . . renew their own pledge to their Master and to one another" (McClendon, *Doctrine*, 389). It is almost as if the gathered disciples are the ones performing the act of renewing the body, are mediating grace through the sacrament, since they are the ones making the pledge. They are the beings, in McClendon's view, who are making use of the *instrumenta*.

same?"[99] is one that indicates that he sees that it might be lost on most contemporary Christians why it is that Christ needs to be embodied—whether in the Eucharist or in the form of the Church.[100] He therefore wonders whether the faith is not built upon "the empty tomb," the idea that we must rely not upon sight but rather upon our belief in the unseen. We return here to Jenson's claim that "bodies are . . . *availabilities* that enable *freedom*,"[101] and explore the relationship between bodies and availability (or *presence*) in Jenson.

Jenson argues that for there to be an objective communication between persons there must be embodiment. He cites Hegel's work as an example of this, noting that in the famous *Phänomenologie des Geistes* Hegel's line of argument is that "were someone to be present to me as subject only and not also as my object in turn, I would just so be that someone's object only and not a subject over against him/her. Thus such a personal presence . . . would enslave me."[102] Jenson claims that Hegel's argument would be true "even were the person the risen Christ."[103] In this vision, community—even with God—cannot be spiritual presence abstracted from bodily presence, but rather spiritual presence that is inextricably linked with bodily presence.[104] Jason Curtis says that for Jenson, like all other beings "Jesus must

---

99. Jenson, *Systematic Theology*, 2:214.

100. See Jenson, "You Wonder Where the Body Went," in *Essays in the Theology of Culture*, 220. See again Hauerwas and Wood, "How the Church Became Invisible." In my own experience, I have found that many members of free churches can dismiss the need for a physical body simply by citing Heb 11:1: "Faith is the assurance of things hoped for, the conviction of things not seen." Many take this to be a lexicographer's definition of the word *faith* and will not allow that belief in something that is readily available to the senses requires anything like "faith." Thus, they would place this definition over against the idea that the Church is the "body" of the Son. We cannot have faith in that which we can see, and so Christ cannot be embodied in the Church, the Eucharist, or anything else if we are to have "faith" in Christ. Jenson admits his awareness of the hesitancy to assign a "body" to the divine in multiple places. One is in the *Systematic Theology*, where he allows with Calvin that "a body requires its place" but confesses that "we find it hard to think of any place for this one" (Jenson, *Systematic Theology*, 1:202).

101. Jenson, "You Wonder Where the Body Went," in *Essays in the Theology of Culture*, 221. The emphasis is Jenson's, and the fact that he italicizes both "availabilities" and "freedom" is indicative of his direction in the essay.

102. Ibid., 220.

103. Ibid. Indeed, it is Christ's body (though not only his body) that is resurrected.

104. As stated in chapter 1, Jenson is aware that this is intellectually offensive. While he believes it is biblical, he confesses that "to say that God has a body is mightily to offend our entire inherited way of thinking about reality," and therefore to ask the question,

be temporally present and must be bodily so in order for his presence to be objectively real. To be temporally present, Jesus must bodily occupy our space, else he is not available to us, and if he is not present, then he is not God."[105] Curtis' description of Jenson's notion of presence seems to be right, and yet we must also note that Jenson affirms Aquinas' understanding that Christ is not locally present, because that would mean he is not in heaven: "the body of Christ does not come to be in the sacrament by spatial motion."[106]

Without the bodily aspect, then, "presence—and it is our salvation that it never quite occurs—would be 'pure' spirit, the nightmare dream of philosophers and the religious. Such a presence would be disembodied spirit."[107] Disembodied spirits are "imprisoning" and "paralyzing," Jenson says, but "a bodily presence is a presence that is both substantive, even a sort of 'thing,' and personal. A bodily presence is an objectively given personally meaningful presence; it is both there as a *res*, an irreducibly given fact, and means for me what the person means."[108]

Jenson's emphasis on the body is, then, meant to emphasize *availability*—an almost vulnerable availability that enables freedom. Reading Jenson again with Curtis we find that

> for one to be present and available to another there must be embodiment; else that person and that communication are both unidentifiable and enslaving. So, if the Christian community is going to address God and others, especially in terms of gospel

---

"'would God really let his body be pushed about on the Supper's table' so that the Church could be the body of Christ?" is to tread into strange waters for many Protestants (Jenson, *Visible Words*, 33, 37).

105. Curtis, "Trinity, Time, and Sacrament," 35.

106. Aquinas, *Summa Theologiae*, III.75.2. Jenson cites this quote in *Systematic Theology*, 1:202.

107. Jenson, *Visible Words*, 21. Jenson includes the claim that "and it is our salvation that it never quite occurs" probably because it is very often the case in the Old Testament that to see God directly entails death. Many have argued that this is the reason that in the New Testament, when angels appear, they must say to paralyzed humans "fear not" before they can deliver a message from the Divine. A disembodied divine presence, that is, is in biblical literature horrifying, and perhaps a death sentence. Jenson points out that while the gospels sometimes have Jesus simply "appearing" in a room (John 20:26), his appearances are "disproportionately appearances to share a meal" (Jenson, *Systematic Theology*, 2:185).

108. Jenson, "Church and the Sacraments," 213. See also Jenson, *Visible Words*, 23–28. Jenson notes here that he's drawing upon a "paradigmatic discussion" that took place in the ninth century between Radbertus and Emperor Charles the Bald.

proclamation, there must be embodiment of all participants. "The word in which God . . . communicates himself must be an embodied word, a word 'with' some visible reality, a grant of divine objectivity. We must be able to see and touch what we are to apprehend from God; religion cannot do without sacrament."[109]

Thus for Jenson the bodily presence of the Son is as important now as it was when Jesus walked the shores of the Sea of Galilee.[110] Indeed, Jenson bets his entire theology upon bodily presence, claiming that "if the gospel is indeed gospel, its speaking is Jesus' presence as himself: in the same body that Mary bore. . . . We must assert: the body Pilate hanged, and the embodiment of gospel-speaking among us, the ensemble of the gospel's sacramental reality, are one thing."[111]

Wholly Present

One of Jenson's emphases, then, is that the description of the Church as the embodied Christ (or even, dare we say, the body of God) has been neglected by Protestants in favor of an emphasis upon the Spirit.[112] However, Jenson's fear of positing a "disembodied spirit" or a "pure spirit"—God without a body such as the Church—is not reflective of a low view of the spiritual aspect as such, but is simply a caution against holding to the existence of a Divine spirit without a body.[113] Just as de Lubac believed that "the Church produces the Eucharist" but felt that he needed to, at that point in history, emphasize that "the Eucharist also produces the Church,"[114] so

---

109. Curtis, citing portions of Jenson, *Visible Words*, 28.

110. McClendon's "this is that" again!

111. Jenson, *Visible Words*, 44.

112. Helpfully, both John Milbank and evangelical thinker Philip Lee bring us back to a core reason that Christians must affirm the bodily aspect as it relates to the Supper, claiming that without it, one can quickly end up in perhaps the worst of all heresies—Gnosticism (Milbank, *Theology and Social Theory*, 389; Lee, *Against the Protestant Gnostics*, 183). As Jenson says, one of modernity's primary problems "is about what constitutes a person. Is a 'someone' indeed not a 'something'? Can a person be present where no *body* is present . . . ?" Here, Jenson says that Catholicism is a helpful correction to "Protestant hesitation to affirm the thing-like presence of Christ as the objects bread and cup," which derives from a "spiritualizing conception of personhood that might be explicitly disavowed by those who trade upon it" (Jenson, *Unbaptized God*, 32).

113. Again, while recognizing that "to say that God has a body is mightily to offend our entire inherited way of thinking about reality" (Jenson, *Visible Words*, 33).

114. De Lubac, *Splendor*, 78.

Jenson believes that both the bodily and spiritual aspects constitute all persons—including the second person of the Trinity; but it is the bodily aspect of God's presence that needs emphasis. Cited earlier, Jenson's "God is a person; and that means he is Spirit and Body" should therefore be taken not only as an affirmation of the body, but also of the Spirit.[115] As has been noted above, in a traditionally Christian account of presence there is an aspect that is more than bodily,[116] and Jenson is consistent with the tradition on this point. Christ's *body* was crucified, was buried, was resurrected, did ascend—but this was not simply so that Christ might leave the Church in a state of awe.[117] If such were the case, it would have made mere rumor of his life, death, burial, resurrection, ascension, and the *miraculous* would not have been *liberating*. Jenson underscores that "had there been no Pentecost, had Jesus risen into the eschatological future while we were simply left behind," the Church would not have been freed to be the body of Christ.[118] But it did not happen so. Instead, he claims that "the church is the 'body' of that Christ whose bodily departure to God's right hand his disciples once witnessed and whose return in such fashion we must still await. The church is the 'Temple' of that Spirit whose very reality among us is 'foretaste' or 'down payment.' Just so the church now truly *is* the people of God and the body of Christ and the temple of the Spirit. For it is what creatures may anticipate from God that is their being."[119]

In the Lucan narrative Jesus' pre-ascension promise to his followers was that when he left them in the flesh their bodies would be "clothed with power from on high" (Luke 24:49). In the Johannine account Jesus puts it this way:

> When the Advocate comes, whom I will send to you from the Father, the Spirit of truth who comes from the Father, he will testify

---

115. Jenson, *Visible Words*, 25.

116. See again the *Catechism of the Catholic Church*, 1373–1374: "Christ . . . who is at the right hand of God . . . is present in many ways to his Church. . . . But 'he is present . . . most especially in the Eucharistic species.' The mode of Christ's presence under the Eucharistic species is unique. It raises the Eucharist above all the sacraments. . . . This presence is called 'real'—by which is not intended to exclude the other types of presence as if they could not be 'real' too, but because it is presence in the fullest sense: that is to say, it is a *substantial* presence by which Christ, God and man, makes himself wholly and entirely present."

117. Jenson, *Systematic Theology*, 2:181.

118. Ibid.

119. Ibid., 172.

> on my behalf. You also are to testify because you have been with me from the beginning . . . I go away, for if I do not go away, the Advocate will not come to you; but if I go, I will send him to you. And when he comes, he will prove the world wrong about sin and righteousness and judgment: about sin, because they do not believe in me; about righteousness, because I am going to the Father and you will see me no longer; about judgment, because the ruler of this world has been condemned. I still have many things to say to you, but you cannot bear them now. When the Spirit of truth comes, he will guide you into all the truth; for he will not speak on his own, but will speak whatever he hears, and he will declare to you the things that are to come. (John 15:26–27; 16:7–13)

Prior to these words, in the Fourth Gospel Jesus even tells the disciples that in spite of the miraculous nature of his works on earth, they will perform "greater works than these" after his ascension (John 14:12). The Spirit, then, gives unto *the Church* genuine power. As Jenson puts it, the pouring out of the Spirit is "to make not individual prophets but a prophetic community."[120] In short, the Spirit comes to enliven a *body* continuously in need of its savior. When God is truly present—which is to say he is present bodily and spiritually—to believers who are truly present, conversion occurs.

Thus is freedom, as Jenson has already noted, found through a person's being joined to a body rather than in being raised above one. In this Jenson agrees with the direction of de Lubac on the subject of the Spirit and the meaning of Pentecost. De Lubac points out that in the sixth century St. Fulgentius of Ruspe, the North African bishop and great lover of the work of Augustine, said of the relationship between the Spirit and the Church that

> the Church, united by the Holy Spirit, speaks in the language of every people. Therefore if somebody should say to one of us, "You have received the Holy Spirit, why do you not speak in tongues?" his reply should be, "I do indeed speak in the tongues of all men, because I belong to the body of Christ, that is, the Church, and she speaks all languages." What else did the presence of the Holy Spirit indicate at Pentecost, except that God's Church was to speak in the language of every people?[121]

---

120. Ibid., 181.

121. Fulgentius of Ruspe, *Sermo 8 in Pentecoste* 1–3, PL 65, 743–44, cited in de Lubac, *Catholicism*, 378.

De Lubac employs Fulgentius' quote about the Spirit not to deny the gift of speaking in tongues—one of the gifts of the Spirit on the day of Pentecost as it is described in Acts 2—but in order to point out that all of God's gifts are meant to enliven the entire *corpus Christi*.[122] Thus, as shown in chapter 3 of this study, in regard to the ceremony of the Eucharist, de Lubac emphasizes that the rite produces a body. He says this, not to marginalize the way in which persons are empowered at the table of the Lord, but as a way of showing that persons are empowered as they are made one with both God and with one another.

Conclusion

In a way similar to de Lubac's use of Fulgentius, Jenson's understanding of God's gifts to us in the Eucharist, his body and his spirit, is that they do not free the Christian from a body but rather incorporate her or him all the more into the *corpus Christi*. Furthermore, only such incorporation into the ecclesial body of Christ frees persons for faithful service to Christ. Thus, as the Church gathers around the bread and wine each Sunday, she is the embodied Christ, present in and for the world in body and spirit. She participates in the meal because she is the body of Christ and, somehow, at the same is the gathered body of Christ because of her participation in the eucharistic meal.

Essentially, I have argued thus far that de Lubac would agree at this point, saying, "Yes, and this is what is meant by 'the Eucharist makes the Church.'" Furthermore, I have said that though he shies away from both the language of sacrament and describing the Eucharist alone as "the heart of the Church," McClendon would add here that "yes, this is what I mean when I describe the Supper as 'a re-membering sign.' Participation in this practice, the Supper, puts back together, or 'reconstitutes,' the church, a body that has been ruptured by sin."

122. I would be remiss if I did not remind the reader at this point that McClendon's "this is that" is founded upon the record of Pentecost in Acts 2, "where Peter reads from the prophets and then says to the audience, this—in other words, what his listeners are seeing—is that—what the prophet was speaking about. So the right way to read prophecy is not just as historical record of the past, but as a disclosure of the meaning and significance of the present. In a sense, the first century (the New Testament period) is the sixteenth century, and the Reformation (and especially the radical Reformation) is our own century." See Ched Myers, "Embodying the 'Great Story': An Interview with James W. McClendon." Online: http://www.thewitness.org/archive/dec2000/mcclendon.html.

Re-membering the Body

In the next and final chapter, I shall argue that a new generation of Baptist theologians, a group that I shall call the "new Baptist sacramentalists," have begun a movement made possible by all three of these theologians. From McClendon these contemporary Baptist theologians learned how to employ the language and history of Baptists in order to emphasize the need for a unity that will be found through participation in practices that he calls the remembering "signs." And yet, gleaning from de Lubac and Jenson (though they cite the former more often than the latter), they learn to take their theologies of the Eucharist further by doing something that McClendon only hints at—by reinterrogating the entire Christian tradition with questions on the unity of the Church and its connection to the Eucharist. Jenson serves here as a more recent (indeed a contemporary) interrogator, and, as we said at the outset of the chapter, has proven to be sacramental in contrast to McClendon, but more prone to ask and answer "Protestant" questions than de Lubac.

5

The Eucharist Makes the (Free) Church

The New Baptist Sacramentalists and Ecclesial Unity

Introduction

IN CHAPTER 2 I claimed that while McClendon "gestures" toward a sacramental understanding of the Supper with a view to ecclesial unity, he stops short of such an understanding. In the third chapter I went on illustrate through the work of de Lubac, a Catholic, what a truly sacramental theology looks like, and further argued that his sacramentalism is what Baptists would call "biblical"—it is due to de Lubac's very detailed engagement with Scripture and the breadth of the tradition that he comes to the conclusion that the Eucharist (the *corpus mysticum*) "makes" the Church (the *corpus verum*). In chapter 4, I argued that Lutheran theologian Robert Jenson comes to the same conclusion, but his role in this study has been to help Baptists understand the Church as the embodiment of Christ, the "real presence" of Christ placed by God in and for the world, but only inasmuch as she regularly participates in the Eucharist.

In this final chapter, I shall argue that there is a surprisingly thick strand of contemporary Baptist theologians who are deeply indebted to McClendon and would agree with the statement that Scripture and the Christian tradition proclaim that the truly "free church" is bound together by the Eucharist. I shall call this group of thinkers the "new Baptist sacramentalists,"[1] and though their work is not monolithic, I will examine

---

1. I use the word *new* here with some hesitation—because sacramentalism has always permeated Baptist theology on some level. One of the Baptist sacramentalists (Philip

some of them together in this chapter, revisiting the work of McClendon along the way since he has influenced all of them either directly or indirectly. In the end, I hope to show that while McClendon gestures toward a sacramental vision and in so doing makes possible the sorts of exercises conducted by these contemporary authors, the only path to seeing the real depth of the connection between the Supper and the unity of the Church will be to engage in a form of what Cameron Jorgenson has called a "Baptist ressourcement,"[2] consulting from all eras those baptist, Protestant, Catholic, and even Orthodox sources that root their arguments in Scripture and subsequently develop a deep connection between the Eucharist and the unity of the Church.[3]

The New Baptist Sacramentalists: A Primer

The new Baptist sacramentalists can be described by way of Steven R. Harmon's *Towards Baptist Catholicity: Essays on Tradition and the Baptist Vision*.[4] In this widely read and controversial text,[5] Harmon opens with a

---

Thompson) has protested my use of this title, and we should recall that de Lubac disowned the title *nouvelle theologie* as a descriptor of his movement for similar reasons. Still, I use the term *new* because the theologians studied here represent a new and vibrant movement within Baptist life, although there have always been Baptists who hold to a sacramental view of the Supper (as I have shown in chapter 2). Also, *new* is employed because prior to the publication of *Baptist Sacramentalism*, Stanley K. Fowler uses the term "Baptist sacramentalist" to describe George Beasley-Murray, Robert Walton, and other British Baptists whose works arose around the middle of the twentieth century (Fowler, *More than a Symbol*, 4). For the purposes of this study, the new Baptist sacramentalists are all contemporary theologians and a generation younger than Beasley-Murray, Walton, and McClendon himself. I would add that the group of thinkers I am considering here has a distinctly North American flavor and that, interestingly, most of them have strong ties to institutions in the American South.

2. Jorgenson, "Bapto-Catholicism," 121.

3. I say "even" Orthodox sources only because, aside from a brief discussion of John Zizioulas in chapter 3, Orthodox sources have been omitted from the scope of this study.

4. Harmon is associate professor of divinity at Beeson Divinity School in Birmingham, Alabama, and vice chair of the Doctrine and Interchurch Cooperation Commission of the Baptist World Alliance.

5. Harmon's book was, for example, the subject of ecumenical panel discussion at the annual joint meeting of the College Theology Society and the region at-large of the National Association of Baptist Professors of Religion, held in Newport, Rhode Island, in May 2008. The program for this meeting can be found online: http://www2.bc.edu/~barciaus/annual.html. It is also the most closely studied text in Jorgenson's study on Baptist identity. On a personal note, I once "caught" my former pastor and current

The Eucharist Makes the (Free) Church

description of what he calls "catholic Baptist" theologians,[6] persons who share with Harmon the idea "that Baptists belong to what the Nicaeno-Constantinopolitan Creed confesses is the 'one, holy, catholic, and apostolic church' and that they must strive after the realization of these marks of the church along with all other denominations."[7] When he lists the "seven identifying marks of a catholic Baptist theology,"[8] he asserts that one thing that these men and women hold in common is their belief in a truly sacramental theology, by which he means "not only a more robust apreciation for the Lord's presence in baptism and the Eucharist than is the case with the symbolic reductionism typical of Baptist theologies of the ordinances influenced by the Zwinglian tradition, but more broadly a theology that understands the sacraments of baptism and the Eucharist as paradigmatic of the relation of God to the material order that is disclosed in the Incarnation."[9]

Harmon makes two other claims that are crucial for our purposes here. First, he underscores the fact that a collection of essays released under the title *Baptist Sacramentalism* in 2003 brings together many of the best of those Baptist voices that articulate a sacramental view not only of the Supper, but of other ordinances and, in some sense, of all reality.[10] Many of the essays in the volume are groundbreaking in and of themselves, but this last chapter will focus upon the work of three contributors—Curtis Freeman, Elizabeth Newman, and Barry Harvey—drawing from their essays in *Baptist Sacramentalism* and from their other works.[11] These theologians

---

Baylor University Chaplain, Dr. Burt L. Burleson, reading this book during hours at work which he reserved for sermon preparation.

6. Harmon, *Towards Baptist Catholicity*, 6.

7. Ibid., 3. For a thorough study of Harmon's book and a movement sometimes referred to as "Bapto-Catholicism," see again Jorgenson, "Bapto-Catholicism," 121.

8. Harmon, *Towards Baptist Catholicity*, 17.

9. Ibid., 13. As an aside, Harmon asserts that the other six marks are the belief that tradition is a source of authority; the belief that there is a place for creeds in liturgy and catechesis; the belief that liturgy is the primary context in which Christians are formed by tradition; the belief that community is a locus of authority; belief in the importance of a constructive retrieval of the Christian tradition; and belief in a "thick ecumenism."

10. It should be noted that some contributors to *Baptist Sacramentalism* do not commit themselves to a sacramental position. Michael A. G. Haykin's essay, for example, is a historical one that perhaps even overreaches in order to emphasize the sacramental strand in Baptist thought, but he nevertheless outlines the positions of sacramentalists and sub-Zwinglian memorialists alike without taking a position himself (Haykin, "'His Soul-Refreshing Presence,'" 177–93).

11. There are a number of lists of Baptist theologians who hold a sacramental view of

contribute essays to the volume that are most specifically concerned with the Supper rather than the other sacraments. Moreover, Harmon identifies Freeman and Newman, among others, as contributing essays that are "especially noteworthy."[12]

The second point of Harmon's introduction that is crucial for the purposes of this chapter is the argument that in embarking upon a serious exploration of the Christian tradition, "catholic Baptists" are emerging thinkers who have followed in the footsteps of James McClendon.[13] Harmon draws from fellow Baptist theologian Mark Medley in order to make this claim,[14] and both Harmon and Medley make the case that if one were to survey the major Baptist thinkers of the eighteenth, nineteenth, and twentieth centuries, only McClendon and Stanley Grenz have seriously engaged the breadth of the Christian tradition and name that tradition as normative.[15] For their part, both Harmon and Medley engage the tradition, cite it as authoritative, and employ it to articulate a sacramental vision of the Supper. Medley, who is frequently cited by Harmon, is the author of an article titled "'Do This': The Eucharist and Ecclesial Selfhood," which might

---

the Lord's Supper. Harmon notes that Molly Marshall, Philip Thompson, Barry Harvey, Curtis Freeman, Elizabeth Newman, and John Colwell are among those Baptists attempting to recover a sacramental understanding of the Lord's Supper (Harmon, *Towards Baptist Catholicity*, 13–14). In the same series as Harmon's book—a series titled Studies in Baptist History and Thought—*Baptist Sacramentalism* features essays by Thompson, Newman, Harvey, and Freeman, but also a host of other authors as well. Most, but not all, of these authors clearly advocate a "sacramental" interpretation of the Supper (see Cross and Thompson, *Baptist Sacramentalism*, 214). See also Ralph C. Wood's call for a "catholicized evangelicalism," which includes a sacramental vision of the Supper and a more prominent place for the Supper in free churches. While some might think Wood's age might prevent him from fitting into the category of "new Baptist sacramentalists," as one who came to see the importance of sacramentalism in the middle of his career, his most sacramental statements come only a few years ahead of his younger contemporaries (Wood, *Contending for the Faith*, 80–81, 187).

12. Harmon, *Towards Baptist Catholicity*, 14.

13. Ibid., 6.

14. Medley, assistant professor of theology at the Baptist Seminary of Kentucky in Lexington, is cited frequently by Harmon when the latter wants to support his arguments on subjects such as the sacraments and the normativity of tradition. His "'Do This': The Eucharist and Ecclesial Selfhood" closely identifies with this study's direction—especially the aim of chapter 3, which seeks to illustrate that de Lubac was correct in saying that "the Eucharist makes the Church."

15. Harmon, *Towards Baptist Catholicity*, 5. Of course, whether the number "two" does justice to Baptist theology from the twentieth century depends on what one believes qualifies a theologian as "major."

The Eucharist Makes the (Free) Church

come closest to affirming what de Lubac meant when he said "the Eucharist makes the Church" without citing the great Jesuit.[16] Medley's voice will therefore play a role in the discussion below, since even though he was not a contributor to *Baptist Sacramentalism*, his work on the Supper in "Do This," published in the same year as *Baptist Sacramentalism*, is clearly sacramental. Helpfully, Harmon's account of Baptist catholicity points us to many others who have similar concerns.[17]

McClendon's Influence

Harmon's description of McClendon's influence upon "catholic Baptists" rings true of the new Baptist sacramentalists. The authors whose sacramental theologies shall be examined in this final chapter not only cite the work of McClendon quite often, they largely cite him favorably.[18] More specifically, as suggested by Freeman, they generally agree that McClendon was right when he suggested that the Supper is not *merely* a symbol, but a "sign of salvation."[19] This is evident in Freeman's work, for example, in that he cites McClendon three times when suggesting that there are crucial differences between symbols and signs. The fact that Freeman was coauthor and coeditor of two documents with McClendon—"Re-envisioning Baptist

---

16. Although, as we will also see with Newman, Medley interacts with Cavanaugh's *Torture and Eucharist* and therefore indirectly with de Lubac.

17. Bearing in mind that Harmon notes that the Baptist catholics—or, for our purposes, the Baptist sacramentalists—are not entirely uniform, I believe that these thinkers have a great deal in common on the Supper, and therefore I will attempt to put them in conversation with one another as well as with McClendon, de Lubac, Jenson, and others from across the tradition.

18. This is not to imply that these writers are in lockstep with McClendon, or again, with one another. Harvey, for instance, notes several "missteps" made by McClendon in his description of the "baptist vision" in his most recent book (Harvey, *Can These Bones Live?*, 52).

19. Though I shall argue that he puts words into the mouth of McClendon in having him call the Supper a "sacrament," Freeman employs McClendon to war against what he calls a "sub-Zwinglian" view (see "'To Feed Upon by Faith,'" 209). For more on the difference between a Zwinglian and a sub-Zwinglian view and the ways in which McClendon and Freeman are involved in this discussion, see the earliest portions of chapter 2 in this study.

Identity"[20] and a volume of historical Baptist documents titled *Baptist Roots*—suggests that he would have been influenced in other ways as well.[21]

The same can be said for the other coauthors of "Re-Envisioning Baptist Identity,"[22] one of whom is Elizabeth Newman. She frequently employs McClendon's "baptist vision"[23] in her reading of Scripture and of the narratives of important figures in Church history.[24] It is perhaps more important, however, to note that in the section of "Re-envisioning Baptist Identity" that deals with the sacraments, Newman and the other coauthors "affirm baptism, preaching, and the Lord's table as powerful signs that seal God's faithfulness in Christ and express our response of awed gratitude rather than as mechanical rituals or mere symbols."[25] Although cited previously in chapter 2, this designation of baptism, preaching, and the Lord's table as "powerful signs" almost certainly gleans from McClendon's earlier designation of these three in particular as the Church's "signs of salvation," wherein signs are also called "powerful practices."[26] That Newman signs her name to a document this closely linked with McClendon's work represents an affirmation of that work.

20. For more on this document, see chapter 2 of this study. As to its authorship, Cameron Jorgenson, Harmon's successor at Campbell University Divinity School, has shown with great care how Freeman, Harvey, and Philip Thompson (who is, importantly, coeditor of the *Baptist Sacramentalism* volumes) began drafting "Re-envisioning Baptist Identity" in the summer of 1996 and that McClendon and Newman, along with Mikeal Broadway, later joined them as the essay's coauthors (Jorgenson, "Bapto-Catholicism," 76).

21. Again, see Freeman, McClendon, and da Silva, *Baptist Roots*; Broadway et al., "Re-envisioning Baptist Identity."

22. Broadway et al., "Re-envisioning Baptist Identity." Though he is not one of the thinkers with whom I will be working at length in the final chapter, *Baptist Sacramentalism* contributor and "Re-envisioning" coauthor Harvey states in *Can These Bones Live?* that McClendon's "encouragement and gentle wisdom and wit were invaluable" to him as a young theologian. Moreover, while he more bluntly notes McClendon's "missteps," like Freeman, Harvey employs McClendon's work on the Supper when he adopts McClendon's description of the meal as a "remembering" and "re-membering" sign in his own texts. Given this study's focus upon the unity of the ecclesial body, this last description will be especially important going forward (for more, see Harvey, *Can These Bones Live?*, esp. 9, 52).

23. I explain McClendon's baptist vision as a way of reading Scripture in chapter 2.

24. For her understanding of Teresa of Avila and the way Newman employs McClendon in order to interpret Teresa's *Interior Castles*, see Newman, "Public Politics of Teresa's Vision."

25. Broadway et al., "Re-envisioning Baptist Identity," 306.

26. McClendon, *Doctrine*, 379.

The Eucharist Makes the (Free) Church

Finally, in a recent interview, Newman states that she was introduced to McClendon's work by Stanley Hauerwas while a graduate student at Duke University, that she met him personally at an American Academy of Religion meeting in the late 1980s, and that, as she noted in the plenary address to the College Theology Society in 2007, after McClendon stood up at a gathering of Baptists at the American Academy of Religion of 1993 and proclaimed that Baptists needed to seek a new venue in which to have theological and ecumenical discussions, he asked Newman and another colleague to explore a relationship with the College Theology Society (Newman was teaching at a Catholic university at the time).[27] This eventually led to the annual joint session of the College Theology Society-National Association of Baptist Professors of Religion (CTS-NABPR), which again was the site wherein the idea for penning "Re-envisioning Baptist Identity" was conceived.[28]

For his part, Mark Medley is neither a contributor to *Baptist Sacramentalism* nor a coauthor or even a signer of "Re-Envisioning Baptist Identity."[29] In brief, he is an even younger, or "newer," Baptist sacramentalist. And yet, he too employs the work of McClendon in his sacramental theology and has presented much of his work at the annual joint sessions of the CTS-NABPR. He is therefore also indebted to McClendon in many ways, a fact that he is well aware of.

We need not overreach, however, in order to establish direct connections between McClendon and Medley. He does indeed cite McClendon in his work, but as the youngest and also the final thinker to be addressed in this chapter on the new Baptist sacramentalists (and therefore in this study), Medley represents an even newer expression of Baptist sacramentalism in North America, an expression made possible by McClendon, but one that will leave a new mark on Baptist ecclesiology. As stated above, Medley's work on the Eucharist bears some similarities to the work of de Lubac as well. A new movement has indeed dawned when, in the thought of a lifelong southerner teaching at a small Baptist seminary in Kentucky (or Virginia or North Carolina, for that matter), we hear echoes of McClendon through statements like "as we re-member Christ in the eucharist,

---

27. Newman, plenary address to the College Theology Society and the National Association of Baptist Professors of Religion, June 2, 2007.

28. Newman, interview by author, April 29, 2009.

29. For a description of Medley's career, see his faculty webpage at the Baptist Seminary of Kentucky: http://www.bsky.org/academics/faculty/dr-mark-medley.

we become the body of Christ,"[30] and of de Lubac when we read that "even as we practice the Eucharist, we are ourselves being *made* eucharistically."[31]

The Supper as a Sign in the Work of the Baptist Sacramentalists

As stated in chapters 1 and 2 of this study, that Baptists have largely said that the Supper is not a sacrament is a claim that is widely agreed upon by sacramentalists and non-sacramentalists alike.[32] Just as those who do not hold to a sacramental view,[33] however, these theologians believe, as Newman puts it, that an important characteristic of the Baptist tradition is the "rich heritage of often going against what the majority believes, and, at times, rightly so."[34] Thus, while one aim of the *Baptist Sacramentalism* volume is to show that the sacramental "strand" has always existed within Baptist life (indeed, editors Cross and Thompson claim in the very first sentence of the book that "many Baptists from the seventeenth century to the present day have held to sacramental views of baptism and the Lord's Supper"[35]), and that this strand is in fact a "surprisingly thick" one,[36] the

---

30. Medley, "'Do This,'" 393.

31. Ibid., 395. Emphasis mine. I'm thinking here of de Lubac's "the Eucharist makes the Church" (de Lubac, *Corpus Mysticum*, 88).

32. Cross and Thompson, *Baptist Sacramentalism*, 1. Newman, professor of theology at the Baptist Theological Seminary at Richmond, is one "sacramentalist" who notes that most Baptists have long been opposed to sacramental language (see Newman, "Lord's Supper," 214–15). Curtis Freeman notes of the historical sacramental theories of Baptists that "for Baptists now as then, sacramentalism is rarely a live option," and that in contemporary Baptist life "it is not an overstatement to say that a 'sub-Zwinglian' theology of the Lord's Supper has become entrenched as a *de facto* orthodoxy among Free Churches" (Freeman, "'To Feed Upon by Faith,'" 196, 206).

33. Bill Leonard, former Dean of Wake Forest Divinity School in Winston-Salem, North Carolina, is one example of a Baptist historian who holds to a purely symbolic view and rightly notes that Baptists rarely advocate a sacramental theology (see again Leonard, *Baptist Ways*, 8). Leonard was commissioned by the Board of Managers of the American Baptist Historical Society to explore Baptist identity in a volume that could replace Robert G. Torbet's *History of the Baptists*—a volume that was issued in three editions and served as an authoritative source for over half a century.

34. Newman, "Lord's Supper," 214. Cf. Cross and Thompson, *Baptist Sacramentalism*, 1.

35. Cross and Thompson, *Baptist Sacramentalism*, 1.

36. Fowler, *More than a Symbol*, 4. Fowler cites Cross as claiming that "Baptists have now generally accepted the word 'sacrament.'" While this may be true in England, where

theologians this study addresses attempt to show that a sacramental (or, in one case, quasi-sacramental) view of both the Supper and the Church are legitimate not necessarily because other Baptists have said so, but primarily because this view is faithful to Scripture and the breadth of the Christian tradition. Furthermore, these Baptists believe a sacramental vision is the only way to true ecclesial unity. Through the Supper, they believe, God draws the Church closer to God's self, and God draws the Church together as the body of Christ. Thus, a "merely symbolic" description of the Supper is not sufficient.

Since, then, the new Baptist sacramentalists find a great deal to criticize in the "just a symbol" description of the Supper, I shall explore further their relationship to McClendon, often beginning with their understandings of symbols and signs.[37] Each has a unique understanding of and relationship to McClendon, however, so I will describe their own understanding of "signs." After exploring this aspect of each of their theologies, I will investigate their ecclesiologies, looking for connections between their understanding of the Supper as a sign and the implications this has for their view of the Church as the unified body of Christ.

McClendon and Freeman

Freeman closes his contribution to the *Baptist Sacramentalism* volume with an assessment and retrieval of McClendon's sign theory. He calls McClendon's work in this area a "fresh reappraisal" and agrees that the Supper, as a practice of the Church, is not "merely symbolic," but a sign that *employs* symbols and in so doing "signifies forgiveness, solidarity, thanksgiving, and the future."[38] In using "signifies" Freeman means to emphasize that "these

---

Cross and Fowler have lived and worked, if meant to describe Baptists in North America this is a spectacular, perhaps unrealistic, claim.

37. In this chapter, I will only occasionally repeat the details of McClendon's sacramental theology and ecclesiology, allowing the work from chapters 1 and 2 to stand. On the other hand, I will repeat the examples that concretize his theories. Here, for example, we would do well to recall this quote from McClendon: "I put a sign on my office door: 'Students are welcome.' It employs some symbols, namely letters and words, in order to *do* something, in this case, to welcome the students who read it" (McClendon, *Doctrine*, 388). For an extensive discussion on the distinction between sign and symbol in McClendon, see 21–25 above.

38. Freeman, "'To Feed Upon by Faith,'" 209. As noted in chapter 2, even in light of the criticisms levied against McClendon, we would do well to retain a deep appreciation for the groundbreaking nature of McClendon's project. As a Baptist from North America

practices are not merely symbolic—they are performative."[39] Thus, the Lord's Supper is a sacrament in that "the Lord is present and active both in the performance of these remembering signs and with the community that performs them."[40] Going further than McClendon, however, Freeman calls for a Baptist liturgy that includes "*paraclesis* (traditionally called *epiclesis*) invoking the presence of the Holy Spirit to unite in mystery this practice with the sacrifice of Christ so God's people may by faith receive nourishment from the Table."[41] Nourishment, that is, is not only symbolized, it is offered and it is "life-giving."[42] In describing the Supper in this way, Freeman believes his understanding of the Supper to be sacramental. To use McCabe's language for a moment, were the nourishment spoken of as "pointed to," the Supper would be a sign *of* nourishment. Since Freeman believes that nourishment is actually offered "from the Table" (might Aquinas have preferred "from God through the Table"?), what we have here is a sign *for* nourishment.[43]

It is Freeman's hope that in carrying forward McClendon's profound, if not extensive, work on the sacraments (or "signs," as McClendon prefers), he can help reverse the trend that for the vast majority of Baptists "the Supper has become an empty relic as the spirituality of unmediated and individualistic piety reigns supreme in American religion."[44] He laments that because of the "merely symbolic" view—and especially the "merely" part of that term—"the Supper consequently suffers from an infrequent and enfeebled practice. As a result many Christians are spiritually starved."[45] We might recall that McClendon comes to the same conclusion in prefacing a series of sermons he preached as interim pastor of a divided Baptist congregation in California. That which McClendon preached three decades ago is Freeman's message today: a move away from the "merely symbolic" view of

---

writing about effectual signs as early as the 1970s, he was truly innovative.

39. Freeman, "'To Feed Upon by Faith,'" 209.

40. Ibid. We shall see below why the final clause of this sentence might trouble some of the other sacramentalists.

41. Ibid., 203.

42. Ibid.

43. For my use of McCabe's sacramental theology in this study, see the end of chapter 2.

44. Freeman, "'To Feed Upon by Faith,'" 209.

45. Ibid.

the Supper, coupled with enacting the practice more frequently, leads to a more spiritually mature and therefore more unified congregation.[46]

Since he follows McClendon so closely, however, we would do well take Freeman's sacramental theology and revisit the criticisms we made of McClendon's sign theory in chapter 2. The reason for doing so is that Freeman calls for a move beyond the "mere symbolism" of most Baptists and employs McClendon in doing so, but it is debatable whether he speaks too quickly for his mentor when he calls McClendon's "signs of salvation" (baptism, the Lord's Supper, and preaching) "sacramental practices."[47] As illustrated above, McClendon himself was very hesitant to use the term *sacrament*, employing it primarily when describing the decisions of Roman Catholic councils and using it very ambiguously in a few other places.[48] In fact, McClendon never refers to the Supper as a "sacrament" in his major works other than when surveying the decisions of church councils, presenting the position of another theologian, or engaging the Catholic Church's appropriation of sacramental language.[49] It is possible that this is a strategic decision by McClendon,[50] since he does note that "there can be but small objection to the language of mystery and sacrament, provided the original sense is retained."[51] And yet, as I stated earlier, one must (*a*) wonder what McClendon thinks the "small objection" would be, and (*b*) note that a "small objection" is still an objection.

---

46. McClendon, *Making Gospel Sense to a Troubled Church*, xix. Though as we noted in chapter 3 when discussing Henri de Lubac's description of the Eucharist as the "heart of the Church," Freeman and McClendon's desires for a more frequent observance of the Supper rub up against "the heart" of free church worship—namely, the sermon. As an example of this, see Freeman's statement that in the view of Baptists like "evangelical pastor and former seminary president Chuck Swindoll," if Christians have communion even on a bimonthly basis "it tends to mean less to the participants." Freeman then notes that for Baptists like Swindoll, most importantly, a move to weekly or monthly communion "would also break the continuity of his ongoing sermon series" (Freeman, "Where Two or Three Are Gathered," 264).

47. Freeman, "'To Feed Upon by Faith,'" 209.

48. See chapter 2 of this book.

49. For McClendon's examples of others using the term *sacrament*, see McClendon, *Biography as Theology*, 77; McClendon, *Ethics* 35, 55, 58, 266; McClendon, *Doctrine*, 113, 339, 386; McClendon, *Witness*, 346.

50. Would McClendon have been concerned about losing his Baptist audience if he used sacramental language too directly?

51. McClendon's understanding of this "original sense" is that "in Latin lands, a *sacramentum* was a pledge or sacred promise" (McClendon, *Doctrine*, 388).

Finally, it should also be noted that McClendon says in two places that in the Supper we have "a rite, not magical nor even (in many usual senses of the term) 'sacramental'—but moral and ethical first of all; a rite aimed at the shaping of the common life of Christian community."[52] Freeman, who seems to want to attribute to McClendon something "closer" to sacramentalism, especially when it comes to baptism,[53] has perhaps confused the work of his contemporaries with that of McClendon himself.[54] After all, Freeman believes with the other new Baptist sacramentalists that Baptists' theology, worship, and church unity suffer as a result of their neglect of the Supper. Thus does he conclude his essay by radically claiming that "a sub-Zwinglian orthodoxy will not satisfy the soul's hunger. Yet there is a way from a low view of the Lord's Supper as private devotion, obligatory ordinance, real absence, and mere symbol to a rich communion worship of common prayer, life-giving practice, real presence, and powerful signs. All God's people are invited to be nourished at the table where is spread a spiritual meal of divine grace to feed upon by faith. Come and dine!"[55]

If Freeman believes that the current Baptist view of the Supper is a "low" one, then he is calling for a "high" one—and not only so that individuals can be made one with God. A move away from a privatistic

---

52. See McClendon, *Ethics*, 219; cf. "Practice of Community Formation," 86–87.

53. I do not make this claim simply based upon Freeman's words in "'To Feed Upon by Faith.'" In response to a paper I gave on McClendon and sign theory at the National Association of Baptist Professors of Religion, Nashville, Tennessee, May 16th, 2008—a paper that evolved into the final sections of chapter 2 of this study—Freeman made a strong case that McClendon's understanding of the Supper is sacramental.

54. Has Freeman so deeply imbibed the work of McClendon that the same critique of McClendon's "sacramental" theology applies to the work of Freeman? I shall answer that question at the end of this section, since Wittgenstein and McCabe have helped us see that even if one uses terms like *sacrament* or differentiates between signs and symbols in order to claim that the Supper "does something," one must take care not to *ultimately* attribute the effects of the sacraments to the actions of the congregation.

55. Freeman, "'To Feed Upon by Faith,'" 210. Coined by C. W. Dugmore, "sub-Zwinglian" is a favorite term of Freeman's, and in using it he tries to distinguish between Zwingli's *actual* sacramental theology, on the one hand, and the symbolism most have *attributed* to him, on the other hand. Theologically speaking, Freeman believes it is important to note that even in his most polemical writings, "Zwingli did not exclude the presence of Christ in the Supper, but preferred to speak of God's omnipresence through the Spirit" (Freeman, "'To Feed Upon by Faith,'" 208). Elsewhere, he uses "sub-Zwinglian" to describe theologians and pastors who have such a thin conception of symbol that they can find little reason to observe the Supper more than two or three times a year, since they believe that any practice that is observed too often leads inevitably to a lack of appreciation of that practice (Freeman, "Where Two or Three Are Gathered," 264).

understanding of the meal toward seeing it and participating in it as "a rich communion of common prayer" would be good for contemporary Baptists, and he points out that there is precedent for this in Baptist history. Baptist leader Thomas Grantham, though Freeman claims he was ultimately "limited by a residual anti-Catholic prejudice," saw the need for unity among Christian separatists in turbulent seventeenth-century England, and this unity, Grantham said, was rooted in the common participation in the flesh and blood of Christ, which these Baptists were "to feed upon by faith."[56] Contemporary Baptists likewise stand in need of an ecclesial unity found only in communal practices like the Supper, "commended to the church, not individual Christians, for performance."[57]

Freeman articulates these concerns outside the *Baptist Sacramentalism* volume, as well. For example, in his "Where Two or Three Are Gathered: Communion Ecclesiology in the Free Church," if the Supper is a "sign of salvation," he asserts, then it is only so if it brings about the participant's unity, or "communion," with God and other members of the body of Christ.[58] In this article Freeman also turns to the Baptist experience in the seventeenth century, contrasting the First London Confession with the contemporary American church's adoption of modernity's hyper-individualism. He notes that "modern Baptists who identify their fellowship with Christ and one another as a bond of only voluntary association do well to study carefully earlier Baptist understandings of the church. For example, the First London Confession declares that the visible saints are 'joyned to the Lord and each other, by mutuall agreement, in the practical injoyment of the Ordinances.'"[59]

Freeman clearly places an emphasis upon the role of the "ordinances" in this quote rather than upon "mutuall agreement" of believers, or their understanding of their "mutuall agreement." Indeed, this is one possible reading of the Confession—if the believers are engaged in "injoyment *of*" the Ordinances, then they could be considered in one sense to be the passive

---

56. Freeman, "'To Feed Upon by Faith,'" 195–96, 202. Indeed, Freeman interacts with de Lubac's work on the Eucharist's replacing the Church as the *corpus verum*, saying that "de Lubac's attention to the 'real' presence located in the Church and the 'spiritual' presence in the eucharist suggests new possibilities and contours for sacramental discussions between Catholics and Baptists" (Freeman, "'To Feed Upon by Faith,'" 196).

57. Ibid., 202.

58. Freeman, "Where Two or Three Are Gathered," 263.

59. Ibid.

characters in the drama of the Supper and baptism while the Ordinances are the active objects being enjoyed.

The Londoners' "mutuall agreement," however, might imply that these early Baptists had already learned to articulate the kind of voluntarism Freeman worries about elsewhere.[60] When he points out in "'To Feed Upon'" (by way of de Lubac) that the primary trouble with contemporary free church Christians "is not that [they] forsake to assemble (Heb 10:25), but that they understand their assembly as just another voluntary association"[61] rather than as a manifestation of the *corpus verum*,[62] the implication is that the seventeenth-century Baptists did not have this trouble. I believe Freeman's is the best reading, but it seems not unfair to ask whether Freeman projects his own sacramentalism upon the views of the seventeenth-century Baptists, as I have argued he does with McClendon.

Freeman might make this sort of projection, but it is most important to state here that he is himself a sacramentalist. As a solution to the "trouble" of seeing themselves as a voluntary association, Freeman suggests that Miroslav Volf is correct when he suggests that free church Christians continue to regard the "hierarchical" aspect of the hierarchical churches with suspicion, but come to appreciate their affirmation that

> Baptism and the Lord's Supper are constitutive of the church. Just as "by one Spirit we are baptized into one body" (1 Cor 12:13), so "because there is one bread, we who are many are one body" (1 Cor 10:17). Baptism and the Supper are not simply acts of obedience. They are the means whereby Christians are joined into the body of Christ through the Spirit. The sacraments therefore belong to the *esse* of the church, not merely the *bene esse* as Free Churches typically maintain. Through them, but not apart from them, persons are made Christians and are sustained in faith and union with Christ and His body.[63]

Freeman believes that he and McClendon affirm a sacramental understanding of the Supper with a view to the unity of the Church. Of those two, however, only Freeman views the Supper in the full sense of the term *sacrament* and therefore as a crucial component of the unity of the Church.

---

60. Freeman, "'To Feed Upon By Faith,'" 196.
61. Freeman, "Where Two or Three Are Gathered," 263.
62. Freeman, "'To Feed Upon By Faith,'" 196.
63. Freeman, "Where Two or Three Are Gathered," 266–67.

The Eucharist Makes the (Free) Church

Freeman is clear that the Supper is a means through which God re-members the Church—a sign *for* unity, to use McCabe's helpful distinction yet again.

McClendon and Newman

Newman also sees the need for a sacramental understanding of the Supper in connection with the call for a thicker conception of unity, striving for "an account of the Lord's Supper that might allow Baptists (and perhaps some others) to embrace a more sacramental understanding of this practice, and thus . . . a more catholic understanding."[64] Newman is careful to add immediately that by "catholic" she means "toward wholeness," indicating her concern to direct "Baptists closer to the Church universal, in the sense that Catholic, Orthodox, and many Protestants (for example, United Methodists, Episcopalians, Lutherans) regard this practice as a sacrament."[65] At the same time, she is not completely clear about what she means by "sacramental" until the close of the article, concluding there that "one of the reasons we can, in fact, call the Lord's Supper a sacrament is because it is not an empty sign but a *living, effective sign*. In receiving Christ's own sacrifice of love, his forgiveness, via the eucharist, we enter into communion with Christ and the body of Christ, the Church."[66] In a way similar to McClendon, then, for Newman the Supper is preeminently a "sign," though unlike McClendon she does not hesitate to call the Supper a sacrament.

Newman's quests for sacramentalism and the unity of the Church cannot be separated. That is, she wants to be clear that she is not calling Baptists to affirm a sacramental vision that they do not genuinely believe in just so that they might have "more in common" with other ecclesial groups. Rather, Newman argues that a sacramental understanding of the Supper is the best way toward establishing "consistency with the gospel and the building of unity in the Church."[67] She recognizes that "'everybody believes this' is not in itself a sufficient reason to accept" the sacramental viewpoint[68]—noting

---

64. Newman, "Lord's Supper," 214.

65. Ibid.

66. Newman, "Lord's Supper," 226. We will explore this definition below. Since she is trying to affirm a doctrine of the real presence but not transubstantiation, we should ask whether it is significant that Newman says that "we receive Christ's own sacrifice of love" rather than "we receive Christ's body."

67. Ibid., 214.

68. Ibid.

Baptists' rich history of going against the theological grain of the Church universal, and often rightly so.[69] Baptists ought to understand the Supper as a sacrament, she believes, precisely because she believes it to be the result of "biblical understanding of words and deeds."[70]

With McClendon and Freeman (and de Lubac and Jenson), then, Newman sees it as "scriptural" that through the Eucharist God not only pulls persons toward God's self, but at the same time "builds up" the Church. Newman, however, provides clarity not often given by Freeman and McClendon; her sacramental theology is directed at the wholeness of the Church universal as well as the local congregation. In order to support this aim, she calls Baptists to move away from what she believes to be the fringe of the tradition in their view of the Supper as "mere symbol,"[71] but at the same time calls Catholics to move away from a rigid insistence upon the doctrine of transubstantiation, claiming that "if only the Roman Catholic Church has embraced this position,"[72] then their view is itself not "*fully catholic.*"[73] Moreover, in terms of authority, Newman believes that "real presence" is dogmatic in status while "transubstantiation" remains "only" a doctrine,[74] and because of this belief about the distinction between doctrine and dogma she hopes that Catholics will be open to ecumenical conversations about communion.[75]

In order to make the claim that transubstantiation is a doctrine not "fully catholic," Newman seems to invoke the fifth-century theologian Vincent of Lérins, whose "rule" or "canon" for determining what is catholic is "that which has been believed everywhere, always and by all."[76] While the Catholic Church's position on transubstantiation is that "the Church of

---

69. Ibid. She raises this point in the midst of a discussion on the Supper.

70. Ibid., 223.

71. Indeed, she joins John Milbank, Robert Jenson, and others cited earlier in expressing the concern that Gnosticism is actually one of the chief threats of any non-sacramental ecclesial group (if there could be such a thing). See page 112, note 120 above.

72. Newman, "Lord's Supper," 219.

73. Ibid., 214. I shall examine below whether Newman's understanding of "catholic" is a legitimate one.

74. Ibid., 219. And again, is this correct?

75. Ibid.

76. Vincent of Lérins, *Commonitorium*. Does de Lubac invoke this rule when he says in *Catholicism* that the social aspect of the Supper "is the constant teaching of the Church, though . . . in practice it is too little known" (de Lubac, *Catholicism*, 82)? This passage is quoted on page 1 of this study.

The Eucharist Makes the (Free) Church

God" has always believed in "this change . . . called transubstantiation,"[77] Newman calls this doctrine into question. Doing so within an essay that calls Baptists to explore a new theory of the real presence allows her to tacitly affirm Baptists' early and now traditional dissent from the Catholic position. Baptists and other separatists have long reacted to what they believe are unbiblical views and practices of the Supper, and have even given their lives in doing so.[78]

Newman believes that Anabaptists and early Baptists reacted to the Catholic practices as "unbiblical" in order to (*a*) preserve the notion that Jesus' sacrifice on the cross occurred once and for all, and to (*b*) jettison an increasingly mechanical understanding of God's grace.[79] That is to say, the Anabaptists and early Baptists believed that if transubstantiation were taken to its logical conclusions, then after the substances of the bread and wine became the substances of Christ's "real" body and blood, when one participated in the Eucharist one was masticating Christ, "crucifying" him each time she or he participated in the meal. This most radical wing of the Protestant Reformation not only believed the alleged "re-crucifixion" to be grotesque—or worse, blasphemous—they thought that the popular belief that this re-crucifixion needed to happen repeatedly as a way of having one's sins forgiven "mechanically" or automatically (that is, without any faith, remorse, or repentance on the part of the participant) was a false one. To illustrate this, Newman tells the story of an Anabaptist martyr who, when asked just prior to her execution about the nature of Christ's presence in the Supper, responded, "What God would you give me? One that is perishable and sold for a farthing?"[80] This same martyr also told a priest that morning that if the bread truly was Christ's body, then he daily crucified Christ in consuming the bread.[81]

This study has posited several times, however, that if (an important qualifier) this reaction to the Catholic practice was a necessary and legitimate one, as the years passed this reaction became an overreaction. The early Anabaptists and Baptists certainly attached a different understanding of "presence" to the Supper than did the Catholics, using the language of "sign" and "symbol," but as posited earlier, their understanding of presence

---

77. *Catechism of the Catholic Church*, 1374, 1376.
78. Newman, "Lord's Supper," 215.
79. Ibid., 217.
80. Ibid.
81. Ibid., 216.

was no sub-Zwinglian "real absence." As shown above, Newman shows that Balthasar Hubmaier, for example, maintained a robust account of the Lord's Supper as a "sign," one constituted by the "symbols" of the bread and wine.[82] These signs, which for Hubmaier are "the body of Christ in remembrance,"[83] help believers remember Christ's sacrifice, but they also in some sense make Christ present and generate believers' activity.

Just as Freeman, then, so does Newman argue that it is later in the history of the free churches that, in attaching words like *merely* to "symbol," they gradually shifted their view until "*symbol* became emphasized over against *reality*."[84] After making this argument, Newman claims that this increasingly "low" view of the Supper resulted in the Supper being practiced less often. If for Baptists Jesus' presence in the Supper was no different from His presence in all other forms of Christian worship—or worse, if Jesus was not present in the Supper at all (again, the "sub-Zwinglian" view)—there was little motivation to go to the trouble of practicing the rite more than a few times a year. Newman, therefore, claims that a lack of frequent practice of the Supper was a direct result of the sacramental theology of these reactionaries. As she puts it, "as *symbol* was emphasized over against *reality*, the practice itself atrophied."[85]

Newman believes that the need to reaffirm the regularity and the sacramental nature of the practice has risen anew, especially so that the Church might see itself as one body instead of a collection of like-minded individuals. Like McClendon, Freeman, and others mentioned above, however, Newman goes even further than a call for more frequent practice. In her view, not only did the misunderstandings of the terms *symbol* and *sign* lead to the atrophy of the practice of the Supper, the decrease in practice has led inevitably to the atrophy of ecclesial unity.[86] Her solution: a view of the doctrine of the "real presence" that is not beholden to the doctrine of transubstantiation (which she believes to be bound by an Aristotelian metaphysics[87]), and one that is directed toward invoking the presence of

82. See chapter 1.

83. Hubmaier, "Simple Instruction."

84. Newman, "Lord's Supper," 217.

85. Ibid. At this point in the work, can we go as far as to state our agreement with Flannery O'Connor's statement to author Mary McCarthy about the Eucharist that "if it's just a symbol, then to hell with it"? For this O'Connor quote, see her letter to "A" dated December 16, 1955, in Fitzgerald, *Habit of Being*, 125.

86. See page 139 above.

87. Newman, "Lord's Supper," 219.

the One who unifies the members of the Church with Himself and with one another.

In order to articulate this vision, Newman does not employ the sign theory of J. L. Austin as directly as does McClendon, but she does invoke the very similar thought of philosopher William H. Poteat, who employs Austin along the way in arguing that symbols and signs are not less "real" than the objects they represent, or "re-present."[88] Rather, symbols and signs function to *do* something. Newman points out to the reader that in the biblical vision of reality, speech, or the Word, "creates or brings into being the world in which we dwell."[89] Moreover, she says that "as creatures in God's image, we could say that our words, like God's, are deeds. They create the worlds in which we dwell."[90]

This last sentence constitutes quite a large claim. If for Newman the Church and indeed all people have in some sense been given the power to "create" with words, it will be helpful at this point for the reader to recall the language of McClendon in his "Baptism as a Performative Sign." There, after offering the reader a rather simplified explanation of speech act theory as described by Austin, he insists that all communities, including the Church, employ words and speech acts that, whether written or verbalized, have the ability not only to describe something but to do something. He notes, for example, that "something happens" when a man says "'I (hereby) take this woman to be my wife' [spoken in a wedding ceremony]."[91] By "something happens," McClendon presumably means that the status of the persons in front of the minister changes. They pass from the state of being "single" to the state of being "married." In the same article, McClendon goes on to note that "Christian baptism, as it is understood by the Baptist theologians just surveyed, and as it ought to be understood, is a performative sign . . . It is also a 'word' from the church to the candidate, a 'word' in which the church says something like: 'We receive you as our brother in Christ.' And it is a 'word' from the candidate to the church, a 'word' in which the

---

88. For a thorough account of Austin, McClendon's understanding and use of Austin's speech act theory, and its relevance to sacramental theology, see the earliest pages of chapter 2.

89. Newman, "Lord's Supper," 222.

90. Ibid., 223.

91. McClendon, "Baptism as a Performative Sign," 409.

candidate says something like: 'Brethren, I take my place in your midst. Receive me!'"[92]

While McClendon says throughout his work that analyzing the "speech acts" of the Church is not the same as analyzing the speech acts of any other community (since the former are the acts not only of humans but also of God[93]), he believes that in order to understand the Church one must interpret her speech acts as well as her texts. In chapter 2, I argued that while in his best moments McClendon is aware that speaking of signs as belonging to the Church alone poses difficulties, at times God disappears as one of the actors in the drama of the Supper. For McClendon, this seems to happen when he on the one hand emphasizes that in baptism and (however briefly) in the Supper there is a "double agency"—so that "in the Lord's Supper, the deacons feed the flock, and Christ *eo ipso* feeds the flock"[94]—and yet on the other hand, in his extended treatments of the Supper, emphasizes that in the Supper "disciples . . . renew their own pledge to their Master and to one another."[95] Often, as I argue in more extended fashion in chapter 2, it is as if the gathered disciples are the ones performing the act of renewing the body. They are making the *pledge* (which, according to McClendon, is the best meaning of the term *sacrament*).[96] They, and not God, seem to be the beings that are making use of the *instrumenta*, the bread and the wine. I then concluded at that point that for McClendon, revisiting the work of Aquinas and Herbert McCabe on causation and instruments would have been a helpful addition to his work on signs.

If, for Newman, a similar understanding of words and speech acts provides "a way beyond the real versus mere symbol impasse of understanding the Lord's Supper,"[97] it is necessary to examine whether she is vulnerable to the same criticisms as McClendon. According to her, a biblical understanding of words and signs as deeds "provides 'space' to perceive

---

92. Ibid., 410. Though in chapter 1 I acknowledged McClendon's qualifier about the danger of linking speech act theory to the sacraments of the Church because of the presence of God as an actor, we showed on pages 74–75 that in this article and in his extended treatment of the sacraments in *Doctrine* McClendon does not formally recognize God as one of the actors.

93. McClendon, *Doctrine*, 389.

94. Ibid.

95. Ibid., 142. For a full account of the critiques made of McClendon's account of presence, see chapter 2.

96. McClendon, *Doctrine*, 388.

97. Newman, "Lord's Supper," 223.

The Eucharist Makes the (Free) Church

of Christ as really present when the community gathers to celebrate the Lord's Supper, but in a way that does not abstractly locate that reality in the substance of the bread and wine."[98] Like McClendon, Newman first turns to the marriage analogy to explain what she means, but she follows up an explanation of marriage with her own understanding of what happens in the consecration (if we may use that word) of the elements in the practice of the Supper:

> At a marriage ceremony when the minister says, "I pronounce you husband and wife," the status of the individuals changes. That they are no longer single but are now married means that the words were in fact deeds that brought about a new reality. So also we can say that the words "this is my body" and "this is my blood," pronounced in the communal context of the celebration of the Lord's Supper, are deeds, bringing about a new reality.[99]

Since she follows McClendon so closely here, at this point we must ask if God has disappeared as an actor in the drama of the Supper in Newman's eucharistic theology. That is to say, if we pressed McClendon on whether he was emphasizing that the disciples make the "pledge" (*sacramentum*) in his understanding of the Eucharist, and that they are therefore the persons who "convey grace," then we must ask Newman here if God is involved in changing the status of the persons getting married or in altering the elements of the bread and the wine—especially in light of her claim that "as creatures in God's image, we could say that our words, like God's, are deeds. They create the worlds in which we dwell just as God's Word (Logos) created and continues to create the world."[100]

Newman follows her own very bold language with a qualifier: "God's words/deeds are prior, our own words/deeds remain in the position of

---

98. Ibid. Of course, according to the thesis of the chapter, the author believes that Newman would be one of those authors participating in a "Baptist *ressourcement*" wherein she engages the tradition in such a way that earlier thinkers such as Augustine, Aquinas, Luther, and even de Lubac help her read Scripture. Clearly, in distancing herself from the doctrine of transubstantiation, Newman places herself at odds with de Lubac (though, as we discussed in chapter 2, the Jesuit himself was accused by the Church of denying transubstantiation). According to Newman, however, this break is not an ultimate one. Newman is working under the assumption that transubstantiation is doctrine and not dogma, and presumably under the assumption that she is a participant in the Christian "tradition," where "tradition" is characterized in part by "argument."

99. Ibid., 224.

100. Ibid., 223.

response."[101] Just as "God waits for Mary to say 'yes' to his invitation to bear God's Son," and the result of his call and Mary's answer is "the beginning of a new creation," so Newman believes that as a result of the words pronounced at the Supper a new creation comes into being.[102] This is perhaps similar to McClendon's theory of "double agency," or it might even be an illustration drawn from her reading on Aquinas' understanding of causation (also sometimes referred to as "double agency"), but it seems that just as with McClendon, a direct allusion to Aquinas would be helpful here—especially given her claim that human words function "*just as* God's Word" does.[103]

As in chapter 2, I am referring here to Aquinas' clear delineation that God is always the principal actor in the sacrament, and that the minister and elements are always secondary actors, or instrumental "causes" of grace. For Thomas "the instrumental cause works not by the power of its own form, but only by the motion whereby it is moved by the principal agent: so that the effect is not likened to the instrument but to the principal agent . . . it is thus that the sacraments cause grace: for they are instituted by God to be employed for the purpose of conferring grace."[104]

Newman's "just as" is misleading, then, implying (perhaps unintentionally) the Church's equality with God in this respect. This can also be seen more clearly if we reexamine the language of Jenson on what "happens" in the Supper (though we earlier criticized him for making some similar mistakes):

> In the Supper . . . we all receive one and the same Body of Christ. . . . And because in this way the members of the church are joined together to one Body of Christ, they are also joined with one another and become one Body whose head is Christ. So also, when in the Supper we receive the body and blood of Christ, we are intimately joined with Christ himself . . . and through Christ we are united to the Father. . . . Thus we are made fellows (*koinonoi*) with the Father, the Son, and the Holy Spirit. All these result from the . . . communion (*koinonia*) of the body and the blood of the Lord.[105]

---

101. Ibid.

102. Ibid.

103. Ibid. Emphasis mine. The term "just as" is what is troubling here. After all, if Newman simply stated that "our words function as God's words," this could imply metaphor.

104. Aquinas, *Summa Theologiae*, III.62.1.

105. Jenson, *Systematic Theology*, 2:221.

The Eucharist Makes the (Free) Church

Though prior to this description Jenson has made certain to point out Jesus' statement that as long as we participate in the Supper, *we*, his followers, "proclaim his death," here the description of the Church also contains some more passive elements—"we all receive," are "joined together," and "through *Christ* are united to the Father." In other areas of his ecclesiology, Jenson has been criticized for deifying the Church in an inappropriate manner, but here it is God—which includes *Logos* (Word)—who is the principal actor or creator.

It may come as a surprise to Baptist readers that we have modified Newman's language with that of Aquinas (a Catholic) and Jenson (a Lutheran whom Catholics accuse of going too far in identifying the Church with Christ). And yet, the careful rendering provided by Aquinas, for example, is exactly what is needed if we are to clear up what the Church means and has meant by the term *sacrament*, and how the Eucharist in particular is a sacrament that "causes grace" in enacting the Church's unity. For Aquinas, as Paul Fiddes points out, the minister and the elements are "causes" of grace, even "efficient causes" in the Aristotelian sense,[106] but they are secondary efficient causes of grace, while God is always the primary efficient cause.[107]

For Newman, if God has given the Church the power to create through words/deeds, the Eucharist is a gift from God to the Church for the purpose of creating unity in the body of Christ. Just as bride and groom are made one by the words "I now pronounce you husband and wife," through the Eucharist "we become one with God and with each other."[108] Newman roots this claim about the Supper and ecclesial unity in 1 Corinthians—the same text so pivotal for McClendon, de Lubac, and Jenson before her. Unlike McClendon, however, she uses the language of sacrament and does so unambiguously:

> "The cup of blessing," wrote St. Paul, "which we bless, is it not a communionwith the blood of Christ? The bread which we break, is it not a communion with the body of Christ? Because there is one bread, we who are many are one body, for we all partake of the one loaf" (1 Cor 10:16–17). One of the reasons we can, in fact,

---

106. Fiddes, "*Ex Opere Operato*," 227–28, 236. This is not to say that Fiddes expresses full agreement with Aquinas on what he calls a "potentially misleading" aspect of Aquinas' work. Fiddes claims, among other things, that Aquinas' understanding of "double agency" (remember, McClendon uses this term in *Doctrine*) too easily and all too directly involves God in our evil acts (Fiddes, "*Ex Opere Operato*," 228).

107. Ibid., 227–28, 236.

108. Newman, "Lord's Supper," 227.

call the Lord's Supper a sacrament is because it is not an empty sign but a *living, effective sign*. In receiving Christ's own sacrifice of love, his forgiveness, we enter into communion with Christ and the body of Christ, the Church.[109]

Christ is thus "really present" at communion for Newman (I would add that in this quote there is also a word about the Church "receiving," perhaps balancing the earlier passages we cited, for which we critiqued her for making the Church the primary actor in the Supper). Newman, however, wants to affirm a doctrine of the real presence while distancing herself from a doctrine of transubstantiation. She does not affirm the idea that as a result of saying "this is my body," Christ's presence in the Eucharist is necessarily "localized" (she also claims by way of Nicholas Lash that this is not the official teaching of the Catholic Church, either, but that it has filtered into Catholic belief at the popular level).[110] In fact, as she stated earlier, she believes that it is precisely the view of "localization" that led some Protestants to the belief that if "real presence" were true, then Christ was being masticated anew every time the Eucharist was offered.

For Newman, a "localized" Christ is far from the point of affirming a doctrine of the real presence. In fact, though she does not cite de Lubac, like the Jesuit she implies that it is an overemphasis upon theories like transubstantiation that has led to an overly privatistic understanding of the rite, and that rather than place too much emphasis on *how* the Supper is the body of Christ for the individual communicant, Baptists would do well to focus on the fact that in the Supper, as some have put it since Augustine, "we become what we receive." For Newman, that is, like de Lubac, in the Eucharist we receive the Body of Christ, and therefore become the body of Christ. If "man is what he eats,"[111] she says through Alexander Schmemann, in partaking of the Body of Christ "we become the real presence of Christ for the world."[112]

Newman's "new theory of the real presence," then, avoids dealing directly with the doctrine of transubstantiation and the ways in which the substances of the bread and the wine change. Instead, she focuses upon the change that takes place in the participants. The "real presence of Christ" at the Lord's Supper is, in fact, the Church. One might be, even should

---

109. Ibid., 226.
110. Ibid., 223.
111. Ibid., 224.
112. Ibid., 227.

The Eucharist Makes the (Free) Church

be, reminded at this point of de Lubac's great revelation that in the early Church it was the Church, not the Eucharist, that was preeminently described as the *corpus verum*. Perhaps even more closely related is Laurence Paul Hemming's statement, also raised earlier, that "knowing *that truth of faith* [that "what is substantially bread and wine is by the power of God alone transubstantiated into the body and blood of his Son"], we can by perfect eating of the sacrament be ourselves transformed into what it is we eat, a transubstantiation of its own kind."[113] While Newman could not agree with the first half of Hemming's claim, for her the Lord's Supper is a sign that is meant to point the body of Christ toward communion with God and in so doing "build up" the ecclesial body of Christ, the "real presence" of Christ. Moreover, by "body of Christ" she means "local congregation" and "Church universal"; this Church is "brought into being and extended" by God through her participation in the Eucharist.[114]

McClendon and Medley

Medley's work also closely identifies with this study's emphasis on the deep connection between ecclesial unity and churchly practices such as the Eucharist. Indeed, he opens his "'Do This': The Eucharist and Ecclesial Selfhood" with the thesis that "knowing the triune God and learning how to see and act rightly are inseparable from participating in the Christian community and its practices,"[115] and for him, the Eucharist is one of those practices named as Christian.[116] Moreover, it is important to note that in using the word *practices*, Medley has in mind the work of McClendon and especially the work of McClendon's student (and later, spouse) Nancey Murphy.[117]

---

113. Hemming, "Transubstantiating Our Selves," 436.

114. Newman, "Lord's Supper," 224.

115. Medley, "'Do This,'" 383.

116. Ibid., 387. Medley actually draws his list from Luther's treatise *On the Councils and the Churches*: (1) proclamation of God's word and its reception in faith, confession, and deed; (2) baptism; (3) the Lord's Supper; (4) the office of the keys; (5) ordination/offices; (6) prayer/doxology/catechesis; and (7) way of the cross/discipleship. Though he has this working list of what he calls "sacramental practices," he does not define what he means by "sacrament" in this work.

117. Medley, "'Do This,'" 386. He cites both McClendon and Murphy when he adds that a renewed emphasis on "practices" has recently aided discussions between Baptists and Catholics in a significant way. Moreover, in his *Imago Trinitatis*, Medley writes that "by 'practice' I mean socially established human activities carried in traditions that form people in a particular way of life. The cultivation of a people who follow the way of Jesus

Re-membering the Body

Just as understanding the word *practice* is important for understanding Medley's larger argument on the Eucharist and the Church, it is important to look at what he means by "participating in . . . practices."[118] Medley's understanding of participation is evident in his use of the Trinitarian theology of theologians such as Jürgen Moltmann, Colin Gunton, John Zizioulas, and especially Catherine LaCugna, all of whom "explore the profound significance of the doctrine of the Trinity for the Christian life."[119] In particular, these thinkers employ the idea that in being made in the image of the triune God—one being, but also three persons engaged in an eternal, "divine perichoretic dance of participation"[120]—humanity was created to be one and many.

Though for Medley the oneness of humanity has been shattered by sin and will not be regained through "a natural progression nor a blossoming of human nature through effort and struggle," he believes that in the Eucharist, ecclesial unity "becomes an actual possibility because we can participate in God's life by God's creative, reconciling, and sustaining grace."[121] We might recall for a moment the work of de Lubac on this point: sin is that which has shattered the image of a humanity created in the image of the triune God, a race of persons who were meant to be "members of one another" (Eph 4:25) rather than in isolation.[122] In a way similar to de Lubac, Medley sees participation in the Eucharist as a solution to sin, "a practice which subverts a false anthropology of will and right by the public *leitourgia* in which persons are made members of God's very Body."[123] Indeed, just as "the Eucharist makes the Church" for the Jesuit, we find that Medley, in line with much of the tradition, reads 1 Cor 10:17 in a causative fashion.[124]

Christ include the following practices: baptism, Eucharist, worship, the interpretation and proclamation of Scripture, reconciliation, hospitality, evangelism, feeding the hungry, and caring for the marginalized" (168).

118. Medley, "'Do This,'" 383.

119. Ibid., 384.

120. Ibid.

121. Ibid., 385.

122. De Lubac, *Catholicism*, 33.

123. Medley, "'Do This,'" 388. Of course, in speaking of the Church as "God's very Body" we have an instance wherein Medley uses something similar to the language of Jenson's "body of God" and de Lubac's adoption of Algerius's "the Lord's body" (de Lubac, *Corpus Mysticum*, 89).

124. Dix, *Shape of the Liturgy*, 251. Again, we have said a number of times that Dix points out that there is a thick strand of the tradition that reads Paul here as saying that

The Eucharist Makes the (Free) Church

In reading the text in this way, the Church is called by God back into participation in the triune life, and that means participation in and among one another. In coming to this passage—indeed, in coming to the Lord's table—equipped with a perichoretic understanding of Trinity and creation (even if the laity do not use such words as *perichoretic*, they can understand the language of Paul when he calls us to be "members of one another"), we arrive expecting and indeed we experience "ecstatic communion not only with God but also with other persons and all of creation."[125]

The claim that at the Supper we experience "communion" with God invites unpacking, especially in light of the way in which we explored the notions of presence found in the work of Freeman and Newman. It is important to note that Medley seems to follow Anglican theologian David Ford on the matter of Christ's presence in the Supper, eschewing "the debate about how Christ is present in the bread and the wine of the Eucharist."[126] For Medley, "the important thing about the Eucharist is the real participation of Christ in the practice and how the Eucharist enables our participation in a godly life."[127]

How does Christ participate in the Eucharist? The answer, for Ford and Medley, lies in Jesus' face. The key for understanding the Eucharist and the way in which our participation in the Eucharist is for us salvific "is 'the face,' both the face of Christ (1 Cor 4:6) and also our own human face (2 Cor 3:18)."[128] Salvation for Ford is coming "face to face with Jesus Christ," and precisely what we find in the Eucharist is "the community of the face, the face of other people and the face of Christ."[129] That is, in the eucharistic meal Christians encounter Christ and one another. Similarly, for Medley, in coming to the table

> one does not stand alone as an isolated, autonomous, self-sufficient individual. . . . The Eucharistic celebration of facing others speaks to the sacramental character of relationships. By being genuinely attentive to another "face," one may possibly meet the eternal God. One might say that just as the perichoretic character of the ecstatic relations within God's life opens out space for

---

"the church is the Body of Christ *because* it receives the sacrament which is His Body."
125. Medley, "'Do This,'" 385.
126. Ibid., 389.
127. Ibid.
128. Ibid., 388.
129. Ibid., 392.

us to live and participate in the reality of God, the perichoretic character of mutual and just relationships between persons opens out space to meet God in the depth of the in-between, in personal encounter.[130]

Thus does Medley see the believer's participation in this practice, as stated above, as a solution to sin—in coming to the table with faces and hands opened toward God and one another, we are saved from ourselves and our own selfish desires, learning to see our neighbor as someone whom we indwell in a sense, someone of whom we are "a member" (to use Paul's language again), rather than as someone with whom we are to compete. Participation in this rite, then, is salvific precisely in that, as stated earlier, it subverts a false anthropology.[131]

It is difficult to miss Medley's continuity with the other theologians addressed in this study and with the larger Christian tradition. Aquinas said, "we have the sacraments because of sin."[132] For de Lubac, the Eucharist is the remedy for the sin of pride. McCabe defines sin as "the disunity of people, their deep disunity."[133] Finally, and perhaps most significantly for our purposes in this work, for McClendon the Supper is a "sign of salvation," and what we are being saved from is our sin, which is in part defined as "rupture"—rupture of the relationship between God and humans.[134]

Also apparent here is that Medley's thinking on "the real presence" is in line with some other theologians we have examined in this study. The *ecclesial* body, the Church, is indeed the "real presence" of Christ, or better, becomes the real presence of Christ, in its participation in the eucharistic rite. And yet, exactly how Christ is present in the elements in order to bring about this unity remains unclear. Medley never offers a critique of Ford's avoidance of the debate about the manner of Christ's presence, or His "real participation." Moreover, he implies that his notion of Christ's presence follows Ford's when he says that in the Eucharist, "to eat Jesus' food is to recognize the gift of himself behind it; it is to receive from him the gift of his essential being—that presence, that face, before which we find again and again our true identity."[135]

130. Ibid., 393.
131. Ibid., 388.
132. Aquinas, *Summa Theologiae*, 3.61.1 and 3.61.3.
133. McCabe, *God Matters*, 79.
134. McClendon, *Doctrine*, 132.
135. Medley, "'Do This,'" 391.

The Eucharist Makes the (Free) Church

Is it for Medley that if we "recognize" and engage Jesus' face in the Eucharist, then we have encountered his real presence? This does not quite seem to be the whole of Medley's argument. After it becomes apparent that to encounter Jesus in the Eucharist is to encounter his "face" in the ecclesial body ("the fullest facing of all") and, more vaguely, in the elements, Medley says that when one speaks of eating Christ in the Eucharist one implies that we eat "the life of Christ, by absorbing everything about him into our ordinary lives. When we feast at the Eucharist, we consume Christ entirely—his attitudes, his outlook, his values, his example—and we allow him to transform and challenge our everyday lives."[136]

Medley is describing something similar to what Augustine (and de Lubac, Jenson, and Newman following Augustine) means when he says that Christ spoke to him the words, "I am your food, but instead of my being changed into you, it is you who shall be transformed into me."[137] Though here Medley uses some quite contemporary terms in order to describe the understandings of an ancient figure (did, or does, Christ "have values" in the sense that Medley and others use this phrase?), he seems to be saying that in absorbing Christ through the Eucharist the Church becomes the body of Christ. As in Newman, that is, the Church becomes what it consumes. For Medley, this means that through its participation in the Eucharist, the Church becomes a body with Christ's attitudes, outlooks, and values.[138]

Medley's major work is perhaps still to come. The youngest of the authors examined in this chapter—indeed, in the entire study—Medley's initial offerings seem to give the signal that he will continue to explore the relationship between the sacraments and the unity of the Church. And yet, while he occasionally uses terms like *sacrament* and *sacramental*, he does not define *sacrament* in either his *Imago Trinitatis* or in "'Do This.'"[139] He does allude to a biblical character performing a "sign action" in *Imago Trinitatis*, but the allusion is at best indirectly related to the sacraments. A

---

136. Ibid., 395.

137. Augustine, *Confessions*, 7.10.16.

138. Newman, "Lord's Supper," 197. Medley, "'Do This,'" 393. The question might be raised again, however, that if the Church is consuming the body of Christ in the Eucharist, in what sense is the Eucharist the body of Christ?

139. Medley, "'Do This,'" 387. Although Medley is more prone to call human relationships "sacramental" (indeed, this is the only sense in which he uses the term *sacramental* in his major work, *Imago Trinitatis*) than he is to use the term in relation to the Eucharist, he does have a list of what he calls "sacramental practices" here.

clearer definition of *sacrament* and a bit more on his understanding of presence is hoped for in the future, especially since his work on participation in the life of the triune God has much to offer the ecclesial body in her quest for unity. As it stands now, it is at least clear that Medley is comfortable with the language of sacrament and is concerned for a deepening of the Church's unity through Christians being invited into the perichoretic life in the Eucharist.

McClendon and Harvey

Barry Harvey shares with Freeman, Newman, and Medley a deep appreciation of McClendon's insights, but adopts a slightly more critical approach to McClendon.[140] While Harvey adopts the terms *remembering* and *re-membering* in his *Can These Bones Live?* and in his contribution to the first *Baptist Sacramentalism* volume, titled "Remembering the Body: Baptism, Eucharist, and the Politics of Disestablishment," he more bluntly notes what he calls McClendon's "missteps"[141] and helps the reader make several distinctions by retrieving the thought of the Thomist Herbert McCabe, who claims that when discussing the "signs" of the Church we must differentiate between "sign *of*" language and "sign *for*" language.[142] In the end, Harvey is able to critically adapt some of McClendon's important work for his own constructive project. I will briefly describe these features in the paragraphs below.

---

140. See Harvey, *Can These Bones Live?*, esp. 141–44. As an aside, in light of his own work with MacIntyre, one can imagine McClendon saying, "Yes, keep going," much like Augustine, when grappling with the concept of *creatio ex nihilo* in the *Confessions*, hoped that he had cleared the path so that his future readers could go further.

141. Harvey, *Can These Bones Live?*, 52. Harvey mentions only one misstep in McClendon's "baptist vision," but if what Harvey calls a misstep really does constitute an error it is an important one, for the baptist vision is the interpretive key to much, if not all, of McClendon's systematic works. To cite Harvey's critique in full, the "chief liabilities lie in part with the univocal force he attributes to the 'is' in the proposition 'the church now is the primitive church and the church on judgment day' . . . The challenge of following Christ in our time and place is a question that cannot be resolved simply by identifying ourselves directly with those called by Jesus during his lifetime. To begin with, our situation is not identical to that of the first disciples, and we must attend to the difference between the two times if we are to be faithful to the commands of Christ."

142. McCabe: "the most important effect of Wittgenstein on sacramental theology was to shift us from speaking of 'signs *of*' to speaking of 'signs *for*'" (*God Matters*, 165).

The Eucharist Makes the (Free) Church

The way in which Harvey employs McClendon's understanding of the Supper as "a re-membering sign" can be likened to the way in which William Cavanaugh appropriates Jesuit theologian Henri de Lubac's claim that "the Eucharist makes the Church,"[143] a theological note similar to Hemming's that will be examined more closely below. While Harvey adopts a more critical stance toward McClendon than Cavanaugh does toward de Lubac, for both Harvey and Cavanaugh, largely through her own fault the Church has been "dismembered" by the nation-state and other institutions,[144] and for both of them the contemporary Church would do well to consult a sacramental theology from a previous generation.

Harvey and Cavanaugh both point out that in exchange for religious toleration, the Church has allowed the role of religion to become caring for "souls," while allowing that the bodies of persons could be claimed for the purposes of the state. While in Cavanaugh's book *Torture and Eucharist* the setting is Pinochet's Chilé in the 1970s, Harvey most often focuses upon the manifestations of the Church's dismemberment in North America. Whatever the contemporary setting, both of these contemporary thinkers believe that only churchly practices such as participation in the Eucharist will enable Christians to be a body capable of resisting the claims made on their bodies and pocketbooks by competing gods. Harvey claims,

> The ecclesial practices that re-member the body of Christ propel human beings beyond the boundaries within which the twin authorities of state and market seek to confine them by binding them together in a new political association that has a center but no boundaries. Hence Paul can write to the Galatians that "as many of you as were baptized into Christ have clothed yourselves with Christ. There is no longer slave or free, there is no longer male and female; for all of you are one in Christ Jesus" (Gal 3:27–28). In similar fashion he regards the sharing of bread and wine as causally constitutive of Christ's body: "Because there is one bread, we who are many are one body, for we all partake of one bread" (1 Cor. 10.17).[145]

It cannot be overstated at this point that when calling for unity, Harvey not only uses McClendon's language of "re-membering," but he sees it as

---

143. For his part, Harvey employs both Cavanaugh and de Lubac in his contribution to *Baptist Sacramentalism*. Newman also employs Cavanaugh in her piece.
144. Harvey, "Re-membering the Body," 96–97.
145. Ibid., 111.

crucial to remind the contemporary reader of Paul's words to the divided Corinthians, just as McClendon, Freeman, and Newman have done. "This" is "that," he seems to be saying with a nod to the late McClendon.

And yet, where McClendon is hesitant to apply the term *sacrament* to the Supper, Harvey uses the term freely in relation to the Eucharist. Moreover, he emphasizes the way in which the Eucharist not only unites the participants with God but also the way in which it knits the participants to one another. In this way, he makes certain to point out that for him, the Eucharist is not "merely" a sign *of* ecclesial unity, but a sign *for* ecclesial unity. Harvey borrows from Herbert McCabe's famous distinction at this point.

As related in chapter 2, McCabe, a Catholic theologian who like McClendon worked in the twentieth century and gleaned a great deal of insight from the philosophical work of Ludwig Wittgenstein, points out that "the most important effect of Wittgenstein on sacramental theology was to shift us from speaking of 'signs *of*' to speaking of 'signs *for*.'"[146] An example of "signs *of*" language in everyday life, McCabe says, is the phrase "a red sky at night is a sign of good weather," wherein the color of the sky points primarily to something else (good weather).[147] Simply put, "the essence of the 'signs *of*' position is that the meaning of a sign is to be found somewhere *else*, a sign stands for something and stands in for something." Harvey believes that this is the way in which McClendon typically employs the term *sign* when he speaks of the Church's remembering signs. The Lord's Supper, baptism, and proclamation recall for the Church the great historic signs of the New Testament—the Last Supper, Christ's death, Christ's burial, the resurrection, and Pentecost. The Church is brought together to remember these events through the remembering signs, which are "signs *of*," pointers to, these great events. The remembering signs also function to remind believers of the great truths of the faith. McClendon believes (with Yoder) that "the *primary* meaning of the Supper" is economic sharing and it is therefore a practice that reinforces primitive socialism, the Supper is a "sign *of*" Christian unity—it does not itself effect the unity of the body but points to the economic sharing that ought to take place because of a previously instantiated unity. As McCabe puts it, for Aquinas the Supper is both as a sign *of* salvation and as a sign *for* salvation. Aquinas, when speaking about

---

146. McCabe, *God Matters*, 165, cited by Harvey, *Can These Bones Live?*, 204.
147. Ibid.

signs, was "not asking 'what is it instead of,' what is the extra thing it stands for?" but rather "'what is it *for*?' How do we use it?"¹⁴⁸

Harvey offers that the sign of the Eucharist is to be used *for* members' unity with God, and importantly, *for* their unity as the body of Christ—it is the way "Christians are re-membered by God to the risen Christ and to one another, and become the true body of Christ."¹⁴⁹ For Aquinas, the sacraments are in some sense *instrumenta*, comparable on a human level to the saw, for example. The saw, a tool which might serve little or no purpose in the hands of certain persons, can be used by a skilled carpenter to make a beautiful piece of furniture. In the carpenter's hands, that is, it becomes an effective instrument used for the purpose of furniture-making. Similarly, for McCabe the eucharistic bread and wine function in the Church as a powerful instrument *for* unity. The Church's conception of Christian unity—based on Paul's belief that "we who are many are one body for we partake of the one loaf" (1 Cor 10:17)—is rooted in divine communication through signs. The bread in this instance is not solely a sign *of*, a pointer to, the Church's unity (though it may do that as well); it is a sign *for* unity in that it communicates God himself and creates the unity of the body of Christ.

The Eucharist, then, is a sign *for* unity in Harvey's work, and therefore a sacrament in the fullest sense, a view most evident in his *Can These Bones Live?* In a chapter titled "Sacramental Sinews" wherein he appropriates the work of McCabe directly, Harvey complains that the "sign *of*" perspective most readily emerges particularly from free church traditions. These communities assert that "the water, bread, and wine represent Christ's death for our act of remembrance and therefore are simply the outward expression of an interior 'spiritual' experience."¹⁵⁰ Harvey laments that this mindset means that these traditions typically "talk about the baptism and Eucharist as 'just' a sign or symbol."¹⁵¹

Harvey may think that McClendon falls short in not using the language of sacrament, but he does not bring McCabe to bear directly upon McClendon's work, perhaps since he knows that McClendon similarly

148. McCabe, *God Matters*, 166, cited by Harvey, *Can These Bones Live?*, 204. Like McCabe, McClendon employs Wittgenstein on language extensively throughout his work. Again, one is tempted to ask, had McClendon read McCabe? Would he have liked it? Would he have employed the language of sacrament less ambiguously?

149. Harvey, *Can These Bones Live?*, 215.

150. Ibid., 202.

151. Ibid.

disdains such "sub-Zwinglian" language, to borrow one of Freeman's favorite terms.[152] Indeed, as stated above, since for McClendon symbols are so crucial to the makeup of signs, the term *mere symbol* is an oxymoron. Moreover, he says repeatedly that the signs of the Church "are effectual."[153] And yet, as is also stated above, McClendon most often stops short of employing "sign for" language. Where he talks of the Supper as one of the "signs *of* salvation,"[154] which is one proper way to speak of it, the reader is left to wonder if he is pushing for a sacramental understanding or not.

Conclusion: The Future of Baptist "Sacramental" Theology

I have posited in this study that the scholarly writing of some of the new Baptist sacramentalists takes on a truly sacramental direction, while McClendon's, though he takes care to say that "something happens" in the Supper, does not. Bearing in mind that McClendon first called the Supper "a re-membering sign" wherein the term *sign* indicates that "something happens" and the term *re-membering* means that what "happens" is that the Church is, in the Supper, "reconstitute[ed], being made part of the whole,"[155] and bearing in mind that McClendon disdains disunity in the body of Christ and that, perhaps most importantly, he proposed from the pulpit of a divided church that participating in the practice of the Supper more frequently would aid them in their quest for unity, one might ask whether or not we are theologically "splitting hairs" at this point. Another question that comes to mind is, why does it matter?

The answer to the first question, I believe, is no. As stated above, in the end McClendon remains uncomfortable using the language of "sacrament," whereas, as we have seen in this final chapter, the new Baptist sacramentalists use such language freely and easily—almost as easily as de Lubac himself. In fact, we have seen that contemporary Baptists like Freeman cite the work of de Lubac along the way, while Freeman, Newman, Medley, and many others from among the new Baptist sacramentalists interact with the work of Cavanaugh, and therefore indirectly with de Lubac, in their essays.

---

152. McClendon, *Doctrine*, 382, 388.
153. Ibid.
154. Ibid., 388. Emphasis mine.
155. McClendon, *Doctrine*, 402.

The Eucharist Makes the (Free) Church

That most of the new Baptist sacramentalists interact with these sources does not make their theologies "sacramental" necessarily, but it does suggest some new directions in Baptist sacramental theology and ecclesiology. Whether there is long-term viability to their project remains to be seen, but I have argued here that the project exists at all is possible because of the fresh direction taken by James Wm. McClendon Jr. Harmon's book suggests as much when he claims that although "present and future generations of Baptist theologians would benefit from a more intentional adoption" of the broader tradition, unlike Baptist giants Strong, Mullins, and Conner, McClendon's own level of engagement with Catholic sources represents a turn in Baptist theology.[156] I do wish that he had engaged, for example, sources such as Augustine, Aquinas, or even de Lubac on the subject. Indeed, though McClendon points us to the larger tradition, he sometimes misses opportunities to make obvious references to that very tradition. For example, McClendon never mentions Aquinas' work when raising the subject of "double agency" in *Doctrine*, and never mentions Augustine in relation to his sign theory. Nevertheless, his willingness to read outside of his own "baptist" tradition is one thing that leads to his "higher" understanding of the Supper.

McClendon's understanding of the Supper as a re-membering sign, along with the fact that all three of the "new Baptist sacramentalists" that we have examined affirm that the Eucharist is a sacrament that not only unites us to God but to one another,[157] leads us back to the second question: Why does it matter whether we posit a purely symbolic view of the Supper or a sacramental one? In order to answer this question, we turn once more to the work of Cavanaugh, the contemporary Catholic whose work is so influenced by de Lubac and was examined at the end of chapter 3 of this study. Through his retrieval of the doctrine of the threefold body of Christ—the historical body (which walked the shores of Galilee and is now at the right hand of the Father), the ecclesial body (preeminently referred to as the *corpus verum*, or true body of Christ, in patristic literature), and the eucharistic body (the *corpus mysticum*, or mystical body of Christ)—Cavanaugh argues that for the patristics the Eucharist (*corpus mysticum*) makes the Church (*corpus verum*) in erasing the gap between the Church and

---

156. Harmon, *Towards a Baptist Catholicity*, 147.

157. See Newman, "Lord's Supper," 226; Freeman, "'To Feed Upon by Faith,'" 197; Medley, "'Do This,'" 387. Again, Medley is more prone to call human relationships "sacramental" than he is to use the term in relation to the Eucharist.

the historical body. Cavanaugh says that in the oldest understandings of the threefold body, "the sacramental body and the church body are closely linked, and there is a 'gap' between this pair and the historical body. The Eucharist and the Church . . . are together the contemporary performance of the historical body, the unique historical event of Jesus."[158]

Cavanaugh, like de Lubac, affirms the doctrine of transubstantiation. And yet he shares de Lubac's concern that while the doctrine of transubstantiation is true, centuries of arguing over transubstantiation have obscured the fact that the eucharistic body was once known preeminently as the *corpus mysticum*, which "made" the faithful, pleading Church the *corpus verum* in pulling her toward the historical, ascended body of Christ. De Lubac and Cavanaugh want to make the point that for the early Church (and, of course, for the contemporary Church, too, though it is largely unaware of the fact), "the Eucharist makes the Church," and this means that without the Eucharist, the Church is *not* the Church, not the body of Christ (and perhaps not any body, but rather a loosely affiliated collection of individuals brought together by a common belief).

This is what a "re-sourcing" of Scripture and the Christian tradition looks like in relation to the Eucharist in the eyes of de Lubac and Cavanaugh. Theologian-pastors like Augustine, Paschasius Radbertus, and Rabanus Maurus, to name a few, believed that through the Eucharist, participants are made the ecclesial body of Christ—"because there is one bread, we who are many are one body, for we all partake of the one loaf" (1 Cor 10:17)—and that "we . . . are one body" means that the "we" in question have been made "members of one another" (Eph 4:25). If we may use the language of McClendon's "baptist vision," de Lubac believes that what was true "then" is true "now"—"the renewal of Christian vitality is linked at least partially to a renewed exploration of the periods and of the works where the Christian tradition is expressed with a particular intensity."[159]

Since the biblical narrative promises that division will remain a problem until Christ's return, and since this study has shown that the Eucharist is a, if not the, primary solution to disunity in the eyes of the New Testament authors and earliest theologians, I argue that the movement that I have dubbed "the new Baptist sacramentalism" will have staying power insofar as it does what de Lubac suggests—continually explore Scripture and the tradition, posing new and relevant questions to texts that are inspired

---

158. Cavanaugh, *Torture and Eucharist*, 212.

159. De Lubac, *Mémoire*, 94.

and tested, and creatively employing the "obviously biblical" (to use Jenson's language) sacraments anew in the twenty-first century—especially the Eucharist as a sign *for* unity (thank you, McCabe). As Newman suggests in her essay, this is not a "Catholic" thing to do, but a very Baptist one— "Baptists have a rich heritage" of turning to ancient texts and as a result making "new" (or renewing) theological claims if they believe the times call for such action. Indeed, this is one thing for which McClendon is praised in the earliest pages of Harmon's text—engaging the broader tradition in spite of the fact that his teachers had not done this and his contemporaries were not doing this.

McClendon has pointed Baptists in the right direction in his appreciation for the broader tradition, and in so doing has pointed Baptists to a more fulsome understanding of the Supper. The times call for a new group of Baptists who will affirm that a purely symbolic understanding of the Supper is not only unbiblical and out of step with the best of the Christian tradition, it encourages a move away from a powerful practice—indeed, a sacrament—which, Sunday after Sunday, re-members the body of Christ, a body that spends much of its week being pulled in many different directions or, in some cases, torn completely apart. The Eucharist makes the Church. Indeed, the new Baptist sacramentalists, through continuing their habit of re-sourcing Scripture and the tradition, can help Baptists see that the Eucharist makes the *free* church.

Bibliography

Abingdon, Robert M. Review of *Ethics: Systematic Theology, I*, by James Wm. McClendon. *Faith and Philosophy* 7 (1990) 117–23.
Allen, Diogenes. "The Rehabilitation of Pilgrim's Progress." *Perspectives in Religious Studies* 27 (2000) 103–15.
Anscombe, G. E. M. "On Transubstantiation." In *Ethics, Religion, and Politics*, 107–12. Minneapolis: University of Minnesota Press, 1981.
Aquinas. *Summa Theologiae*. New York: Benziger, 1948.
Athanasius. *Against the Arians*. In *Select Treatises of St. Athanasius in Controversy with the Arians*, edited and translated by John Henry Newman. New York: Longmans, Green, 1903.
Augustine. *Confessions*. Translated by John K. Ryan. New York: Image, 1960.
Austin, J. L. *Sense and Sensibilia*. New York: Oxford University Press, 1964.
Balthasar, Hans Urs von. "The Achievement of Henri de Lubac." *Thought* 51 (1976) 7–49.
———. *The Theology of Henri de Lubac: An Overview*. San Francisco: Ignatius, 1983.
Barron, Robert. "Considering the Theology of James Wm. McClendon, Jr." *Modern Theology* 18 (2002) 267–76.
Barth, Karl. *Church Dogmatics IV.2: The Doctrine of Reconciliation*. Edinburgh: T. & T. Clark, 1958.
Battle, Michael, editor. *The Quest for Liberation and Reconciliation: Essays in Honor of J. Deotis Roberts*. Louisville: Westminster John Knox, 2005.
Beckwith, Sarah. *Christ's Body: Identity, Culture, and Society*. London: Routledge, 1993.
Bergsten, Torsten. *Balthasar Hubmaier: Anabaptist Theologian and Martyr*. Edited by William R. Estep. Translated by Irwin J. Barnes and William R. Estep. Valley Forge: Judson, 1978.
Blough, Neal. "The Church as Sign or Sacrament: Trinitarian Ecclesiology, Pilgram Marpeck, Vatican II and John Milbank." Online: http://www.goshen.edu/mqr/pastissues/jano4blough.html.
Bonhoeffer, Dietrich. *No Rusty Swords: Letters, Lectures and Notes, 1928–1936*. Edited by Edwin H. Robertson. Translated by Edwin H. Robertson and John Bowden. New York: Harper & Row, 1965.
Braaten, Carl. "Robert William Jenson: A Personal Memoir." In *Trinity, Time and Church: A Response to the Theology of Robert W. Jenson*, edited by Colin E. Gunton, 1–9. Grand Rapids: Eerdmans, 2000.
Braaten, Carl, and Robert W. Jenson, editors. *Christian Dogmatics*. 2 vols. Philadelphia: Fortress, 1984.

Bibliography

Bradshaw, Paul, editor. *The New Westminster Dictionary of Liturgy and Worship.* Philadelphia: Westminster John Knox, 2002.

Broadway, Mikael N. "Bibliography of McClendon's Writings." *Perspectives in Religious Studies* 27 (2000) 11–20.

Broadway, Mikael N., et al. "Re-Envisioning Baptist Identity: A Manifesto for Baptist Communities in North America." *Baptists Today* 15 (1997) 8–10.

Brown, Dale. Review of *Ethics: Systematic Theology, I*, by James Wm. McClendon. *Brethren Life and Thought* 33 (1988) 250–51.

Brown, Raymond. *An Introduction to the New Testament.* New York: Doubleday, 1997.

Burrell, David. Review of *Biography as Theology*, by James Wm. McClendon. *Journal of the American Academy of Religion* 53 (1975) 624.

Calvin, John. *Institutes of the Christian Religion.* Edited by John T. McNeill. Translated by Ford Lewis Battles. 2 vols. Philadelphia: Westminster, 1960.

Catechism of the Catholic Church. New York: Doubleday, 1995.

Cavanaugh, William T. "Consumption, the Market, and the Eucharist." In *Hunger, Bread and Eucharist*, edited by Christophe Boureux, Janet Martin Soskice, and Luiz Carlos Susin, 88–95. London: SCM, 2005.

———. *Theopolitical Imagination.* London: T. & T. Clark, 2002.

———. *Torture and Eucharist: Theology, Politics, and the Body of Christ.* Malden, MA: Blackwell, 1998.

Certeau, Michel de. *The Mystic Fable.* Chicago: University of Chicago Press, 1992.

———. *The Practice of Everyday Life.* Translated by Steven Rendall. Berkeley: University of California Press, 1984.

Chadwick, Henry. *The Early Church.* London: Penguin, 1967.

Chantraine, Georges. "Cardinal Henri de Lubac (1886–1991): Influence on Doctrine of Vatican II." *Communio* 18 (1991) 297–303.

Charry, Ellen. *By the Renewing of Your Minds: The Pastoral Function of Christian Doctrine.* New York: Oxford University Press, 1997.

Clark, Neville. *An Approach to the Theology of the Sacraments.* London: SCM, 1956.

Companion to the Catechism of the Catholic Church: A Compendium of Texts Referred to in the Catechism of Catholic Church. San Francisco: Ignatius, 1994.

Congar, Yves. *Un people messianique.* Paris: Cerf, 1975.

Conner, Walter T. *Christian Doctrine.* Nashville: Broadman, 1937.

Cross, Anthony R., and Philip E. Thompson, editors. *Baptist Sacramentalism.* Carlisle, UK: Paternoster, 2003.

Curtis, Jason M. "Trinity, Time, and Sacrament: Christ's Eucharistic Presence in the Theology of Robert W. Jenson." *Journal for Christian Theological Research* 10 (2005) 21–38.

Daley, Brian. "The *Nouvelle Théologie* and the Patristic Revival: Sources, Symbols, and the Science of Theology." *International Journal of Systematic Theology* 7 (2005) 362–82.

D'Ambrosio, Marcellino. "Ressourcement Theology, Aggiornamento, and the Hermeneutics of Tradition." *International Catholic Review* (1991) 533–47.

Dix, Gregory. *The Shape of the Liturgy.* London: A. & C. Black, 1945.

Dockery, David S. Review of *Ethics: Systematic Theology, I*, by James Wm. McClendon. *Criswell Theological Review* 3 (1988) 224–25.

Durnbaugh, Donald F. *The Believers' Church.* Scottdale, PA: Herald, 1968.

Essick, John D. Inscore. "Messenger, Apologist, and Nonconformist: An Examination of Thomas Grantham's Leadership among the Seventeenth-Century General Baptists." PhD diss., Baylor University, 2009.

Ewell, Rosalee Velloso. "The Roman Wheel: A Theological Method of Organization." *Perspectives in Religious Studies* 27 (2000) 113-20.

Fawcett, John. *Christ Precious to Those that Believe.* 4th ed. Minneapolis: Klock & Klock, 1979.

Fiddes, Paul. "*Ex Opere Operato*: Re-thinking a Historic Baptist Rejection." In *Baptist Sacramentalism 2*, edited by Anthony R. Cross and Philip E. Thompson, 219-38. Milton Keynes: Paternoster, 2008.

Finger, Thomas. *A Contemporary Anabaptist Theology: Biblical, Historical, Constructive.* Downers Grove, IL: InterVarsity, 2004.

Fitzgerald, Sally, editor. *Habit of Being.* New York: Farrar, Straus & Giroux, 1979.

Forde, Gerhard. "Robert Jenson's Soteriology." In *Trinity, Time and Church: A Response to the Theology of Robert W. Jenson*, edited by Colin E. Gunton 126-38. Grand Rapids: Eerdmans, 2000.

Fowler, James W. Review of *Biography as Theology*, by James Wm. McClendon. *Christian Century* 92 (1975) 244-45.

Fowler, Stanley K. *More than a Symbol: The British Baptist Recovery of Baptismal Sacramentalism.* Waynesboro, GA: Paternoster, 2002.

Freeman, Curtis W. "The 'Coming of Age' of Baptist Theology in Generation Twenty-Something." *Perspectives in Religious Studies* 27 (2000) 21-38.

———. "'To Feed Upon by Faith': Nourishment from the Lord's Table." In *Baptist Sacramentalism*, edited by Anthony R. Cross and Philip E. Thompson, 194-210. Waynesboro, GA: Paternoster, 2003.

———. "Where Two or Three Are Gathered: Communion Ecclesiology in the Free Church." *Perspectives in Religious Studies* 31 (2004) 259-72.

Freeman, Curtis W., James Wm. McClendon Jr., and C. Rosalee Velloso da Silva. *Baptist Roots: A Reader in the Theology of a Christian People.* Valley Forge, PA: Judson, 1999.

Gadamer, Hans Georg. *Truth and Method.* Translated by Joel Weisenheimer and Donald G. Marshall. 2nd ed. New York: Continuum, 2002.

Gaillardetz, Richard R. *The Church in the Making: Lumen Gentium, Christus Dominus, Orientalium Ecclesiarum.* New York: Paulist, 2006.

Garrett, James Leo. "Walter Thomas Conner." In *Baptist Theologians*, edited by Timothy George and David S. Dockery, 419-24. Nashville: Broadman, 1990.

George, Timothy. "The Sacramentality of the Church: An Evangelical Baptist Perspective." In *Baptist Sacramentalism*, 21-35. Waynesboro, GA: Paternoster, 2003.

———. "The Spirituality of the Radical Reformation." In *Christian Spirituality: High Middle Ages and Reformation*, edited by Jill Raitt, Bernard McGinn, and John Meyendorff, 334-71. New York: Crossroad, 1987.

Gill, Jerry H. Review of *Understanding Religious Convictions*, by James Wm. McClendon and James M. Smith. *Christian Scholar's Review* 6 (1976) 206-8.

Grantham, Thomas. *Christianismus Primitivus.* In *Baptist Roots: A Reader in the Theology of a Christian People*, edited by Curtis W. Freeman, James Wm. McClendon Jr., and C. Rosalee Velloso da Silva, 88-97. Valley Forge, PA: Judson, 1999.

Grenz, Stanley J. *Beyond Foundationalism: Shaping Theology in a Postmodern Context.* Louisville: Westminster John Knox, 1995.

Bibliography

Gritsch, Eric A., and Robert W. Jenson. *Lutheranism: The Theological Movement and Its Confessional Writings*. Philadelphia: Fortress, 1976.

Gunton, Colin E. "Creation and Mediation in the Theology of Robert W. Jenson." In *Trinity, Time and Church: A Response to the Theology of Robert W. Jenson*, edited by Colin E. Gunton, 80–93. Grand Rapids: Eerdmans, 2000.

Hanigan, James P. Review of *Ethics: Systematic Theology, I*, by James Wm. McClendon. *Christian Scholar's Review* 17 (1987) 97–98.

Harmon, Steven R. *Towards Baptist Catholicity: Essays on Tradition and the Baptist Vision*. Milton Keynes: Paternoster, 2006.

Harper, Brian. "The Church as a Social Ethic: The 'Baptist' Theology of James W. McClendon." PhD diss., Baylor University, 1995.

Harvey, Barry. "Beginning in the Middle of Things." *Modern Theology* 18.2 (2002) 251–61.

———. *Can These Bones Live? A Catholic Baptist Engagement with Ecclesiology, Hermeneutics, and Social Theory*. Grand Rapids: Brazos, 2008.

———. "Doctrinally Speaking: James McClendon on the Nature of Doctrine." *Perspectives in Religious Studies* 27 (2000) 39–60.

———. "Re-membering the Body: Baptism, Eucharist, and the Politics of Disestablishment." In *Baptist Sacramentalism*, edited by Anthony R. Cross and Philip E. Thompson, 96–116. Waynesboro, GA: Paternoster, 2003.

Hauerwas, Stanley. *A Community of Character*. Notre Dame: University of Notre Dame Press, 1981.

———. *In Good Company: The Church as Polis*. Notre Dame: University of Notre Dame Press, 1995.

———. "Only Theology Overcomes Ethics: Or, What 'Ethicists' Must Learn from Jenson." In *Trinity, Time and Church: A Response to the Theology of Robert W. Jenson*, edited by Colin E. Gunton, 252–68. Grand Rapids: Eerdmans, 2000.

———. *The Peaceable Kingdom*. Notre Dame: University of Notre Dame Press, 1983.

———. *The Truth about God: The Ten Commandments in Christian Life*. Nashville: Abingdon, 1999.

———. "What Could It Mean for the Church to Be Christ's Body? A Question without a Clear Answer." In *In Good Company: The Church as Polis*, 19–31. Notre Dame: University of Notre Dame Press, 1995.

Hauerwas, Stanley, and Ralph C. Wood. "How the Church Became Invisible: A Christian Reading of American Literary Tradition." *Religion and Literature* 38 (2006) 61–93.

Hauerwas, Stanley, Nancey C. Murphy, and Mark Thiessen Nation, editors. *Theology Without Foundations*. Nashville: Abingdon, 1994.

Haykin, Michael. "'His Soul-Refreshing Presence': The Lord's Supper in Calvinistic Baptist Thought and Experience in the 'Long' Eighteenth Century." In *Baptist Sacramentalism*, edited by Anthony R. Cross and Philip E. Thompson, 177–93. Waynesboro, GA: Paternoster, 2003.

Haymes, Brian. "Towards a Sacramental Understanding of Preaching." In *Baptist Sacramentalism*, edited by Anthony R. Cross and Philip E. Thompson, 263–70. Waynesboro, GA: Paternoster, 2003.

Hemming, Laurence Paul. "Transubstantiating Our Selves." *Heythrop Journal* 44 (2003) 418–39.

Hollon, Bryan. "Ontology, Exegesis, and Culture." PhD diss., Baylor University, 2006.

Bibliography

Holmes, Stephen R. "Towards a Baptist Theology of Ordained Ministry." In *Baptist Sacramentalism*, edited by Anthony R. Cross and Philip E. Thompson, 247–62. Waynesboro, GA: Paternoster, 2003.

Horton, Michael Scott. *People and Place: A Covenant Ecclesiology*. Philadelphia: Westminster John Knox, 2008.

Hubmaier, Balthasar. "Several Theses Concerning the Mass." In *Balthasar Hubmaier: Theologian of Anabaptism*, edited and translated by H. Wayne Pipkin and John Howard Yoder, 72–75. Scottdale, PA: Herald, 1989.

———. "A Simple Instruction." In *Balthasar Hubmaier: Theologian of Anabaptism*, edited and translated by H. Wayne Pipkin and John Howard Yoder, 314–38. Scottdale, PA: Herald, 1989.

Irenaeus. *Against the Heresies*. In vol. 7 of Patrologia graeca. Edited by J.-P. Migne. 162 vols. Paris, 1857–1886.

Jasper, R. C. D., and G. J. Cuming, editors and translators. *Prayers of the Eucharist: Early and Reformed*. Collegeville, MN: Liturgical, 1975.

Jenson, Robert W. "About *Dialog*, and the Church, and some Bits of the Theological Biography of Robert W. Jenson." *Dialog* 11 (1972) 38.

———. "Always to Care, Never to Kill: A Declaration on Euthanasia." In *First Things* 20 (1991) 45–47.

———. *America's Theologian: A Recommendation of Jonathan Edwards*. New York: Oxford University Press, 1988.

———. "The Church and the Sacraments." In *The Cambridge Companion to Christian Doctrine*, edited by Colin Gunton, 207–25. Cambridge: Cambridge University Press, 1997.

———. *Essays in the Theology of Culture*. Grand Rapids: Eerdmans, 1995.

———. "How the World Lost Its Story." *First Things* 36 (1993) 19–24.

———. "The Homosexual Movement." *First Things* 41 (1994) 15–21.

———. "The Inhuman Use of Human Beings." *First Things* 49 (1995) 17–21.

———. *On Thinking the Human: Resolutions of Difficult Notions*. Grand Rapids: Eerdmans, 2003.

———. *Story and Promise: A Brief Theology of the Gospel about Jesus*. Ramsey, NJ: Sigler, 1989.

———. *Systematic Theology*. 2 vols. New York: Oxford University Press, 1997–99.

———. "Toward a Christian Theory of the Public." *Essays in Theology of Culture*, 132–46. Grand Rapids: Eerdmans, 1995.

———. *The Triune Identity: God according to the Gospel*. Philadelphia: Fortress, 1982.

———. *Unbaptized God: The Basic Flaw in Ecumenical Theology*. Philadelphia: Fortress, 1992.

———. *Visible Words: The Interpretation and Practice of Christian Sacraments*. Philadelphia: Fortress, 1978.

Jorgenson, Cameron. "Bapto-Catholicism: Recovering Tradition and Reconsidering the Baptist Identity." PhD diss., Baylor University, 2008.

Kant, Imanuel. *Religion Within the Limits of Reason Alone*. Translated by Theodore Green. New York: Harper & Row, 1960.

Kantorowicz, Ernst. *The King's Two Bodies: A Study in Medieval Political Theology*. Princeton: Princeton University Press, 1957.

Kärkkäinen, Veli-Matti. *An Introduction to Ecclesiology: Ecumenical, Historical, and Global Perspectives*. Downers Grove, IL: InterVarsity, 2002.

Bibliography

Knowles, David. *The Evolution of Medieval Thought*. London: Addison Wesley Longman, 1962.
Knox, David B. "The Nature of Worship." *Churchman* 71.2 (1957).
Langan, John P. Review of *Understanding Religious Convictions*, by James Wm. McClendon and James M. Smith. *Theological Studies* 37 (1976) 354–56.
Langlands, Bryan. "Discipline and Eucharist: Foucault, Cavanaugh, Disciplined Bodies and the Re-creation of the Body of Christ." ThM thesis, Duke Divinity School, 2006.
Lee, Philip. *Against the Protestant Gnostics*. New York: Oxford University Press, 1987.
Leonard, Bill. *Baptist Ways: A History*. Valley Forge, PA: Judson, 2003.
Lindbeck, George. *The Nature of Doctrine: Religion and Theology in a Postliberal Age*. Philadelphia: Westminster, 1984.
Longbottom, Don. Review of *Ethics: Systematic Theology, I*, by James Wm. McClendon. *Conrad Grebel Review* 6 (1988) 271–73.
Lubac, Henri de. *Catholicism: Christ and the Common Destiny of Man*. Translated by Lancelot C. Sheppard and Elizabeth Englund. San Francisco: Ignatius, 1988.
———. *Christian Resistance to Anti-Semitism: Memories from 1940–1944*. Translated by Elizabeth Englund. San Francisco: Ignatius, 1990.
———. *The Church: Paradox and Mystery*. Staten Island, NY: Alba House, 1969.
———. *Corpus Mysticum: The Eucharist and the Church in the Middle Ages*. Edited by Laurence Paul Hemming and Susan Frank Parsons. Translated by Gemma Simmonds with Richard Price and Christopher Stephens. Notre Dame: University of Notre Dame Press, 2006.
———. *The Drama of Atheist Humanism*. Translated by Edith M. Riley, Anne Englund Nash, and Mark Sebanc. San Francisco: Ignatius, 1983.
———. *Mémoire sur l'occasion de mes écrits*. Namur: Culture et vérité, 1989.
———. *The Motherhood of the Church*. Translated by Sergia Englund. San Francisco: Ignatius, 1981.
———. *The Mystery of the Supernatural*. Translated by Rosemary Sheed. New York: Crossroad, 1998.
———. *Scripture in the Tradition*. Translated by Luke O'Neill. New York: Crossroad, 2000.
———. *The Splendor of the Church*. Translated by Michael Mason. San Francisco: Ignatius, 1986.
———. *Theological Fragments*. Translated by Rebecca Howell Balinski. San Francisco: Ignatius, 1989.
Lumpkin, William. *Baptist Confessions of Faith*. Rev. ed. Valley Forge, PA: Judson, 1969.
Luther, Martin. *The Large Catechism*. Translated by Robert H. Fischer. Philadelphia: Fortress, 1959.
———. "The Pagan Servitude of the Church." In *Martin Luther: Selections from His Writings*, edited by John Dillenberger, 249–359. Garden City, NY: Doubleday, 1961.
MacIntyre, Alasdair. *After Virtue*. 2nd ed. Notre Dame: University of Notre Dame Press, 1984.
———. *Dependent Rational Animals: Why Human Beings Need the Virtues*. Chicago: Open Court, 1999.
———. *Three Rival Versions of Moral Enquiry*. Notre Dame: University of Notre Dame Press, 1990.
———. *Whose Justice? Which Rationality?* Notre Dame: University of Notre Dame Press, 1988.

Bibliography

Marion, Jean-Luc. *God Without Being*. Chicago: University of Chicago Press, 1991.
Mascall, E. L. *Corpus Christi: Essays on the Church and the Eucharist*. London: Longmans, Green, 1965.
McBeth, H. Leon. *The Baptist Heritage*. Nashville: Broadman, 1987.
McCabe, Herbert. *God Matters*. London: Geoffrey Chapman, 1987.
McCall, Duke, editor. *What Is the Church? A Symposium of Baptist Thought*. Nashville: Broadman, 1958.
McClendon, James Wm. "Balthasar Hubmaier, Catholic Anabaptist." *Mennonite Quarterly Review* 65 (1991) 20–33.
———. "Baptism as a Performative Sign." *Theology Today* 23 (1966) 403–16.
———. "The Baptist and Mennonite Vision." In *Mennonites and Baptists: A Continuing Conversation*, edited by Paul Toews, 211–24. Winnipeg, MB: Kindred, 1993.
———. *Biography as Theology*. Nashville: Abingdon, 1974.
———. "The Concept of Authority: A Baptist View." *Perspectives in Religious Studies* 16 (1989) 101–7.
———. "The Doctrine of Sin and the First Epistle of John: A Comparison of Calvinist, Wesleyan, and Biblical Thought." ThD study, Southwestern Baptist Theological Seminary, 1953.
———. *Doctrine: Systematic Theology*. Vol. 2. Nashville: Abingdon, 1994.
———. *Ethics: Systematic Theology*. Vol. 1. 2nd ed. Nashville: Abingdon, 2002.
———. "Evangelical Ethics." *Modern Churchman* 29 (1987) 42–48.
———. "How Is Christian Morality Universalisable?" In *The Weight of Glory*, edited by D. W. Hardy and P. H. Sedgwick, 101–15. Edinburgh: T. & T. Clark, 1991.
———. *Making Gospel Sense to a Troubled Church*. Cleveland: Pilgrim, 1995.
———. "Narrative Ethics and Christian Ethics." *Faith and Philosophy* 3 (1986) 383–96.
———. *Pacemakers of Christian Thought*. Nashville: Broadman, 1962.
———. "The Practice of Community Formation." In *Virtues and Practices in the Christian Tradition: Christian Ethics after MacIntyre*, edited by Nancey C. Murphy, Brad J. Kallenberg, and Mark Thiessen Nation, 85–110. Harrisburg, PA: Trinity, 1997.
———. "Protestant Theology: USA." In *The Blackwell Encyclopedia of Modern Christian Thought*, edited by Alister E. McGrath, 524–31. Oxford: Blackwell, 1993.
———. "The Radical Road One Baptist Took." *Mennonite Quarterly Review* 74 (2000) 503–10.
———. "What Is Baptist Theology?" *American Baptist Quarterly* 1 (1982) 24–28.
———. "What Is a Southern Baptist Ecumenism?" *Southwestern Journal of Theology* 10 (1968) 73–78.
———. "Why Baptists Do Not Baptize Infants." In *The Sacraments: An Ecumenical Dilemma*, edited by Hans Küng, 7–15. New York: Paulist, 1966.
———. *Witness: Systematic Theology*. Vol. 3. Nashville: Abingdon, 2000.
McClendon, James Wm., and James M. Smith. *Understanding Religious Convictions*. Notre Dame: University of Notre Dame Press, 1975. Rev. ed. published as *Convictions: Diffusing Religious Relativism*. Valley Forge: Trinity, 1994, 2002.
McCue, James F. "The Doctrine of Transubstantiation from Berengar of Tours through Trent: The Point at Issue." *Harvard Theological Review* 61 (1968) 385–430.
McPartlan, Paul. *The Eucharist Makes the Church: Henri de Lubac and John Zizioulas in Dialogue*. Edinburgh: T. & T. Clark, 1993.
———. *Sacrament of Salvation: An Introduction to Eucharistic Ecclesiology*. Edinburgh: T. & T. Clark, 1995.

Bibliography

Medley, Mark. "'Do This': The Eucharist and Ecclesial Selfhood." *Review and Expositor* 100 (2003) 383–401.

———. *Imago Trinitatis: Toward a Relational Understanding of Becoming Human*. Lanham, MD: University Press of America, 2002.

Migne, J.-P., editor. *Patrologia Graeca*. 162 vols. Paris: Migne, 1857–1886.

———. *Patrologia Latina*. 217 vols. Paris: Migne, 1857–1886.

Milbank, John. "Enclaves, or Where Is the Church?" *New Blackfriars* 73 (1992) 341–52.

———. *The Suspended Middle: Henri de Lubac and the Debate Concerning the Supernatural*. Grand Rapids: Eerdmans, 2005.

———. *Theology and Social Theory: Beyond Secular Reason*. Oxford: Blackwell, 1990.

Moody, Dale. "The New Testament Significance of the Lord's Supper." In *What Is the Church? A Symposium of Baptist Thought*, edited by Duke McCall, 79–96. Nashville: Broadman, 1958.

———. *The Word of Truth: A Summary of Christian Doctrine Based on Biblical Revelation*. Grand Rapids: Eerdmans, 1981.

Mouw, Richard J. Review of *Ethics, Systematic Theology, I*, by James Wm. McClendon. *Reformed Journal* 37 (1987) 22–27.

Mullins, Edgar Young. *The Axioms of Religion*. Philadelphia: American Baptist Publication Society, 1908.

———. *Christian Religion in Its Doctrinal Expression*. Nashville: Sunday School Board of the Southern Baptist Convention, 1917.

Murphy, Nancy C., Brad J. Kallenberg, and Mark Thiessen Nation, editors. *Virtues and Practices in the Christian Tradition: Christian Ethics after MacIntyre*. Harrisburg, PA: Trinity, 1997.

Newman, Elizabeth. "The Lord's Supper: Might Baptists Accept a Theory of Real Presence?" In *Baptist Sacramentalism*, edited by Anthony R. Cross and Philip E. Thompson, 211–27. Waynesboro, GA: Paternoster, 2003.

———. "Outside the Castle Walls: The Public Politics of Teresa's Vision." In *Faith in Public Life*, edited by William Collinge, 62–80. Maryknoll, NY: Orbis, 2008.

Niebuhr, H. Richard. *Christ and Culture*. New York: Harper & Row, 1951.

Ottati, Douglas F. Review of *Ethics: Systematic Theology, I*, by James Wm. McClendon. *Religious Studies Review* 69 (1990) 105–10.

Patterson, Bob. "Original Sin Revisited: McClendon, Niebuhr, and Feminist Theology." *Perspectives in Religious Studies* 27 (2000) 71–82.

Payne, Ernest. *The Fellowship of Believers: Baptist Thought and Practice Yesterday and Today*. London: Kingsgate, 1954.

Pinnock, Clark. "The Physical Side of Being Spiritual: God's Sacramental Presence." In *Baptist Sacramentalism*, edited by Anthony R. Cross and Philip E. Thompson, 8–20. Waynesboro, GA: Paternoster, 2003.

Pipkin, H. Wayne. *Zwingli: The Positive Value of His Eucharistic Writings*. Leeds, UK: Yorkshire Baptist Association, 1986.

Preston, Geoffrey. *Faces of the Church: Meditations on a Mystery and Its Images*. Texts prepared by Aidan Nichols. Edinburgh: T. & T. Clark, 1997.

Quasten, Johannes. *Patrology*. Vol. 3. Utrecht: Spectrum, 1960.

Raitt, Jill, with Bernard McGinn and John Meyendorff, editors. *Christian Spirituality: High Middle Ages and Reformation*. New York: Crossroad, 1989.

Ratzinger, Joseph. *Called to Communion: Understanding the Church Today*. San Francisco: Ignatius, 1996.

Bibliography

———. "The Ecclesiology of the Constitution *Lumen Gentium*." In *Pilgrim Fellowship of the Faith: The Church as Communion*, 123–52. San Francisco: Ignatius, 2005.

———. "Eucharist, Communion, and Solidarity." Lecture for the closing of the Eucharistic Congress at Benevento, June 2, 2002. Published in *L'Osservatore Romano*, English ed. (Baltimore, MD), November 13, 2002.

Rempel, John D. *The Lord's Supper in Anabaptism: A Study in the Christology of Balthsar Hubmaier, Pilgram Marpeck, and Dirk Philips*. Waterloo, ON: Herald, 1993.

Rossi, Philip J. Review of *Ethics: Systematic Theology, I*, by James W. McClendon. *Theological Studies* 48 (1987) 567–69.

Rowland, Tracey. *Culture and the Thomist Tradition: After Vatican II*. London: Routledge, 2003.

Sattler, Michael. "On Congregational Order." In *Baptist Roots: A Reader in the Theology of a Christian People*, edited by Curtis W. Freeman, James Wm. McClendon Jr., and C. Rosalee Velloso da Silva, 48–49. Valley Forge, PA: Judson, 1999.

Schillebeeckx, Edward. *The Eucharist*. Translated by N. D. Smith. New York: Sheed & Ward, 1968.

Schmemann, Alexander. *The Eucharist: Sacrament of the Kingdom*. Crestwood, NY: St. Vladimir's Seminary Press, 1987.

Stackhouse, Max. "Rejoinder to James Wm. McClendon, Jr." *Journal of the American Academy of Religion* 56 (1988) 555–56.

———. Review of *Ethics: Systematic Theology, I*, by James Wm. McClendon. *Journal of the American Academy of Religion* 55 (1987) 615–17.

Stassen, Glen. "Anabaptist Influence in the Origin of the Particular Baptists." *Mennonite Quarterly Review* 19 (1962) 332–48.

Stephens, W. Peter. "The Theology of Zwingli." In *The Cambridge Companion to Reformation Theology*, edited by David C. Steinmetz and David Bagchi, 80–99. Cambridge: Cambridge University Press, 2004.

Steuer, Axel D., and James Wm. McClendon, Jr. *Is God God?* Nashville: Abingdon, 1981.

Stiver, Dan R. *The Philosophy of Religious Language: Sign, Symbol & Story*. Malden, MA: Blackwell, 1996.

Stortz, Martha Ellen. Review of *Ethics: Systematic Theology, I*, by James Wm. McClendon. *Currents in Theology and Mission* 16 (1989) 458.

Stout, Jeffrey, and Robert MacSwain, editors. *Grammar and Grace: Reformulations of Aquinas and Wittgenstein*. London: SCM, 2004.

Strong, Augustus H. *Systematic Theology: A Compendium and Commonplace Book Designed for the Use of Theological Students*. New York: A. C. Armstrong, 1899.

Stroup, George W. Review of *Ethics: Systematic Theology, I*, by James Wm. McClendon. *Homiletic* 12 (1987) 23–24.

Thompson, Philip E. "Sacraments and Religious Liberty." In *Baptist Sacramentalism*, edited by Anthony Cross and Philip Thompson, 36–54. Waynesboro, GA: Paternoster, 2003.

Tilley, Terrence W. *Postmodern Theologies: The Challenge of Religious Diversity*. Maryknoll, NY: Orbis, 1995.

———. "Why American Catholic Theologians Should Read 'Baptist' Theology." *Horizons* 14 (1987) 130.

Torbet, Robert G. *A History of the Baptists*. Valley Forge, PA: Judson, 1982.

Vincent of Lérins. *The Commonitorium of Vincentius of Lerins*. Edited by Reginald Stewart Moxon. Online: http://www.fordham.edu/halsall/ancient/434lerins-canon.html.

Bibliography

Volf, Miroslav. *After Our Likeness: The Church as the Image of the Trinity*. Grand Rapids: Eerdmans, 1997.
Wainwright, Geoffrey. "Eucharist and/as Ethics." *Worship* 62 (1988) 123–38.
Walton, Robert C. *The Gathered Community*. London: Carey, 1946.
Wayland, John. "The Lord's Supper, Administration Of." In *Encyclopedia of Southern Baptists*, edited by N. Cox, 2:794. Nashville: Broadman, 1958.
Westmoreland-White, Michael L. "Reading Scripture in the Baptist Vision: James Wm. McClendon and the Hermeneutics of Participation." *Perspectives in Religious Studies* 27 (2000) 61–70.
Whitt, Jason. "Transforming Views of Baptist Ecclesiology: Baptists and the New Christendom Model of Political Engagement." PhD diss., Baylor University, 2008.
Wilken, Robert Louis. "Is Pentecost a Peer of Easter? Scripture, Liturgy and the *Proprium* of the Holy Spirit." In *Trinity, Time and Church: A Response to the Theology of Robert Jenson*, edited by Colin Gunton, 158–77. Grand Rapids: Eerdmans, 2000.
Williams, A. N. "The Future of the Past: The Contemporary Significance of the *Nouvelle Théologie*." *International Journal of Systematic Theology* 7 (2005) 347–61.
Williams, Daniel H. *Retrieving the Tradition and Renewing Evangelicalism: A Primer for Suspicious Protestants*. Grand Rapids: Eerdmans, 1999.
Wood, Ralph C. *Contending for the Faith: The Church's Engagement with Culture*. Waco, TX: Baylor University Press, 2003.
———. "James Wm. McClendon's Doctrine: An Appreciation." *Perspectives in Religious Studies* 24 (1997) 195–99. Reprinted in *Nexus Libri* (Fall/Winter 1997–98) 1–3.
Wood, Susan K. "Robert Jenson's Ecclesiology from a Roman Catholic Perspective." In *Trinity, Time and Church: A Response to the Theology of Robert Jenson*, edited by Colin Gunton, 178–87. Grand Rapids: Eerdmans, 2000.
———. *Spiritual Exegesis and the Church in the Theology of Henri de Lubac*. Grand Rapids: Eerdmans, 1998.
World Council of Churches. *Baptism, Eucharist and Ministry*. Faith and Order Paper 111. Geneva: WCC, 1982.
Yeago, David S. "Catholicity, Nihilism, and the God of the Gospel: Reflections on the Theology of Robert W. Jenson." *Dialog* 31 (1992) 18–19.
Yoder, John Howard. *Body Politics: Five Practices of the Christian Community before the Watching World*. Nashville: Discipleship Resources, 1992.
———. *For the Nations: Essays Public and Evangelical*. Grand Rapids: Eerdmans, 1997.
———. *Fullness of Christ*. Elgin, IL: Brethren, 1987.
———. "The New Humanity as Pulpit and Paradigm." In *For the Nations: Essays Public and Evangelical*, 37–50. Grand Rapids: Eerdmans, 1997.
———. *The Politics of Jesus*. Grand Rapids: Eerdmans, 1972.
———. "Sacrament as Social Process: Christ the Transformer of Culture." *Theology Today* 48 (1991) 33–44.
Zizioulas, John. *Being as Communion*. Crestwood, NY: St. Vladimir's Seminary Press, 1985.
Zwingli, Huldrych. "An Exposition of the Faith." In *Zwingli and Bullinger*, edited by Geoffrey W. Bromiley, 245–79. Philadelphia: Westminster John Knox, 1953.

Index

Augustine, 1n2, 3n11, 10, 14n3,
    15n10, 25n73, 45, 51, 52n202,
    62n16, 63n20, 64, 66n38–40,
    69–70, 74, 81, 81n124, 84,
    84n145, 86n151, 87, 93,
    104n35, 108–9, 113n76, 122,
    145n98, 148, 153, 154n140
  on signs, 66
Aquinas, Thomas, 1n2, 3, 11, 21n48,
    38n130, 39n135, 50n189,
    51–53, 62n16, 66n47, 75, 77,
    101, 119, 134, 144, 145n98,
    146–47, 152, 156–59
Austin J. L., 14, 23, 143

baptism, 16–17, 23–26, 27n80,
    28, 32n101, 33, 35–36, 43,
    45n167, 50, 55n218, 60n5,
    85n148, 94, 99, 99n7, 101,
    112n68, 115, 127, 127, 130,
    132, 135–36, 138, 143–44,
    149n116, 150n117, 154,
    156–57
Baptist, 5n16, 6, 8n30, 10, 11n42,
    13n2, 15, 17, 22, 27–30,
    48–49, 57, 60, 65, 79, 92, 100,
    117n98, 126, 129n18, 130,
    154n141, 159, 160
baptist vision, 27–30, 49, 65, 92, 126,
    129n18, 130, 154n141, 160
Beasley-Murray, George, 126n1
Beckwith, Sarah, 73n79, 75, 78
Benedict XVI, see Ratzinger, Joseph
Berengar, 44, 67–68, 75–76, 103
body of Christ (see also *corpus Christi*), 1, 2n8, 3–5, 8n30,
    10–11, 19–20, 24–25, 34–35,
    38–39, 41–45, 47–49, 51,
    54, 57, 59–60, 63, 67–68,
    70–88, 90–94, 96–98, 100n11,
    102–5, 108n52, 109–10, 113,
    115–17, 119, 121–23, 132–33,
    137–40, 142, 146–49, 153,
    155, 157–61

Calvin, John, 1n2, 18–19, 57, 63n20,
    118
Cary, Jeffrey,
Cavanaugh, William, 3, 4, 10n35,
    20, 34n108, 35n108, 41n147,
    67n42, 68–69, 73n80, 76–79,
    82n131, 87–96, 104n31,
    114n82, 129n16, 155, 158–60
corpus Christi, 3n13, 75, 78, 123
corpus mysticum, 3, 10n35, 26n73,
    34n109, 41n146, 44n160,
    49n185, 57n230, 60n6, 61,
    62n16, 64, 65n34, 66n38,
    67–68, 69n56, 71n71, 72n73,
    73–74, 76–78, 80–82, 84n146,
    85, 86n151, 103n25, 109n54,
    125, 132n31, 150n123, 159,
    160
corpus verum, 3, 10n35, 67, 73, 76,
    78, 82, 92, 96, 125, 137n56,
    138, 149, 159–60
Council of Trent, 68, 112

De Lubac, Henri, 1–10, 26, 30, 33–34,
    37, 38, 41–42, 44, 48, 49n185,
    51, 52n202, 57–88, 92–93,
    95–98, 99n7, 100, 101n15,

173

Index

De Lubac, Henri (*continued*)
    102–3, 104n31, 105–6,
    108–10, 111n63, 112, 113n74,
    116–17, 120, 122, 124–25,
    126n1, 128n14, 129, 131,
    132n31, 135n46, 137n56, 138,
    140, 145n98, 147, 148–55,
    158–60
Dix, Gregory, 37, 48, 51, 70, 73n79,
    74n83, 78–80, 89n170, 111,
    113n75, 150n124

ecclesiology, 6, 10, 12, 34, 55, 60–61,
    69, 87n153, 92n188, 94–95,
    97, 98n3, 101–2, 106n41, 107,
    108n51, 131, 133n37, 137,
    147, 159
Essick, John Inscore, xii, 20n46
eucharistic unity, 2, 4, 22, 65
ex opere operato, 66n41, 147

Fiddes, Paul, 66n41, 147
Fourth Lateran Council, 75
frequency of eucharist/communion
    daily communion, 15, 41, 69,
        41, 93
    monthly communion, 135n46
    weekly communion, xi, 8, 135n46
Fulgentius, 122–23

Gadamer, Hans-Georg, 7
Grantham, Thomas, 8n30, 20–21,
    56, 137

Harmon, Steve, 2n5, 5n17, 66,
    110n62, 126–30, 159, 161
Harvey, Barry, 5n17, 35n112, 54n212,
    55n218, 127, 128n11, 154–57
Hauerwas, Stanley, 44n164, 73n80,
    115n83, 118n100, 131
Hegel, George, 118
Hemming, Laurence Paul, 80, 85–86,
    149
Hubmaier, 8n30, 19, 22n52, 142

individualism, 21, 78–82, 137

Jenson, Robert, 1n1, 4, 6, 10–11,
    14n4, 30n94, 42, 48, 52n202,
    64, 74n85, 83, 84n141,
    97–125, 129n17, 140, 146–47,
    150n123, 153, 161
Jorgenson, Cameron, 126–27, 130n20
Judson College, xi, 112n71

LaCugna, Catherine, 150
liturgy, 2n4, 37n125, 39n137, 48n182,
    51n197, 70n62, 73n80, 74n84,
    79n110, 81n123, 89n171,
    111n63, 112, 114n78, 127n9,
    134, 150n124
Luther, Martin, 1n1, 11, 18, 57,
    101, 111n62, 113, 145n98,
    149n116

MacIntyre, Alasdair, 7–8, 40–42,
    100n8
Marpeck, Pilgrim, 8n30, 105n40
McCabe, Herbert, 38n133, 139n135,
    44n161, 48, 50–51, 52n205,
    59, 114, 134, 136n54, 139,
    144, 152, 154, 156–57, 161
McClendon, James, 2–6, 8–17, 21–65,
    68n49, 71–72, 76n101, 79, 85,
    90–92, 94, 96–98, 100–101,
    103n24, 111n63, 112–13,
    117n98, 120n110, 123–31,
    133–136, 138–40, 143–49,
    152, 154–61
Medley, Mark, 5n17, 128, 129n16,
    131, 132n30, 149, 150–54,
    159
Mullins, Edgar Y., 16–17, 25, 52–53,
    54n212, 159

Newman, Elizabeth, 5n17, 12, 13n2,
    15n11, 26n74, 45n165,
    55n218, 127–32, 139–49, 151,
    153–54, 155n143, 156, 158,
    159n157, 161

Paul, 3, 5, 32–35, 65–66, 70, 73, 74,
    83–84, 91, 99n70, 101, 103–4,

174

107–9, 113, 147, 150n124,
151, 155

Pinochet, 88–89, 95, 155
Potts, David E., xi
Private eucharists, 78–81, 100, 114–17, 136

Radbertus, 68, 74, 76, 119n108, 160
Ratzinger, Joseph, 86–88
Rempel, John D., 8n30

sacrament, 1, 2n5, 3n13, 4n15, 5, 6n19, 8–21, 24–26, 32, 48, 51–64, 66–67, 70, 71n68, 72, 73n80, 75, 76, 78–79, 83, 85–86, 96–112, 116–21, 123–64
Schmemann, Alexander, 1n2, 128
sign(s), 1n1, 2–3, 9–10, 12–16, 18–19, 21–30, 35–42, 44, 49, 49–60, 65–66, 71, 72n72, 76n101, 79, 82, 85n149, 106, 113n74, 114, 117n98, 123, 129–30, 132–37, 139, 142, 148–49, 152–59, 161
Simons, Menno, 41
speech act, 24, 31, 56
speech act theory, 14, 22, 24n63, 25, 143, 144n88
Strong, Augustus H., 16, 25–26, 159
symbol(s), 2n5, 12–13, 15–19, 21–27, 29, 36, 45, 48, 53, 54n212, 57, 71n68, 75, 80, 90, 98–99, 110–11, 116, 126n1, 127, 129–30, 132n33, 133–36, 140, 142–44, 157–59, 161

Thompson, Philip, 5n17, 9n30, 20, 126n1, 128n11, 130n20, 132
tradition, 2–16, 22, 25–26, 28n86, 30n94, 37, 38n130, 40n140, 42, 45–46, 48, 51, 53, 59–67, 73n78, 96, 99n7, 100–105, 109, 111, 114n77, 117, 121, 124–29, 132–34, 140–41, 145n98, 149n117, 150–52, 157, 159, 160–61
transubstantiation, 10, 28n86, 44, 67–68, 71, 73, 79, 81n126, 85–86, 92, 139n66, 140–42, 145n98, 148–49, 160
trinity, 4, 5n17, 11, 44, 45n164, 83, 105–6, 108–9, 119n105, 121, 150

unity, 1–14, 16, 18–23, 30–33, 34n108, 38n130, 42, 44–46, 49–51, 53–57, 60, 62, 65, 67–69, 71–78, 80, 85, 91–92, 94–100, 106, 108, 112, 114–15, 117, 124–26, 130n22, 133, 137, 139, 142, 147, 149–50, 152–58, 161

Vatican 1, 77, 82n129
Vatican 2, 10, 72, 73n77, 87, 106, 107n47

Walton, Robert C., 21–22, 126n1
Whitt, Jason, 92n187
Wittgenstein, Ludwig, 50, 136n54, 154n142, 156–57
Wood, Ralph C., xi, 5n17, 73n79, 113n76, 118n100, 128n11
Wood, Susan K., 63n17, 98n3, 105–10

Yoder, John H., 43, 45, 49, 50, 68n49, 71, 156

Zwingli, Ulrich, 2n5, 13n2, 17, 21n48, 48, 110, 127, 129n19, 132n32, 136, 142, 158

www.ingramcontent.com/pod-product-compliance
Lightning Source LLC
Chambersburg PA
CBHW020851160426
43192CB00007B/873